Making the Case for Race in Middle School

Making the Case for Race in Middle School

Supporting Adolescents and Teachers in Critical Racial Consciousness and Advocacy

Tina M. Durand
Foreword by Paul Gorski

ROWMAN & LITTLEFIELD
Lanham • Boulder • New York • London

Published by Rowman & Littlefield
An imprint of The Rowman & Littlefield Publishing Group, Inc.
4501 Forbes Boulevard, Suite 200, Lanham, Maryland 20706
www.rowman.com

86-90 Paul Street, London EC2A 4NE, United Kingdom

Copyright © 2025 by Tina M. Durand

All rights reserved. No part of this book may be reproduced in any form or by any electronic or mechanical means, including information storage and retrieval systems, without written permission from the publisher, except by a reviewer who may quote passages in a review.

British Library Cataloguing in Publication Information Available

Library of Congress Cataloging-in-Publication Data

Names: Durand, Tina M., 1968– author.
Title: Making the case for race in middle school : supporting adolescents and teachers in critical racial consciousness and advocacy / Tina M. Durand.
Description: Lanham, Maryland : Rowman & Littlefield, 2025. | Includes bibliographical references. | Summary: "Making the Case for Race in Middle School advances the argument that providing youth with the opportunity to think critically about the pervasive dynamics of race in society, and in their own lives, is an essential element of teacher pedagogy in a multiracial democracy"— Provided by publisher.
Identifiers: LCCN 2024027127 (print) | LCCN 2024027128 (ebook) | ISBN 9781475858587 (cloth) | ISBN 9781475858594 (paperback) | ISBN 9781475858600 (epub)
Subjects: LCSH: Middle school education—Social aspects—United States. | Critical pedagogy—United States. | Culturally relevant pedagogy—United States.
Classification: LCC LB1623.5 .D87 2025 (print) | LCC LB1623.5 (ebook) | DDC 373.236—dc23/eng/20240812
LC record available at https://lccn.loc.gov/2024027127
LC ebook record available at https://lccn.loc.gov/2024027128

∞™ The paper used in this publication meets the minimum requirements of American National Standard for Information Sciences—Permanence of Paper for Printed Library Materials, ANSI/NISO Z39.48-1992.

Contents

Foreword   vii
Paul Gorski

Preface and Acknowledgments   xi

1. (Re) Framing the Case of Race in Schools: Unmasking the Irony   1
2. The Salience of Race and Identity in Middle School: "The World Isn't Black and White" for Students of Color   19
3. The Salience of Race and Identity in Middle School: "There's Just Nothing Really There" for White Students   53
4. Starting with Our (White) Selves: Teachers, Teaching, and Race in Middle School   81
5. Centering Race in Critical Multicultural Praxis: Pedagogical Possibilities and Classroom Strategies   109
6. Do What's in Your Power to Do: (Re) Claiming our Agency in Making the Case for Race in Middle School   153

Notes   165

Index   187

About the Author   193

Foreword
Paul Gorski

"I didn't join this club to do the same old Black History Month celebration," Aaron said to Principal Filmore.

An eighth grader, Aaron, and several of his classmates had fashioned the Black Student Alliance (BSA) after the one at the high school that they, as Fair Lane Middle School students, would be attending the following year. They did their due diligence. They studied the rules governing the establishment of a student organization. They recruited Ms. Barnes, a language arts teacher, to be their sponsor. They completed a club proposal form. They delivered that form to the assistant principal, Ms. Lawrence.

Ms. Lawrence was hesitant at first. She responded in the half-pleading, half-condescending way white adults who enjoy celebrating diversity but feel uneasy in the face of antiracism sometimes do in these situations. She suggested that they create something entirely softer: a general diversity club, maybe, or almost anything without the words "Black" and "Alliance" in the name.

Never underestimate a middle schooler. Leave it to youth to get right to the heart of things while too many adults—white adults, especially—project their racial disease or their downright determination to protect systems of advantage onto them. Aaron and his friends refused the whitewashing, Ms. Lawrence relented, and the Fair Lane BSA was born.

They recruited Ms. Barnes as their sponsor largely because she was one of the few Fair Lane teachers who encouraged honest conversations about race and racism in her classes. This is what they wanted: a space for students to have open conversations about what it meant to be Black in their school and the larger community. They wanted a space for real talk about the racism they experienced at Fair Lane and in their broader lives. They wanted to *do something* about the racism.

In their experience, most Fair Lane teachers, as kind as they might be interpersonally, tended toward Ms. Lawrence's approach to race. *Let's celebrate diversity and share one another's cultures, but make sure white people are comfortable while we do it.* If they encouraged conversations about racism in class at all, it was in the past tense, as though the civil rights movement or President Obama's election had put an end to racial injustice. Most of their teachers avoided conversations about race and racism in the present tense altogether, even when learning opportunities arose naturally in their classes. Everything was about interpersonal *respect* or *surface-level cross-cultural exchange*, neither of which posed any real threat to institutionalized racism.

Aaron and his classmates were not fooled. They knew they were not safe from racism even at their school. They often watched as teachers seemingly refused to address racist incidents that happened right in front of them, or as teachers stumbled their way through trying to address these incidents, often making matters worse. They experienced the impact of racial discipline disparities. With a few exceptions, they felt largely invisible in the curriculum or represented only in tokenistic, not-quite-honest ways. They were going to talk about these things in the BSA. They were going to advocate for change.

In fact, they found the white students who attended BSA meetings also to be enthusiastic about talking openly about race and racism, even if they arrived with little knowledge or used language clumsily. Their read of the situation was that white adults at their school were projecting their unease not only onto Black and Brown students but also onto white students, demonstrating low expectations of the conversations everybody at Fair Lane was capable of having.

Let's be honest. If Black and Brown students need to carve out their own spaces in our schools to find comfort and camaraderie, then we, the adults, have failed them already. If they need to invent a mechanism to do the antiracism work we ought to be doing, it's time to take serious stock of our understandings and commitments. That's what Aaron and his classmates were doing at Fair Lane, what students of color are doing in many places. They were doing what the adults refused to do, never knew they were supposed to do, or worried they'd be punished for doing.

With February just a few months away, the BSA pitched to Ms. Barnes an event in which they would share their work with the rest of the school. Usually, the annual Black History Month assembly featured a local historian who shared stories about "notable," mostly long since passed, Black people from the region: inventors, doctors, athletes, politicians, and artists. Year after year, it was the same sort of tokenizing, painstakingly depoliticized approach that frustrated Aaron and his BSA cofounders. Sure, it was cool to hear about interesting people from history, they told Ms. Barnes, "But we're Black right now, and we have to deal with racism right now." They wished the school community would talk about *that*.

So this is what the BSA proposed as a replacement for the same old assembly. They would organize a panel that would include two Black students—one each from the middle and high school BSAs—and a few local activists who would talk about racism in schools and the broader community. They would share their personal experiences and describe how students can get involved in change efforts.

Along with Ms. Barnes, they shared their idea with Principal Filmore. He seemed dumbfounded when they shared how they experienced the assembly over the last couple of years, which was not too different from how they experienced the overall curriculum at Fair Lane. Mr. Filmore quickly deflected from that conversation, suggesting instead that they collaborate with the local historian to identify local people who had participated in civil rights activism. Aaron tried to explain again that they wanted to focus on the present, on what needs to change *now*, rather than the past. Ms. Barnes made their case, too.

Mr. Filmore was unmoved. "We need to offer something that will appeal to everyone," he said. "We've found over the years that this program, introducing notable Black figures from our region's history, appeals to everyone." That's where it landed: Fair Lane would proceed with the same old assembly.

And Aaron and the other BSA leaders who sat in that room with Mr. Filmore knew exactly who his "everyone" was and who his "everyone" wasn't.

This is a recurring, painfully predictable scenario. The question is never the readiness or willingness of youth. My experience is that most students are desperate for honest conversations and deep learning on race and racism. We, the adults—perhaps the white adults in particular—project our own misgivings onto youth. We might talk a big game about high expectations, but we too often fall prey to our own discomforts when it comes to racial justice and the consciousness of young people. When it comes to equity and justice, we mostly enact grossly low expectations.

Here's the good news. When I've worked with middle schools or even elementary schools where educators were looking for productive ways to have the kinds of conversations Aaron and his classmates felt desperate to have, when we've focused not on white adult discomforts and emotionalities but on the interests, joys, and demands of students, it always has led to feelings of liberation for the educators—at least for the ones who had resisted for misguided pedagogical or "age-appropriate" reasons rather than for racist ideological reasons. We free ourselves to be better, more just educators when we examine what keeps us so constrained. We find that the people we're pretending to "protect" from deeper consciousness and real conversations are the ones with the most to gain in personal growth, in the joy of authentic connection, in beloved community; this includes us.

Sure, as a matter of strategy, we should account for the challenges that may arise when we get serious about antiracism. We know that there are well-organized, well-funded parent and community groups ready to pounce at any sign we mean business with our antiracist commitments. We can build support networks, have one another's backs, and interpret the inevitable blowback as proof we're doing the right thing. We know that most educators—perhaps especially elementary and middle school teachers—were not prepared in their licensure programs to facilitate conversations about racism in their classrooms. That's not their fault; it's a failure of those programs. So we need some knowledge- and skill-building, and not just of the soft and fluffy *let's sing a song of unity while we ignore racism* variety that often fills books about fostering diversity appreciation in pre-adolescents. We know, or we'll learn quickly, that we will trip over ourselves repeatedly because there is no perfection or predictability when it comes to antiracist conversations or actions. So we need to offer ourselves grace.

What I love most about *Making the Case for Race in Middle School*, and why I'm excited that you've chosen to read it, is that Tina M. Durand doesn't hide the messiness. This isn't one of those "here are five strategies" books that fail to provide context or that dodge opportunities to give readers an ideological nudge. It starts with the premise that we *can* engage middle school students in antiracist conversation and action, which we *ought to* do. There are strategies and actions and practical ideas. But Durand also provides all the contextual stuff we need. How do we prepare ourselves to do it well? What sorts of complexities should we predict? She pushes us ideologically, because nobody can sustain an antiracist practice while gripping stubbornly onto racist ideological blockages. All the critical ingredients are here. All the usual fluff is not.

I invite you, as you flip through the pages toward chapter 1, to consider who the Aarons are in your school, and who are the Ms. Lawrences and the Mr. Filmores. And consider, when you take stock of what you're willing or not willing to do in the name of antiracism, who are you as an educator, and who, exactly, are you protecting?

Paul Gorski, founder of the Equity Literacy Institute and
coauthor with Katy Swalwell of *Fix Injustice, Not Kids and*
Other Principles for Transformative Equity Leadership

Preface and Acknowledgments

For all my adult years, I have identified professionally as a teacher. The exciting and dizzying pace of the academic school year, where the weeks are filled with preparing lessons, activities, lectures, group activities, and grading—lots of grading—is an opportunity to be creative, instructive, and innovative. To inspire, and to be inspired. Reflecting on the hundreds of students I have taught and built relationships with, initially as an early elementary teacher in public school, and currently as a university professor of applied human development, there is a constancy in the magic they bring to the classroom. So I must first acknowledge the many, many students who have trusted me, guided me, enthralled me, tested me, perplexed me, challenged me, and learned alongside me throughout my awesome and ever-evolving pedagogical journey. Being able to bring forth and share what I have learned, what I value, and who I have become as a teacher in this book would not have been possible without the wonderful support, feedback, and flexibility of my acquisitions editor at Rowman & Littlefield, April Snider. April, I could not have done this without you!

My identity as a teacher, and especially as a university professor, has meant something significant in my family. Being a first-generation college student makes some aspects of this remarkable since the insatiable curiosity of wanting to know and understand more from professional sources runs counter to the way I was socialized as part of an interdependent, Italian family, where insights and ways of knowing come from trusted family members and people in your life, and from lived experience, not necessarily from books. Being the first person in my family to receive a PhD underscores this point. For always believing in my potential, and for their tolerance when I (occasionally!) wax pedantic in the way only academics can, I thank my very special family.

But there's something very *un*remarkable about my relatively recent transition to social justice teaching that focuses on race, racism, equity, and anti-oppressive practice: I am a White, cisgender, straight, able-bodied woman. Being a member of several dominant, intersecting identities means, among other things, that I had the privilege to become "woke" (yes, "woke"—more on that in this book) through a process that unfolded gradually. Put simply, as White people, our initiation into race and pursuit of antiracism or antiracist teaching is often a choice that begins as an intellectual activity, not as lived experience, as it is for people or teachers of color. Coming to see myself and my role as an actor in an inequitable, racialized system is the result of deep reflection, graduate and professional study and coursework, and intentional reading, but has been greatly nurtured by dialogue, listening, and ongoing engagement with multiracial colleagues, friends, and university students. In particular, my close colleague—Grace Kim has influenced me the most, as I continue to grapple with the contradictions inherent in striving to be a culturally humble, White, antiracist educator. Grace, you once pointed out to me that we have different racial realities on campus, but you were patient, generous, and loving enough to believe we could navigate them together as cross-racial allies and friends. For challenging me, for inspiring me, for mentoring me, for our endless problem-solving (and problem-posing!) around equity issues, for our late-night texts, and for crying and laughing out loud with me, I thank you, my friend.

To the graduate students who were part of my research team over the past five years, Anna Skubel, Ronnie Blackwell, and Efe Shavers, who engaged in the brainstorming, conversations, conference presentations, writing, and data collection with passion, commitment, and diligence, you are also an essential part of this work. And of course, I am deeply humbled by the racial-ethnically diverse middle school students who participated in the studies that will be presented in this book, and who shared their school and identity-based experiences with honesty, bravery, interest, and candor. To the parents and families who allowed their children to participate in research studies that made explicit reference to school climate, race, and identity, I thank you. You serve as evidence that empathy and support for this work do indeed exist in the communities in which schools are situated.

To those in my larger academic community at the Wheelock College of Education & Human Development at Boston University, the majority of whom also consider issues of diversity, equity, and inclusion as core values, I thank you for being "my people," especially during the extraordinarily challenging events of the past several years.

Most importantly, I thank my amazing husband Jon. You are my person. Thank you for loving me in all the special ways that you do. Thank you for being patient and understanding of the mental energy and focus that planning, grading, and writing a book require. Know that I acknowledge all the times I've responded "I can't talk right now," as you've approached me while I'm writing on my laptop, but also know that I always feel your connection. Thank you for your constant support and encouragement. If I don't tell you enough, living and sharing my life with you is my greatest joy and my greatest privilege.

Chapter 1

(Re) Framing the Case of Race in Schools

Unmasking the Irony

> I don't know if this is important . . . but we learn the capitals of every single country in the world. Except for in Africa. My teacher wanted to teach it, but it's a [state] thing. They said that there are too many countries, but then there's like the same amount of countries in Europe, and we had to learn all capitals from that. So, I feel like that might be kind of motivated somehow racially. I'm not completely sure. (Zandra,[1] biracial, seventh-grade student)

The salience of race in schools is both tangible and elusive, and fundamentally ironic. This chapter will outline several important ways that this is the case. As Zandra's opening quotation illustrates, many early adolescent students notice this ambiguity, but they aren't "completely sure" about it. Toward this end, this book advances the argument that providing students with the space and opportunity to think critically and reflexively about the pervasive dynamics of race in society, and in their own lives, is an essential element of being a teacher in a democracy that is both richly diverse, but profoundly inequitable.[2] Moreover, early adolescence is proposed as a developmentally exciting and fruitful time for teachers to engage in this work with middle school students, whose emerging capacity for abstract thinking and perspective-taking skills enable them to benefit from what renowned Brazilian educator Paulo Freire called a humanizing, critical pedagogy.[3] This is one in which students become co-investigators in dialogue with their teachers, with the goal of developing "conscientização," or critical consciousness, which is learning to recognize and act against oppressive social conditions. Because race and racism are among the most charged issues in society and are often avoided as topics of conversation or instruction—in school or otherwise—they are the intentional focus of this book.

Among many things, implementing this kind of pedagogy requires intentionality and reflection, and teachers must have incisive resources and support as they continue to learn and grow in this endeavor. What is embedded in this statement must be named, however, and that is the majority of teachers in the United States are racially White.[4] This does not mean that White people cannot be successful teachers of race and anti-racism; in fact, we know that many White teachers engage in this work with courage, skill, and sensitivity every day in classrooms across the country, in communities with other allies. But it does necessitate that embedded whiteness in teachers' ideologies, consciousness, and understandings about race—inevitable due to our dominant socialization in a white supremacist society—must be interrogated.[5] Put simply, if you are a White person, you have been socialized to believe that your race has no meaning;[6] by extension, this sense of "racelessness" is embedded in the pedagogical training that prospective teachers receive in teacher education programs, which are decidedly white and Eurocentric[7] in tone, imbued with the belief that having good intentions and a set of "best practices" constitute the essence of effective teaching.[8] This book aims to facilitate meaningful reflection and praxis (i.e., the melding of theory and practice) among teachers regarding the role of race in schools; for example, to grapple with the irony that as visible as White teachers and administrators are in schools and in our collective memories, for most White people, this phenomenon is not considered remarkable or noteworthy—it's just "the way things are," or "the way it's always been."

ESSENTIAL PREMISES AND ASSUMPTIONS AROUND THE PLACE OF RACE IN SCHOOL

Race, teaching, and whiteness? Proposing links between these areas runs counter to the view that good teachers need only carefully hone the best practices noted above so that they can work for "all children." But the purported best practices as they are often presented in teacher preparation programs and professional development seminars are themselves culturally derived, making this infinitely more complicated.

Hence, as we embark upon the historically contested topic of race in the school curriculum, it is important to clarify a set of essential premises that undergird the arguments and strategies set forth in this book. Specifically, five assumptions frame and tie together the discussions across chapters, and they are outlined below. If the concepts or ideas are new to you, the citations provided in each section are excellent sources of additional reading.

- Systemic racism is endemic to U.S. (and global) society and has both ideological, material, and affective dimensions.[9] Racism is often defined by scholars as a system of advantage based on race; that is, it is not only a personal ideology based on racial prejudice but also a system involving institutional policies and practices that have historically benefited White people, at the expense of people of color.[10] Racial disparities between White people and people of color[11] in virtually all societal institutions—healthcare, economic, criminal justice, housing, employment, government, media, and education—are extensive and well documented (albeit not uniformly distributed across racial-ethnic groups), not just by academic scholars but also by federal organizations and nonprofit agencies.[12] Racialized cultural messages (both tacit and explicit), regarding the superiority of White, Euroethnic[13] people, are often the means by which such discrepancies are communicated and justified; to use psychological terms, these messages become internalized by both Whites and people of color through our collective socialization. This process of absorbing ideas, beliefs, or attitudes into our consciousness implicates the affective dimension of systemic racism, with the potential to influence our interactions.[14] Since the practice of teaching is fundamentally relational, this bears importantly on teacher-student interactions and on the teacher-student relationship.

- Following from the above, like all societal institutions, white supremacy and whiteness are the foundation upon which U.S. schools are built.[15] This concept has a particular meaning and does not imply that schools are filled with teachers who are extremists committing horrific acts of violence, although vitriolic, prejudicial, and discriminatory sentiments among teachers have been documented, both on social media platforms and in classroom observations.[16] White supremacy refers to the social order based on the racial hierarchy in the United States, fueled by the belief in the inherent superiority of White Europeans over non-Whites. The construct of whiteness is not synonymous with individual White people, but can be thought of as the collective consciousness and ways of being in the world in which people—generally White people—maintain white supremacy.[17] As it bears upon the focus of this book, this means that race already permeates the classroom, even when it may not be the main "topic," and that White teachers, especially, are implicated in the process of addressing it with students with insight and intentionality.

- By legitimizing the salience of race in the classroom, this book does not refer to what is often considered the "celebratory" approach to "multiculturalism," where students participate in annual cultural fairs or multicultural days, or share ethnocultural traditions or artifacts, such as food or clothing, with the school community.[18] There is nothing inherently wrong with such practices if they are conducted in a context in which equity (i.e., fairness, not equality or sameness) is centered, and where the experiences of students outside of white, Eurocentric norms are neither tokenized nor trivialized. However, this book argues for a critical multicultural approach to the teaching of race in school, whereby teachers and students engage together to identify, name, and begin to challenge the norms that keep inequitable practices in place, and the ways that such norms have come about and evolved throughout history.[19] As we will see in later chapters, early adolescent students are astute in identifying such racialized inequities in their schools as well as in society, but need more knowledge, scaffolding, and support in doing so in order to develop an understanding of what they see or *don't* see, as illustrated in the opening quotation from 12-year-old Zandra.

- It is a truism in teacher education in the United States that children should be treated as individuals and that teachers must accommodate students' learning styles or behavioral profiles in the classroom. Within the field of applied developmental psychology, this has often meant that we seek to understand the ways that continuity in developmental norms is mediated by individual sources of variability, such as age, temperament, or personality. Notwithstanding the relevance of these individual differences, renowned scholar and teacher educator Geneva Gay argues in her book *Culturally Responsive Teaching* that issues of race, ethnicity, and culture are often minimized or discounted as legitimate sources of difference in the classroom, and the ways in which students' individuality is deeply entwined with these aspects of the self is neither understood nor acknowledged.[20] Further, she poses the compelling rhetorical question of how educators "can recognize and nurture the individuality of students if they do not know them" (p. 30).[21] The central premise of this book—that race, ethnicity, and culture are highly salient aspects of youths' identity constructions and lived experiences in both school and life, and hence, must be legitimized as important—takes inspiration from this question. The voices of students that are featured in this book provide compelling examples of the ways young adolescents are coming to understand the salience of these factors in their identity constructions, which are themselves influenced by their racial and ethnic positionality or by other dimensions of difference (e.g., gender, family context).

- A disposition that will be challenged in this book is that the practice of teaching is *neutral*, along with the conventional ethos that good teaching transcends race, ethnicity, or culture, and is devoid of context. The presumed neutrality of teaching will be challenged in two primary areas: process and content. Regarding the process, as stated earlier in this chapter, it is important to recognize that the practice of teaching itself is a cultural construction; that is, both the content and form of what are often considered pedagogical "best practices" are derived from middle-class, white, Euroethnic interactional and discourse styles, as well as expectations for student behaviors. When examining the content of what is taught, we must acknowledge the well-documented fact that the U.S. public school curriculum writ large is deeply Eurocentric.[22]

Let us consider teacher neutrality in the context of what has been referred to as a global racial reckoning over the past few years, in response to high-profile police killings of Black female, male, and trans people, as well as the racial-ethnic and class-based inequities revealed through the COVID-19 pandemic, to name two prominent examples. As schools and teachers have sought to address these issues in the classroom with young people, a powerful narrative and backlash against teachers addressing content that is characterized as "political" has emerged in the national discourse. However, as an educator, not addressing these issues of racial violence or inequity, and the many ways these impact the lives of students—especially those from historically marginalized groups—is *just as political* an act as not responding.[23] What is advanced throughout this book is an argument for a justice-oriented pedagogy with young people, where race is centered in all its complexity (e.g., dimension of identity, source of historic oppression, and site for learning and understanding), and where teacher neutrality on this issue is abandoned with intention and purpose. In its finest form, teaching is an act of care and an act of love. If we want students to learn from us, they must first trust us, and this requires authenticity. When issues of inequity (racial or otherwise) present or reveal themselves, students must know where we stand. To be clear, they must see us—their teachers—take a stand on issues around injustice.

The irony here is that despite the current, albeit not new, set of attacks on schools and teachers, the nature of which will be elaborated on later in this chapter, political issues are already at play in schools. Stated more clearly, education is, and has always been, an inherently political endeavor.[24] What is more, race has always been centered in such endeavors, as we discuss next.

SO RACE HAS ALWAYS BEEN RELEVANT IN SCHOOLS? UNPACKING THE CONTRADICTIONS

There are profound contradictions around the salience of race in public schools and in the latest and most overt protestations in favor of the avoidance or outright (legislative) removal of race-based content or equity-oriented conversations in the curriculum. On the one hand, rooted in Enlightenment notions of Western exceptionalism and rational thought, the ideologies of color-blindness, meritocracy, and equal opportunity serve as the dominant ideas that constitute our beliefs about what it means to be an "individual" in a free society, or even more strikingly, what it means to be "American."[25] These ideologies, or mainstream "common sense" ideas that govern a society, are embedded in all societal institutions in the United States—including schools.[26] Ideologies are largely transmitted through hegemonic means; that is, without force or coercion, in ways that seem regular, inevitable, or natural, such as through representations, content, myths, stories, or practices that can be simply characterized as "how we've always done it," or "the way things are." In the ideologies above, one's race (ostensibly) doesn't matter—in school or otherwise.

What is important to notice and deconstruct is the way that the hierarchical, social categories that structure society—specifically, those that have a material impact on our lived experiences and opportunities—are rendered invisible and irrelevant in such ideologies. In their book *Unraveling Assumptions: A Primer for Understanding Oppression and Privilege*, Karen Suyemoto, Roxanne Donovan, and Grace Kim suggest that we might think of social categories such as race, ethnicity, gender, ability, sexuality, and social class as "master statuses" for a society, in that they relate to power, privilege, and oppression, and the ways that one's status or position within each is organized within a hierarchy (i.e., comprised of dominant and subordinate groups).[27] In contrast, ideologies like meritocracy tell us that we need only put forth our best effort and "work hard" to claim our rightful share of the American "melting pot."

Viewed in this way, we can see why acknowledging race-ethnicity and having conversations about race and racism in school are maligned in the public eye, because they are an affront to our shared "humanity," or might detract from a child just being an "individual." Similarly, we can locate the fear that acknowledging racial differences will "divide" us as rooted in these ideologies. The irony is that dominant and subordinate groups are already divided across virtually all life outcomes and institutional contexts and the lived experiences and stories of individuals and communities of color have been historically silenced.[28] As educators, acknowledging and attending to this as it bears upon our work and interactions with young people is tantamount to being an equity-oriented educator and to the implementation of a humanizing pedagogy. To quote scholar and author Bettina Love, "a curriculum that is rich in the stories and lives of Black, Brown, and people of color humanizes not only students of color but White students as well."[29]

It is important to consider the ways in which the recent, 2023 Supreme Court rulings in *Students for Fair Admissions, Inc. v. University of North Carolina* and *Students for Fair Admissions, Inc. v. President & Fellows of Harvard College* reify, reassert, and map onto each of these ideological belief systems (i.e., color-blindness, equal opportunity, meritocracy, and individualism). In this historic decision, which has implications for K–12 education,[30] the Court effectively eliminated the use of race-conscious admissions programs at colleges and universities in the country, reversing several decades of legal precedent that allowed for a "narrowly tailored" consideration of race as one of many factors in deciding which qualified applicants to admit. Instead, the majority opinion asserted that college admissions must use color-blind criteria because not doing so violates the premises of what Justice Clarence Thomas characterized as the Constitution's "color-blind rule" . . . where "all men are created equal, are equal citizens, and must be treated equally before the law."[31] In what history might reveal to be one of her most impactful quotes, Justice Ketanji Brown Jackson, the Court's first Black female justice, countered in her dissent as it applied to the UNC case, "today, the majority pulls the ripcord and announces 'color-blindness for all' by legal fiat. But deeming race irrelevant in law does not make it so in life."[32]

Although examining the nuances in both the majority and dissenting opinions of the Court on this case—and there are many—is beyond the scope of this discussion, the decision is a powerful testament to a profound reluctance that exists among many in the body politic to acknowledge race as a determining factor in one's life.[33] Indeed, while there is legal debate regarding the ruling's short- and long-term impact on institutional policies and practices as they regard educational access and opportunity, it is not an overstatement to say that young people lie at the center of this issue. Its psychological and emotional impact will be deeply felt—especially among groups that have been historically marginalized in higher education settings, particularly those considered more elite.[34] Will we, as teachers, acknowledge this reality for our students in the face of such a monumental ruling, or in the face of other national or local examples in which injustice or harm is at stake, with courage, critical analysis, and empathy? Or disempowered by the weight of presumed teacher neutrality, along with the fear of retaliation if we choose to engage, will we retreat to silence? A central objective of later chapters in this book is to address these challenges with candor, practicality, and a sense of possibility, especially as they regard the work and advocacy of White teachers, who work in vastly different schools, communities, and geographic regions.

This brings us to the other side of the irony and contradiction around the role of race in schools that were presented as a framework for this chapter. Despite the ways that color-blindness, equal opportunity, meritocracy, and individualism work together to create what sociologist and scholar of race Eduardo Bonilla-Silva calls an "impregnable yet elastic wall" (p. 74)[35] that serves to mask the racial reality in the United States, the case that race is important in U.S. schools has already been made, fomented in the crucible of whiteness. Specifically, the historical reality is that race and inequitable, racialized policies and practices have permeated U.S. schooling since its inception.[36] To be clear, an insidious case for race in schools is illustrated in the following list of institutional policies and practices:

- Historic racial segregation, desegregation, and gradual resegregation of U.S. schools.[37]
- Deculturalization in the schooling of Black, Native American, Asian, Latinx, and Hawaiian children.[38]
- Contentious legislation (e.g., English-only mandates) and maligned practices regarding bilingual and dual-language education.[39]
- Overrepresentation of children of color (especially Black children) in special education programs.[40]
- Overrepresentation of White teachers and White administrators.[41]
- Disproportionately harsh school discipline and criminalization of youth of color, resulting in the school-to-prison pipeline.[42]
- Eurocentric curriculum and stylistic features of teacher-student interactions and modes of instruction that are themselves Eurocentric.[43]

To say that race is irrelevant in the examples provided above would be both fallacious and willfully obtuse. Although the list is far from exhaustive, it illustrates some of the most powerful, insidious, and pervasive ways that schools have systematically disenfranchised Black and Brown children, and in fact, have enacted harm upon them,[44] while whiteness and Eurocentrism remain intact. It is not the objective of this book to provide an in-depth discussion and analysis of each practice and phenomenon above; indeed, each is replete with rich and voluminous scholarly and applied source material that does just that. But seeking out such scholarship in order to transform teaching from what Freire[45] described as a mechanistic implementation of a "traditional" curriculum that is not connected to life, to an intellectual activity designed to foster critical knowledge and awareness about the world, is one of many strategies around the teaching of race that will be presented in chapter 5, especially as they are necessary for White practicing teachers, in particular.

So let us sum up the contradictions around the place of race in schools that have been articulated in this section. Dominant ideologies like colorblindness, equal opportunity, and meritocracy reinforce and give currency to the idea that race *doesn't* matter—in schools or otherwise. Yet, prominent institutional practices and policies in schools lay bare the reality that race *does* matter, especially as it regards the preservation and maintenance of whiteness and white supremacy in schools. If you are a teacher, reflecting upon these (and other) fundamental contradictions around race may be disempowering, emotional, and overwhelming. This book does not aim to erase these contradictions, which exist as part of our historical and contemporary reality. Instead, it aims to underscore the ways that as an educator, navigating them with courage and grace in contextually relevant ways is an awesome responsibility, and one with transformative potential.

As educators, we must be ready to make the case that race matters in schools because it matters in *students' lives*. It matters if we see schools as places where hateful speech, harassment, or violence are challenged, not avoided.[46] It matters if we see schools as places that acknowledge and affirm the racial, ethnic, and cultural identities of all students, rather than places where such differences are homogenized or maligned. It matters as we seek to prepare students to be empathetic and civic-minded and to examine the world with curiosity, critical thinking, and a sense of possibility. It matters if we seek to prepare students to thrive in a nation in which the racial, ethnic, and cultural diversity of our people is both our history and very much our destiny. As articulated in Lisa Delpit's book, *Teaching When the World is on Fire*,[47] it matters "when the world is on fire" around issues of race, as well as other topics that have enormous relevance to young people, such as gender, sexuality, climate change, school violence, or student loan debt.

As a teacher, to absolve oneself of the responsibility to address issues like race and racism with students has an impact on them as learners and as people. Avoiding conversations about race or staying silent on issues of racial injustice is fundamentally insulting, disaffirming, and alienating to Black and Brown students.[48] But it is also a disservice to White students, who need to understand the destructive power of racism, its role in our country's history, and the way white identity as both (raceless) and superior is a product of this. Yet, they also need to learn about the work of White abolitionists and the components of White anti-racist allyship, both in the past and in the present.

Scholars—especially scholars of color—have pointed out that the current fervor or "fire" around the teaching of race in schools is not new. Rather, it is merely the newest manifestation of a predictable backlash of white anger, resistance, and rage that has been launched throughout history in the face of significant racial progress.[49] For example, the landmark *1954 Brown v. Board of Education* ruling that ended legal segregation in schools was met with massive and sustained white resistance that decimated the pipeline of Black principals and teachers.[50] The election of Barack Obama in 2008 and 2012 unleashed a fresh set of explicitly racist representations and narratives into the public discourse that coalesced in examples such as the birther movement, as well as a dramatic rise in nationalist, alt-right hate groups.[51]

The most current resistance to the teaching of race, ethnicity, or systemic forms of oppression with young people is the powerful attack on critical race theory (CRT) and "woke"[52] education, and it fits into this predictable pattern of white backlash to institutional initiatives designed to challenge inequity or to change the status quo in a way that benefits historically marginalized racial groups. Because it is important for teachers to be able to respond to the particularity and character of this latest set of attacks with insight and specificity as they seek to engage in conversation and instruction about race in school, a discussion of its evolution and movement into the national consciousness is provided next.

THE ATTACK ON CRITICAL RACE THEORY AND ITS EMERGENCE AS THE NEW "VILLAIN" IN SCHOOLS

CRT is an academic, theoretical framework that began in legal studies several decades ago to examine racial inequity in the historical context and in law.[53] As will be argued here, the current distortion of CRT for ideological purposes is the latest version of tactics used throughout history aimed at upholding white supremacy, led by (mostly) White people who have both institutional and cultural power. Once again, we see schools as the highly politicized site in which this plays out, placing children, families, educators, and communities in the crossfire.

In their recent book, *Critical Race Theory and its Critics: Implications for Research and Teaching*,[54] authors Christina López and Christine Sleeter provide a comprehensive and incisive analysis of the well-organized and well-orchestrated attacks on teaching about race, ethnicity, and diversity-related content in schools that operate under the cover of CRT, which the authors, like others, refer to as the new "villain." These attacks and criticisms are strategic, well-organized, and well-funded by influential conservative think tanks and media outlets, resulting in a manufactured "crisis" in schools, whereby children (read: White children) are being "indoctrinated" with separatist, divisive, radical, anti-American ideas. Such a "crisis" presents as more threatening to White people amidst the disproportionate rise in the population of people of color in the United States, as compared to the White population, and by extension, in U.S. public schools, whose racial demographic is shifting from majority White to majority-ethnic minority.[55]

But why use an academic theory like CRT as a tactic, and how did it happen? Although one individual, Christopher F. Rufo, a senior fellow at the Manhattan Institute, is widely considered to be the architect of this particular strategy,[56] the extraction of CRT from academia and into the public discourse undoubtedly occurred in response to the increased activism around racial injustice that has evolved and gained momentum in the last decade. In 2012, Black women Patrice Cullors, Alicia Garza, and Opal Tometi created Black Lives Matter (BLM) as a media hashtag, speaking and enacting truth to power regarding the acquittal of George Zimmerman in the death of 17-year-old Trayvon Martin. This created a local, national, and eventually global platform in which police brutality and anti-Blackness could be interrogated, yet still occurred amidst and alongside continued lethal violence toward Black, Brown, and Indigenous people at the hands of police throughout the next decade. Such police brutality (which is far more familiar to communities of color than it is to white communities) was at the apex of what has been referred to as the 2020 "summer of racial reckoning" that occurred in response to the killings of Ahmaud Arbery, Breonna Taylor, and George Floyd, as well as the systemic inequities brought to the surface by the COVID-19 pandemic.[57]

This watershed moment in our history precipitated an increased consciousness around racial injustice across the nation. In response, schools began to adopt a more intentional focus on anti-racist teaching and sought to provide teachers with the pedagogical training, knowledge, and curricular materials necessary to focus more squarely on issues of diversity, equity, and inclusion (DEI), and to grapple with the ways that past and present-day racism manifested in peoples' lives.[58] Workplace organizations followed suit and began to prioritize DEI efforts and training in earnest; according to the 2020 Society for Human Resource Management report, job openings for DEI positions rose 55% after the passing of George Floyd.[59]

It is in this context in 2020 that Mr. Rufo obtained materials and transcripts from several employee workshops with DEI and antibias goals (namely, one implemented by Seattle's Office of Civil Rights); in his analysis of training materials, he located the term "critical race theory" as source material. His subsequent writing and blog posts regarding what he found as "segregationism, group-based guilt, and race essentialism" earned him a spot on the *Tucker Carlson Show* on Fox News.[60] On the show, he publicly denounced CRT, referring to it as an "existential threat" to the United States, and called upon then president Trump to take action against it. Shortly thereafter, on September 22, 2020, Trump signed Executive Order (EO) 13950, directing federal agencies to cease and desist from using federal monies to fund "divisive, un-American propaganda training sessions."[61] CRT quickly became a frequent talking point in conservative media outlets, being weaponized as a catchall term for *any* curricular content, classroom lessons, or conversations in schools around diversity, inequity, or injustice, which were purported to "indoctrinate" youth with "left-wing" ideas that promote a hatred of White people and of America. Rufo himself articulated the strategic element of this; in a 2021 interview correspondence with a journalist from *The New Yorker*, Rufo acknowledged the resistance to progressive ideas and actions among conservatives that had been brewing since Barack Obama's presidency, noting:

> We've needed a new language for these issues. "Political correctness" is a dated term, and more importantly, doesn't apply anymore . . . cancel culture is a vacuous term and doesn't translate into a political program, "woke" is . . . too easily brushed aside. "Critical Race Theory" is the perfect villain.[62]

Hence, the assault on diversity and equity content, using the manufactured rhetoric around CRT, took firm hold in the national discourse and continues in our present moment. An anti-CRT agenda has been adopted by school boards across the nation, nonprofit organizations such as Moms for Liberty, and as signature aspects of national and local political campaigns.[63] As of this writing, since 2020, there has been a spate of bills or gag order legislation designed to limit, constrain, or ban the discussion of "divisive concepts" or ideas related to race, gender, religion, or sex in the public K–12 curriculum. The Critical Race Studies Program at UCLA School of Law (CRS) has released a document entitled *CRT Forward: Tracking the Attack on Critical Race Theory*, which presents the work and findings of The Tracking Project, one of the only national databases that has tracked anti-CRT measures enacted at the local and state level in the United States between 2020 and 2022.[64] According to the report, as of December 31, 2022, lawmakers in 28 states have adopted at least one anti-CRT action (e.g., executive directions, policy, resolutions) at the state level; of those 28, 16 have specifically enacted anti-CRT legislation. Anti-CRT measures and rhetoric have primarily targeted K–12 schools, and those formally adopted (226 measures nationally) affect almost half of the nation's 50.8 million public school students. In 2023, UCLA researchers have tracked at least 50 new anti-CRT bills.[65] These practices run alongside an escalation of book bans and censorship in classrooms and libraries nationwide. For example, during the first half of the 2022–2023 school year, PEN America's Index of School Book Bans lists 1,477 instances of individual books banned, affecting 874 unique titles, most of which target stories about people of color and LGBTQ+ individuals, an increase of 28% compared to the months of January–June 2022.[66]

It is an understatement to say that these regressive ideas and actions have the net effect of chilling students' and educators' speech in the classroom, while impinging upon their educational right to learn and discuss the issues that impact our society. As discussed in later chapters, such actions dramatically undermine teacher agency, increase teachers' anxiety and fear about teaching about race and other DEI content, and constitute a lack of public respect and trust for teachers' pedagogical expertise. The argument made in this book is that legislative attempts and actions to remove, censor, or ban such content diminish the quality of education students receive and restricts their exposure to different perspectives and ways of being that are part of a pluralist society like the United States. Further, when we reflect upon the content of most books being banned or examined for removal, we see whose history and perspectives are considered important (White, cis, straight people).

Once again, the backlash is not new. The current attacks on CRT are similar to those waged in the early 1990s against multicultural education in K–12 schools and ethnic studies courses in higher education.[67] Herein, we see the same anxieties that emerge from the ideologies discussed earlier in this chapter: that the United States, rooted in Western political thought, was founded upon the principle of individuals being able to rise above their "inferior" ethnic origins to a shared common culture, in which the ideals of individual liberty and economic freedom are centered. From this view, the role of schools is to uphold these ideals, and attention to racial or ethnic origin is thought to subvert this. It is important to recognize that such claims and ideas make no mention of historic racial inequality, focusing only on the theoretical definition of equality as equal rights of individuals before the law. In doing so, a falsified view of reality is maintained. As Kimberlé Crenshaw, one of the founders of CRT, notes, such claims also rest upon the sentiment that to talk about race or address racial inequity is itself racist and constitutes discrimination against White people, who are made to feel guilty about being White.[68]

What CRT actually *is* and aims to *do* is outlined below, but it is important to remember that it is not a new theory, but one developed decades ago by legal scholars in an academic context. This is a fundamentally grounding point that lends perspective to the public fervor around the deceptive use of the term. Since CRT is being used as a dog whistle to conservative-leaning groups regarding the "dangers" of racial consciousness,[69] an accurate and informed understanding of what CRT consists of is beside the point; that is, truth or accuracy is not important to the way CRT is being deployed to serve this aim. But it is not beside the point for teachers and educators, who must understand what CRT is and what it is not to respond effectively, and to honor students' right to receive an inclusive education that is free from censorship, discrimination, or erasure, and where the complexities in our nation's history and character are interrogated.

WHAT IS CRT, AND IS IT TAUGHT IN K–12 SCHOOLS? ANSWER: LIKELY NOT

CRT has its roots in legal scholarship and is itself an analysis of the ways that racial inequity is embedded in U.S. jurisprudence.[70] In the 1970s, seeking to understand the persistence of racial inequality despite the gains of the civil rights era, early CRT scholars and writers such as Kimberlé Crenshaw, Derrick Bell, Mari Matsuda, and Richard Delgado turned to an examination of the ways that constitutional law upheld and maintained institutional racial inequity—inequity that still exists in the present day.

Specifically, CRT was an interrogation of the presumed neutral principles, impartiality, and objectivity of the law and an illumination of the way the law preserves whiteness and white interests. For example, the belief in equal treatment for all persons, regardless of their different histories or circumstances, provides a rationale for favoring race-neutral approaches that maintain the racially unequal status quo, as opposed to targeted approaches that would address racial inequity.[71] The principle of free speech as a "marketplace of ideas" that is embodied in the First Amendment also becomes more complex with a CRT lens, in terms of whether all groups have the same opportunity and access to articulate their views, which/whose speech is more protected and valued in societal institutions, and who can safely respond to "hate speech," as well as define what constitutes it. Each instance above is determined by whiteness standards of speech.[72]

After the first decade, the application of CRT was broadened to other multidisciplinary areas of study, such as immigration policy, language rights, and Indigenous people's sovereignty and land claims,[73] to name only a few. Regardless of the issue, CRT views the social construction of race in historical context and tied to people's lived realities, centering on how inequality is reproduced and maintained in systemic policies and practices. It is important to recognize that CRT is focused on an institutional analysis of racism, not on individual acts of bigotry or prejudice. Put simply, the focus is on systems, not individuals. Counter to many critics' claims, CRT does not serve as a basis for race-based assumptions about individuals, seek to privilege or divide respective races, or teach White people (especially children) to hate themselves.

The ways that CRT has evolved as a framework to examine racialized disparities in education are outlined by one of the founders of this shift, scholar Gloria Ladson-Billings, in her book *Critical Race Theory in Education: A Scholar's Journey*.[74] For example, educational researchers have used CRT to unmask the ways that white, Eurocentric ideologies are normalized and embedded in all aspects of teaching and school culture,[75] or to illuminate patterns of institutional racism in school practices (e.g., curriculum, school discipline, tracking).[76] CRT has been used to illustrate the ways that traditional conceptions of multicultural education (MCE) in K–12 schools offer only a superficial and uncritical coverage of race, where different racial and ethnic groups are presumed to have "equal opportunity" to share unique aspects of their respective heritages without acknowledging that the practices of Euro-ethnic Whites are normalized and privileged over others.[77]

It is hoped that the abovementioned discussion casts serious doubt upon the possibility that CRT is being "taught" in K–12 schools, due to its theoretical complexity and academic underpinnings. Indeed, even within higher education, CRT as a content area appears most often at the graduate, not undergraduate, level. In a 2022 podcast with the *Harvard EdCast* on the state of CRT in education, Gloria Ladson-Billings makes a blunt statement: CRT is not being taught in K–12 schools.[78] This point has been underscored by many scholars of education and pre-service teacher educators who spend time in schools and classrooms, and an excellent discussion of the myths around CRT is provided in a brief from the National Association of School Psychologists (NASP) entitled *The Importance of Addressing Equity, Diversity, & Inclusion in Schools: Dispelling Myths about Critical Race Theory*.[79] In their aforementioned book, López and Sleeter outline the ways that CRT is being conflated with any DEI initiatives designed to promote a more inclusive school culture, or with any school-based efforts to redress inequities in school practices. The authors clarify further that CRT is *not* the implementation of well-known curricular strategies such as culturally responsive teaching, antibias or anti-racist teaching, ethnic studies, LGBTQ+ studies, restorative justice, or social-emotional learning (SEL).[80]

Although a comprehensive assessment of the extent to which schools and teachers across the country actually employ a more "woke" or equity-oriented pedagogy now, as opposed to pre-2020, would be difficult and well beyond the scope of this book, perhaps it is accurate to say that there has been some increase in teachers' critical consciousness in some areas, and in school districts' attempts to provide more professional development around DEI.[81] Professional organizations such as the American Psychological Association (APA) have increasingly sought to provide guidelines on the use of inclusive language across categories of race, gender, sexuality, age, and (dis)ability that are widely accessible online.[82] A *New York Times* piece entitled "What's Actually Being Taught in History Class," featured the ways that a diverse cohort of history teachers have renewed their commitment to present their students with a less sanitized version of history that includes its more painful and oppressive aspects, as well as more diverse perspectives and experiences.[83]

Notwithstanding this, there are also recent studies with both practicing and pre-service White teachers whose findings reflect their largely uncritical, uninformed, and unreflective stance on topics such as race and racism in the classroom[84]; such findings are consistent with decades of scholarship on the whiteness of teacher education. In a recent piece in *EducationWeek* entitled "No, Public Education Isn't Too Woke. It's Barely Even Awake," Bettina Love comments on the politicization of the term "woke" as a movement that is supposedly taking over U.S. public schools.[85] As Love notes, an honest accounting of the racialized realities of public schooling, such as inequitable funding, access to enrichment or AP classes, disproportionate surveillance and suspensions of students of color, dramatically lower proportions of books that are written by or include people of color, or the isolation (or firing, in more rare cases) of educators who are earnestly engaged in anti-racist teaching, shows how America's public school system is far from "woke." Rather, the inequitable status quo is reinforced and maintained. As Love's article implies, the equity question that lies at the center of this issue is: Who needs to wake up?

This book sits squarely amidst this tension, with the goal of supporting educators—administrators, teachers, counselors, specialists—to be more informed and resilient in the face of political rhetoric—CRT, "woke," or otherwise—that seeks to malign the teaching of race in school. As public educators, we must take responsibility for obtaining a greater awareness and understanding of systemic inequity, as well as progress, and their dramatic impact on people and communities, through the study of race. Deep reflection and authenticity are required to do this successfully.

MAKING THE CASE OF RACE WITH AUTHENTICITY: THE POTENTIAL OF EARLY ADOLESCENCE

As suggested in the title of this chapter, this book calls for *re*-framing the case of race in school. What does this mean, exactly? Succinctly, it means that the salience of race in its many dimensions—such as its social construction and role in U.S. history, aspect of identity, cultural reference point, source of learning, and source of oppression or solidarity—is acknowledged in school curricula in ways that are critically informed and fundamentally authentic. Authenticity means many things in this context, not the least of which is the need for White teachers to first understand the way their racial positionality and socialization influence their teaching practice. Yet, this brings forth the potential for teachers and students to come together in new ways that are grounded in accountability, honesty, trust, and respect, which is the explicit focus of chapters 4 and 5.

But when should the case for race be made? In the arguments against addressing race and racism in school, children's age is often cited as a factor; that is, whether children are "too young" to handle such serious conversations or emotionally loaded content, and that children should just be allowed to be children. Yet the results of the recent *Coming Together: Family Reflections on Racism Study*, designed to examine how racially diverse children ages 6–11 experienced and processed the racialized events of 2020, found that 85% of children who participated were aware of racism and unfair treatment across races, and that many had witnessed or experienced discrimination themselves.[86] To take this a step further, it is also sobering to consider this question: If young children of color can be harmed or killed by racialized violence, especially Black and Hispanic boys, who are significantly more likely to die from police intervention,[87] then shouldn't all children, and especially White children, be learning about it in developmentally appropriate ways?

Although there are now decades of scholarship and testimony from teachers on the benefits of an antibias curriculum and education for children in the early elementary grades, this book focuses with excitement on the spirit of early adolescence, which roughly spans the ages 11–14, during the time students are in middle school—a relatively recent American school initiative and "movement." If you are close to a middle school student, you are likely familiar with such "spirited excitement," which often manifests as a compelling mix of curiosity, self-consciousness, quest for new experiences, and a desire to fit in, as well as with the popularized perceptions of this period as a challenging, conflict-ridden time of uncertainty, confusion, and awkwardness. Of course, it is impossible to easily characterize this developmental period (which is itself a Western construction), because youths' experiences are profoundly influenced by a host of individual and sociocultural factors (e.g., gender, race, ethnicity, social class, family structure, neighborhood, and sexuality). However, it is accurate to say that it is a period of rapid growth and change—what developmental psychologists call a sensitive period. During sensitive periods, individuals are particularly open to not only positive and healthy environmental influences and stimuli that can greatly influence their learning, but also extremely vulnerable to the impact of maladaptive or toxic ones that can dampen or diminish it—the proverbial "double-edged sword."

We focus on the early adolescent period as a pivotal one for the emergence of a deeper consciousness around race—what is referred to as critical racial consciousness because of this kind of developmental significance. During this time, adolescents experience newfound responsibilities and deepening relationships with peers and adults. Trust, and the willingness for adults and kids to "stand up" for each other's best interests, become integral components of what constitutes their idea of both a "good friend" and a "good teacher," as will be illustrated in upcoming chapters. Importantly, as youths transition to adolescence, they embark upon the construction of identity in its multiple dimensions (e.g., gender, sexuality, vocation). More specific to the focus here, this is a time when factors such as race and ethnicity become increasingly salient to youths' identity, sense of self, and competence, and to their cognitive constructions of how the world works and operates.[88]

We know from research on the adolescent brain that early adolescents are particularly sensitized to environmental stimuli—both positive and negative—and that their brains are chemically "primed" to encode both mundane and novel experiences deeply, with great detail and emotion.[89] As such, it follows that contextual factors within the school—such as whether a climate of safety and affirmation is detected (and for whom)—will exert a powerful influence during this period. Put another way, early adolescence is marked by an increase in racial-ethnic awareness that leads youth to become increasingly attuned to its salience in the school environment. For example, perceptions of discrimination and their relative impact begin to set in during the early adolescent period. Alternatively, witnessing teacher or peer advocacy in the face of injustice—racial, cultural, or otherwise—can have a formative impact.

To buttress and lend credence to the rationale for the benefits of engaging in critical inquiry around the topic of race with middle school students, this book does something unique. Specifically, it features the voices of racially and ethnically diverse students across three separate, demographically different communities, in four separate middle schools, drawn from two collaborative research projects that examined students' perspectives on the salience of race, ethnicity, and school diversity, and the importance of race as a dimension of identity.

Although there is some developmental continuity in the ways the youth featured in this book evaluate and talk about race and ethnic-racial identity (ERI)[90] in their schools, the perspectives of White students and students of color vary in very important and intersectional ways. For this reason, the perspectives of each group are mainly discussed in two separate chapters, both of which provide a compelling counternarrative to the persistent claim that the teaching of race is divisive, detrimental, and "anti-American." Together, their narratives provide evidence that young adolescents are unabashedly hopeful in their desire for a better, more inclusive world. Perhaps this finding can serve as inspiration for you to confront the irony of race in school with a renewed commitment, and to stand firmly on the side of a humanizing pedagogy that is unapologetically grounded in the values of racial justice, affirmation, and equity.

Chapter 2

The Salience of Race and Identity in Middle School

"The World Isn't Black and White" for Students of Color

> Imagine a pie chart and it's like cut into different pieces. The biggest part would be, uh, White people, because that's the largest population in the United States. And then, there'd be a bunch of tiny little slivers, and I'd be one of those extremely tiny slivers because I'm probably one of the only student ethnicity in school. It just diversifies everything, and just adds more color, and just kinda proves that the world isn't black and white—it's so many different things. (Abdul, South Asian, seventh-grade student)

What are your initial reactions to Abdul's statement above? What implicit and explicit knowledge about the construct of race is reflected? Does anything surprise you? Are there emotions that you pick up on? As a teacher, what other questions might you ask Abdul? Is the content of his response relevant, both in school and in life? How do you anticipate the way other students might respond, and on which criteria might their responses differ? Do you see his comment as divisive? Inclusive? Perhaps most importantly, does Abdul's comment suggest that he lacks the cognitive capacities to engage with this topic, or to think critically about issues of race, ethnicity, culture, and diversity?

In this chapter and the one that follows, the voices and perspectives of early adolescent students in middle school who are both similar and different from Abdul along many dimensions will provide vivid insights into the questions that are posed above, as well as generate new ones. Specifically, the findings from two collaborative research projects with racial-ethnically diverse adolescents regarding the salience of race, ethnicity, and ethnic-racial identity (ERI)[1] in their school experiences are presented and attest to the significance of these factors in their lives. The narrative themes that will be discussed are the result of more than 60 hours of individual and focus group interviews with 52 middle school students, generated through a team-based, multistage qualitative analysis of hundreds of pages of verbatim transcripts of all recorded interviews. Hence, amidst the cacophony of "expert" (read: adult) voices and perspectives around the teaching of race, equity, and social justice concepts in school, we focus with excitement on those who truly lie at the center of this issue: our youth.[2] As such, the choice to feature students' voices early on in this book is an intentional one.

WHICH YOUTH? THE USE OF RACIAL-ETHNIC TERMINOLOGY

It is important to underscore at this juncture that although the categorical (and often contested) terms "White students" and "students of color" are used in this book to distinguish student groups according to historic dimensions of structural privilege and oppression, racial (for the latter) and ethnic variability exists within each. Yet, the distinction and interplay between race and ethnicity are very different for each respective group. As you consider the themes that will be presented later in this and subsequent chapters, you will notice that racial and ethnic distinctions as sources of variability in the experiences of students of color are highlighted quite often in students' narratives (e.g., how Asian students experienced issues of visibility differently than Black students), but much less so for students who identified as White. This is because White students in the study discussed the salience of their ethnicity far less often or simply did not know their ethnic background if they were asked about it. This is likely a function of the normativity of whiteness, as well as what sociologist Mary Waters has characterized as the "optional" and "symbolic" quality that ethnicity has for White individuals in the United States, who have a degree of choice about whether and how they identify themselves (e.g., as Irish, White, or "just American").[3] Such choices are voluntary and costless, and typically have little impact on their interactions. Hence, references to students of color and White students that are made henceforth should be considered with these complexities in mind.

Race Matters—Moving Toward the Ability to Legitimize the Perspectives of Students

The aim of the research projects presented in this book—to examine students' perspectives and lived experiences with race and identity as revealed through their interview narratives—is grounded in several premises about youth, especially as they bear upon the practice of education and a humanizing pedagogy: (1) that youth deserve attention in their own right, (2) that youth have valuable developmental assets and perspectives that adults can learn from, (3) that it is imperative to listen to youth when they are courageous enough to speak about historically sensitive and personal issues, (4) that youth have "insider" knowledge about their own lived realities, and finally, (5) that the seeds of social justice advocacy in youth are planted through critical dialogue with trusted adults, and with each other.

These premises may resonate strongly with you if you teach, parent, or mentor an early adolescent, and it must be acknowledged that the process of considering or enacting them in practice is often not easy, to say the least (far from it!). As we seek to learn and build stamina in this area, many professional sources of inspiration exist. For example, an unyielding belief in the potential of young people is central to the rich and evolving field of Positive Youth Development (PYD), which has had a meaningful impact on how we, as a society, conceptualize, talk about, and serve adolescents. With its theoretical roots in the related disciplines of positive psychology and developmental psychology, PYD is a strengths-based view of adolescence, where youth are viewed as resources to be developed through the promotion of assets such as character, civic engagement, competence, care, and compassion.[4] Over the past few decades, the concept of PYD has been richly enhanced by the collaborative contributions of practitioners, nonprofit organizations, and policymakers, who have used it as a framework for youth development programming, interventions, and opportunities that capitalize on youths' resilience in contextually relevant ways (e.g., youth living in a rural community may need different supports than those living in an urban community).

Focusing more specifically on the construct of race, the abovementioned premises in support of young people's engagement in the educational process are greatly enhanced by a CRT perspective, and in fact, guided the development of the research projects that will be discussed. Importantly, a CRT-informed methodology calls for the creation of spaces by which students themselves can begin to interrogate what have been called "stock" stories—those imbued with notions of meritocracy, color-blindness, or white superiority that were outlined in the previous chapter—as they regard people's success and life outcomes.[5] Relatedly, the idea of a counter-story is a key tenet of CRT. A counter-story is one that draws explicitly on the lived experiences of groups who have experienced historic marginalization, through personal narratives, family histories, or interactions with culturally affirming adult models that "counter" deficit notions of such groups.[6] Within the context of education, counter-stories also have the potential to disrupt hegemonic, racialized discourses around achievement or dominant school practices, for example. You will see examples of such counter-stories, along with the ways that students grapple with them, embedded in the narratives that will be presented in this chapter.

To sum up, considering students' own voices as integral to the argument being made throughout this book—that race matters in school—rests upon the assumption that what young adolescents have to say is valuable, and that their stories, and counter-stories, can inform strategies for change. Yet, it is absolutely the case that students do not tell a *uniform* story around the ways that race, ethnicity, and ERI are relevant in school and in their lives. Although there are many individual and contextual factors that account for this, broadly framed, the differences in how White students conceptualize, experience, and talk about the salience of race are different from the ways that students of color do. As well established in the scholarly literature and in practice, individuals from marginalized groups (racial or otherwise) will develop an awareness of structural inequality and the salience of social or group identity earlier in life, as a result of experiences with discrimination, parent socialization, or representations (e.g., leadership, media).[7] In contrast, individuals tend to be less aware of a group identity in which they hold privilege. Regarding our focus on race in this book, one way these differences will manifest is in more elaborate narratives from students of color, especially around ERI, as compared with those from White students, who often mused that their race or ethnicity was something that "doesn't feel important to me."

The research projects from which the student narratives are drawn explored the relevance of race, ethnicity, and identity within the broader domain of school climate, defined as the norms, beliefs, values, and interpersonal relationships between students and adults in the school. In simpler terms, school climate refers to the "felt" experience of the school environment. Adding further specificity, scholar Sandra Graham defines the racial-ethnic climate of the school as the degree to which the climate is perceived to be fair, equitable, and supportive of positive interactions between students of different racial-ethnic groups, and whether a sense of belonging is perceived.[8] The racial-ethnic climate of the school has been found to be highly salient to the daily experiences and overall adjustment of students with racially marginalized identities, in particular.[9] Importantly, many studies have shown that youth of color (most notably, Black and Brown youth) consistently rate this dimension of school climate less favorably than their White counterparts.[10] Hence, the promotion of an affirming and supportive racial-ethnic climate in school is an equity issue with great urgency for middle school educators, especially since students' experiences during this time can dramatically influence their success and agency in high school and beyond.[11]

It is in this spirit that this book draws first upon the voices of students of color to make a moving and compelling case for teaching about the constructs of race in middle school, followed by the voices of White students in chapter

3. This order of presentation is yet another intentional choice that is not without its tensions. That is, beginning with the perspectives of students of color is not meant to imply that they (or more broadly, people of color) should bear the burden of leading these conversations; indeed, much has been written about the lack of accountability and reflexivity among White people in this area, who often expect people of color to educate them about race-related topics.[12] Rather, the intention is to center their perspectives with deep respect and humility that recognizes, first and foremost, that their willingness to share their experiences with the research team was both brave and generous. It is also an acknowledgment that throughout history, U.S. schools have struggled to affirm the lived experiences of students of color and to create supportive environments where they can thrive.[13]

Background and Overview of the Research Projects and Participating Schools

The student narratives in this book are based upon two consecutive research projects that aimed to examine variability in early adolescents' experiences with important dimensions of school climate: the academic climate, racial-ethnic climate, sense of belonging, and teacher support. Although these dimensions often overlap and are interrelated—for example, perceptions of teacher support undoubtedly bear upon students' views of the academic climate—our focus in this book is on students' reported experiences with race and ethnicity (i.e., the racial-ethnic climate), as well as their ERI constructions.

The research projects, referred to as Study 1 and Study 2, were conducted over the course of several years. Both were developed and implemented as collaborative partnerships between a large research university and four separate middle schools serving students in grades six–eight, respectively. All participating school districts were interested in being part of the research because they were working on issues of diversity, equity, and inclusivity within their school communities. Data collection for Study 1 was conducted during the 2015–2016 school year, and data collection for Study 2 was conducted during the 2021–2022 school year. Both studies were reviewed and approved by all participating school districts and the Institutional Review Board of the partnering university.

Although both Study 1 and Study 2 shared the same overarching focus, there are important differences between them. Study 1 was conducted in middle schools in two urban school districts within two of the largest cities in the state, respectively, and employed only qualitative methods that included both individual, semistructured interviews and focus groups with students. As can be seen in table 2.1, both participating schools, noted as Schools A and

Table 2.1. Demographic Characteristics of Participating Schools

	School A	School B	School C	School D
Total School Enrollment	791	432	823	942
Race (% total)				
Black	20.7	32.6	4.5	3.5
Hispanic or Latinx	44.2	63.7	4.3	4.7
Asian or Pacific Islander	7.8	0.2	44.3	44.3
Native American	0.1	0.0	0.1	0.0
Multirace	3.0	4.9	6.7	8.2
White	22.1	0.5	40.1	39.4
English-language learner (% total)	39.2	38.0	4.4	5.7
First language not English (% total)	56.0	56.9	35.8	36.5
Low Income (% total)	60.2	64.4	8.7	8.7

Note: Classifications and terminology used above reflect those required by the federal Elementary and Secondary Education Act (ESSA) for school reporting purposes. Data for Schools A and B are based on the 2015–2016 school year. Data for Schools C and D are based on the 2022–2023 school year.

B, contained a majority of Latinx and Black students, with more than 50% of the school population reported as low income. However, their demographic characteristics differed in two significant ways: although White students were a numeric minority in both schools, this was especially the case in School A. Additionally, School B was considerably smaller in size than School A.

Study 2 was designed as a mixed-methods project that was conducted in two middle schools, noted as Schools C and D, which were part of the same suburban metro school district. This project included an anonymous electronic survey on dimensions of school climate that was disseminated to students in both schools, as well as individual, semistructured interviews with a smaller subset of students that delved more deeply into the survey content. Although the schools who participated in Study 2 were similar to those in Study 1 in terms of the relatively small percentages of multiracial and Native American students, they had a very different demographic profile overall. First, both middle schools were relatively large and considered affluent, with very low percentages of low-income students. Both schools contained some racial diversity, but Asian/Pacific Islander students comprised the single largest racial group in each school, followed by White students, with much smaller percentages of Latinx and Black students. Data regarding teachers' racial backgrounds at each of the four participating schools were not available, but all school principals confirmed that it was their understanding that the majority of teachers were White.

The semistructured interviews and focus groups (in Study 1) that were conducted with all student participants were conducted face-to-face with students at each school site, either during a designated time during the school day or after school. Written consent for students to participate in interviews was received from all families/guardians, and students also provided consent on their own behalf at the time of each interview. For their interview or focus group, each student met with one member of the research team, which was comprised of a multiracial-ethnic group (i.e., Black, White, Latinx) that included a university professor and graduate students in the fields of developmental and counseling psychology. The majority of interviews were conducted in English, but three interviews in School B were conducted in Spanish, at the request of students. Although all members of the research team had experience teaching, working, and building rapport with adolescents, students were matched with the same racial-ethnic interviewer whenever possible; because none of the researchers identified as Asian, this was not possible for our Asian student participants. Across both projects, semistructured interviews ranged from 14–60 minutes, with an average of 28 minutes. In Study 1, focus groups ranged from 16 to 51 minutes. All interviews were professionally transcribed verbatim.

Although student interviews were analyzed exhaustively and holistically—that is, the topic of race emerged in many places throughout the interviews—the following specific interview questions tapped students' perspectives on the salience of race in more direct ways, and yielded some of the richest and most detailed information that informed the construction of themes. For clarity, they are listed here:

- So when we started talking, you identified as [self-identified race-ethnicity]. Is being XX important to you? Why or why not?
- Are your race and/or ethnicity important in this school? Does this matter? Why or why not?
- Do you hang out with or have friends with kids from different ethnic, racial, or cultural groups?
- How do you feel about meeting and getting to know kids from different ethnic, racial, or cultural groups?
- Do you think teachers and adults at this school care about or think about kids' ethnicity or race, or does it not matter so much? Tell me more about this.
- Do you think students at this school care about or think about kids' ethnicity or race, or does it not matter so much? Tell me more about this.
- Are there other things about your identity and who you are that are more important than race/ethnicity? Tell me about this.
- One of the things we heard in individual interviews is that this school is very diverse. What do you think about this? (Focus group question)
- Is it important to you to have kids who are of your same race-ethnicity in your classes? Why or why not? (Focus group question)

It is important to contextualize both studies within the larger sociopolitical context in the United States during the periods in which both studies were implemented, particularly regarding the presence of race in the national discourse. The interviews conducted for Study 1 occurred near the end of the tenure of Barack Obama as the 44th U.S. president and during the election campaign of Donald Trump, the 45th president, who many have argued employed overtly racist and anti-immigrant rhetoric, especially against the Black and Brown groups from which many student participants likely identified.[14] The implementation of Study 2 occurred not long after the global impact of both the COVID-19 pandemic and #BlackLivesMatter protests, both of which inspired renewed calls for racial justice. Study 2 interviews with students were conducted during the chaotic period of schools reopening during the pandemic, which shone an additional light on racialized inequities in our societal institutions, not the least of which included schools. Hence, it seems fair to say that while our nation was grappling with its national identity and character in ways that were overtly more polarized and divisive during both study periods, the salience of race remained at the forefront. This undoubtedly influenced the perspectives of our student participants in ways that neither study design directly addressed. Instead, this context underscores the point that early adolescents need and deserve opportunities to discuss important issues that are relevant to their lives. As our study findings will attest, they have much to contribute to the conversation.

Who Were the Students? Study Participants

The student participants from both studies are introduced in table 2.2, using pseudonyms, which will be used for all direct quotations that are presented in the findings. The reader will be reminded that although the 14 students who identified as White are included in the table as part of the full sample across both studies, their perspectives will be addressed separately in the next chapter. In most cases, all demographic information regarding age, grade, gender, place of birth, and race-ethnicity that is presented in the table was self-reported by students at the beginning of each interview; in several cases, racial-ethnic labels were adjusted to preserve student anonymity. Although students were asked to clarify pan-ethnic labels (e.g., Asian/Chinese), they did not use consistent terminology (e.g., "Indian" and "Indian American") and often used race and ethnicity as interchangeable during interviews. This is consistent with the complexity of the psychological experience of group membership as noted by the Ethnic and Racial Identity in the Twenty-first Century Study Group.[15] As can be seen in the table, the students of color from participating schools (38 students) are diverse in terms of race, ethnicity, place of birth, and the way they self-identify, along with the school settings they were part of. These intersectional dimensions of diversity lend depth and richness to students' reported experiences with race, ethnicity, and identity in school, and to the collective story that they tell.

Table 2.2. Demographic Characteristics of Project Participants (n = 52)

Name (Pseudonym)	Age	Grade	Gender	Race-Ethnicity	Place of Birth
School A					
Andre	13	7	Male	Puerto Rican	U.S. mainland
Enzo	12	6	Male	Puerto Rican	U.S. mainland
Evano	15	9	Male	Puerto Rican	Puerto Rico
Catia	14	9	Female	Mexican and Guatemalan	US
Jaden	13	8	Male	Dominican	Dominican Republic
Dev	13	8	Male	Asian/Indian	US
Joel	12	7	Male	White	US
David	13	8	Male	Black/West African	US
Adrian	14	8	Male	Black/Gambian	Gambia
Alfonse	14	8	Male	Puerto Rican	Puerto Rico
School B					
Yolanda	12	7	Female	Puerto Rican	Puerto Rico
Max	13	7	Male	Dominican	Dominican Republic
Alfredo	13	7	Male	Puerto Rican	Puerto Rico
Kara	13	7	Female	Puerto Rican	Puerto Rico
Robert	13	7	Male	Dominican	Dominican Republic
Rosa	13	7	Female	Dominican	Dominican Republic
Colon	13	7	Male	Honduran	Honduras
School C					
Eli	13	8	Male	South American	US
Mata	14	8	Female	Indian and White	US
Abel	13	8	Male	Black/African	US
Suna	14	8	Female	Indian American	India
Ria	13	8	Female	Indian American	US
Reis	13	8	Male	Indian and European	US

Table 2.2. (Continued)

Name (Pseudonym)	Age	Grade	Gender	Race-Ethnicity	Place of Birth
Abdul	12	7	Male	Asian Pakistani	Pakistan
Cam	12	6	Male	Asian/Chinese	US
Joseph	13	7	Male	Hispanic/Spaniard	Spain
Lila	12	6	Female	White	US
Jinda	12	6	Female	Asian/Indian	US
Solomon	13	8	Male	White	US
Trey	13	7	Male	White	US
Vivian	14	8	Female	Asian/Indian	US
Aidan	12	6	Male (for now)	White	US
Nala	13	7	Female	Indian and Eurasian	Germany
Jonah	12	7	Male	Asian/Chinese	US
Nita	13	7	Female	South Asian/Indian	Canada
Zandra	12	7	Nonbinary	Black and White; Mixed	US
Sue	12	6	Female	White	US
Yudi	12	6	Male	South Asian	US
School D					
Agatha	11	6	Female	White	France
Ivan	12	6	Male	White	US
Hope	11	6	Female	Asian/Chinese	US
Mona	12	6	Female	Indian American	US
Misha	12	6	She/her	Indian American	US
Geoff	14	8	Male	White	US
Gia	13	8	Female	White	China
Ana	13	8	She/her	Asian/Chinese	US

Amura	14	8	Female	Asian/Indian	US
Anwar	12	6	Male	Asian/Indian	US
April	12	6	Female	White and Jewish	US
Natalia	13	7	Female	White	US
Aline	13	7	Female	White	US
Brit	13	8	Nonbinary/they	White American	US

Note: The perspectives of four students (Mata, Reis, Nala, and Zandra) who indicated a biracial heritage are considered in this chapter alongside those of students of color. The names of all students are pseudonyms assigned by the researchers.

HOW, AND IN WHAT WAYS, ARE RACE, ETHNICITY, SCHOOL DIVERSITY, AND IDENTITY SALIENT TO STUDENTS OF COLOR IN MIDDLE SCHOOL?

In this section, the ways that race, ethnicity, identity, and being part of a diverse setting were salient to students of color across demographically different school communities are discussed. The findings are organized and presented as six thematic categories. More specifically, these categories are the result of a systematic merging of prior qualitative analyses conducted from both studies that have been published or presented elsewhere as separate reports.[16] An inductive approach was used in all analyses of the student interviews, where initial codes and subsequent categories were derived from the meanings, ideas, and expressed thoughts around race-ethnicity, diversity, and identity that were contained in the interview transcripts; that is, from the words, quotes, and narratives of the student participants, rather than from a predetermined list of topics. Although the categories discussed below cut across both studies and illustrate the shared ideas that emerged regarding students' school-based experiences, critical sources of variability exist and will be highlighted throughout the discussion. To magnify students' voices, each thematic category is illustrated in italics, with a direct student quotation.

"Before I Came to this School, my View on the World was Very, Very Small"

First and foremost, the benefits of school diversity and the opportunity to interact with different racial-ethnic groups was an aspect of their schools that students were proud to share. Specifically, students in all schools noted that being part of an ethnically and racially diverse environment contributed greatly to their growth and learning, providing them with opportunities to explore customs and cultural practices that were different from their own in a very experiential way. They described the content of their learning in concrete terms, such as having opportunities to learn about ethnocultural celebrations, holidays, or traditions, or material aspects of culture, such as food or clothing.

Broadly characterized, the benefits of an ethnically and racially diverse school were cognitive, social, relational, and practical for students. The cognitive benefits were described as providing students with essential and relevant information about "the world," and something that "makes you just more intellectual," as described by Ria. Ria went on to describe the racial-ethnic diversity in School C as integral to promoting inclusivity, as well as a safeguard against being "ignorant" about "how it [the world] works":

I think it's [race-ethnicity in school] important because like if you have many people of like different races, you get to learn more about the world around you ... that makes you more inclusive and literally, it makes you less ignorant about the world and how it works.

Similarly, David commented on how his own perspective, or "view on the world," had been broadened by his enrollment in School B:

Before I came to this school, my view on the world was very, very small. It opened up my eyes a lot more, I learned about a lot more, um, ethnicities and cultures. I also learned more about how people live day to day, and I've learned that a lot of stereotypes about . . . like about ISIS and stuff . . . you can't just blame a whole problem on an entire race.

The quotes from Ria and David above illustrate the potential for school racial-ethnic diversity to be leveraged as a source of inspiration for classroom dialogue or curricular content that helps students to "broaden" their perspective in ways that allow them to learn about "the world" that exists outside of the classroom. However, across all schools, the presence of explicit dialogue around race and ethnicity as sources of learning that might occur in the classroom via structured conversations and/or curricular content was not reported widely, or with specificity, by students. In one of the few examples of this, Vivian commented on the presence of more diverse racial-ethnic representation in literature in her eighth-grade year at School C, noting that "at least in English class, we read a lot of books about main characters who aren't American and aren't White." Similarly, Mata, also from School C, noted that "the only time you would [talk about race or ethnicity] is in Health class, if you were doing something about identity." As will be seen in the discussion of the next theme, many students expressed curiosity or appreciation for the inclusion of DEI content (racial or otherwise) in the curriculum. However, they perceived this to be either a more limited occurrence or a notable absence.

In contrast, the ways that learning about race and ethnicity emerged through social interactions within the peer group were more widely expressed in students' narratives. Students identified a diverse environment as having social benefits, such as the opportunity to meet a wider array of people, as illustrated in Cam's comment, "the most important thing is all the people that come here, there's a lot of different people to be friends with like different races, and all that stuff, like different hobbies, the like, all the different stuff." Put simply, racial-ethnic diversity facilitated wider relational connections. Yet the potential for learning from these connections—that is, not just *having* diverse friends but *learning* from diverse friends—was also noted by students. The following exchange from a focus group that included several recently immigrated, Latinx students at School B—Max, Robert, and

Colon—illustrates the more global learning opportunities that are embedded in schools that include recent immigrant populations, along with students' belief in the potential for ethnoculturally different groups to "connect":

> *Max:* You come here and learn about other people.
>
> *Robert:* Other countries. How it was like in that country.
>
> *Colon:* Like I don't think that when I came, they knew where I was from, like where it's located at. Now, like . . .
>
> *Max:* Like how different each country is from each other. Like, Dominican and Haiti, they're not the same, but, we still have people that connect.

Finally, when discussing the value of racial-ethnic diversity within their school settings, many students in Schools A and B referred to its practical benefits that centered on issues of access, support, and opportunities for learning—sentiments around racial-ethnic diversity that were not present in any of the narratives from students in Schools C and D. For example, Alfredo commented, "it's [School B] not like one of those racist schools that if you don't speak English, they don't want you there." Within these accessible spaces, students viewed their schools as places that gave them the academic skills to be successful in both the short and long term. Teachers were instrumental to this; for example, there was acknowledgment by several students that race or ethnicity sometimes elicited differential instruction from teachers. In many cases, students perceived this to have an adaptive quality, especially around issues of learning English as a second language, whereby sheltered English immersion (SEI) or dual-language classrooms or instruction were available and necessary, according to students. Colon elaborated on this, commenting on the extra support from teachers that he, and other immigrant students, received in terms of not only language, but for learning in general:

> Because I'm coming . . . I don't know if they [teachers] know how it is in there, but they might know that it's like a poor country, where I came, so they might be helping us a lot to learn while we didn't learn back there . . . so they might give us extra supports to like so they can like teach us how to speak the language, pronounce it.

Although the vast majority of students did not articulate a sophisticated understanding of the institutional inequality that is present in U.S. schools,[17] all focus group conversations in Schools A and B included a broad acknowledgment that their schools afforded them opportunities that did not exist in other (native for some) countries, both in the present and historically. The following quote from Enzo, a student in School A, is illustrative of this:

> The good thing about having diverse people here at [school], um, they're giving people a chance. Like say me and [focus group participant] were Puerto Rican kids that never went to school, or maybe went to school up until fifth grade, and we were just living in our houses, but then we came to [present city] and they gave us an actual chance, to gain up our learning, to feel like, you know, we can actually get some learning in, and maybe go up to college. We can master our dreams that we want to do.

Since teachers have long been considered instrumental to students' learning across domains, it seems fair to say that they play an outsized role in helping students—especially those groups who have been historically marginalized by stereotypes surrounding achievement—to "master their dreams," as Enzo so vividly articulated. The implications of this bear importantly on the next theme.

"Like, I Wish They [Teachers] Could Just Stand Up for Me"

The powerful role that teachers played in students' school lives and experiences within the school climate was richly illustrated throughout their narratives. To be clear, the presence of supportive teachers who showed an orientation to students' learning, and whose actions were highly student-centered, was a key dimension of all students' positive experiences across all participating schools. Students described teachers as integral to their success, articulating the ways they encouraged them to do their best work, helped them to solve problems, and provided help for learning. Yolanda described how teachers' commitment to student learning rendered her school the "best one" she had ever attended:

> Um, this school really helped me to learn more, and I think of the other schools that I went to, this is the best school I went to. Because in the other schools I kind of learned, but didn't understand, and I feel like in this school, the teachers explain more, and they help me learn more, and things that I don't know.

Good teachers were also described as caring individuals who were generous with their time and who were both relatable and relational. This is strikingly illustrated in Alfonse's comment that a good teacher "treats you like you're his son. Like he makes you feel kind of special. He connects with you."

The frequency of students' positive appraisals of their teachers, however, was tempered by their descriptions of teacher behaviors that reflected a sense of complacency around issues of race, ethnicity, and cultural diversity. First, it was recognized by many students across all schools that it was meaningful to them when teachers did validate race-ethnicity in the classroom, because "everyone's race is important," as Jinda asserted. A majority of students commented that the school environment should be one where they were allowed to "be proud" of their ethnocultural differences. When asked to clarify how this was facilitated, the most frequently cited examples by students were when different cultural or religious holidays or observances in school practices were acknowledged, or through special events such as cultural fairs that showcased students' cultural traditions (e.g., food, dance, or dress).

However, from the students' views, conversations around race or ethnicity that occurred in more intentional ways within the classroom and school curriculum were more infrequent, confined to particular classes or subjects, mentioned most frequently in Schools C and D, and were limited in scope, as the following comment from Hope suggests:

> So, like, other students can learn how to respect other cultures . . . well, we have lessons on like different people and how they—well, just a couple lessons. It's not like super part of the curriculum. Like teachers just like to add it to their lesson.

In the following exchange between Alfredo, Yolanda, and the interviewer, the students name the absence of their ethnic history in the curriculum more directly, despite the large number of Puerto Rican students enrolled in School A:

> *Alfredo:* You know, like some Puerto Ricans have a lot of history. You know, like boxers, baseball players, are sometimes Spanish.
>
> *Interviewer:* And why should you know about them?
>
> *Alfredo:* Because, they're like, Puerto Ricans, Puerto Rico's heroes, you know? They show that Puerto Rico is like, alive.
>
> *Interviewer:* Do you learn anything about Puerto Rico in school here?
>
> *Alfredo:* No.
>
> *Yolanda:* It's like Alfredo said. We *should* learn about our heroes, and things about places there we've never been before.

Hope's perception that topics or "a couple of lessons" around race and ethnicity were "just added" to the curriculum in a more tangential way, or were absent from the curriculum, as suggested in the case of Alfredo and Yolanda's observations, appeared to make it hard for students to assess whether race and ethnicity were, in fact, important constructs to their teachers. In fact, students in all participating schools were asked a direct question about this (i.e., "do you think your teachers care about things like race and ethnicity in this school?"). Their answers were quite nuanced. On the one hand, many students interpreted the question in terms of its implications for equitable student treatment, which will be elaborated on in the next theme. Catia was one of only a few students who considered this question in terms of the benefits of school diversity for teachers themselves, framing her answer in a positive and hopeful light:

> Teachers value that [racial-ethnic diversity] because they see it as another part of them, I mean, because they see a lot of Hispanics in this school so they really take it- like to take it to heart and they know that, the students they have are Hispanics and they might be Americans or they might be another race and, they're gonna meet a lot of other races. . . . And I've just noticed it in certain teachers because, um, like there are students who don't even speak English and . . . they really like value them, they learn from them. They take like . . . like opportunities from them 'cause they get to learn Spanish, they get to learn their race, they get to learn so much of them.

More frequently, however, students responded to this question in a way that made a distinction between teachers' generalized caring *about* them as individuals and being authentically *engaged* in the teaching of race, ethnicity, or race-related content. This is illustrated by Anwar's comment: "I mean, they [teachers] probably care, but I don't think they like, celebrate or anything . . . or, they care, but they don't really talk about it that much." Similarly, Mona shared this sentiment as she reflected on teachers' ambivalence on this issue, musing, "I don't think it [race-ethnicity] matters that much to teachers. . . . I don't think they really ask about it or want to know in depth."

In the quotation that was featured in the opening of chapter 1, Zandra takes this ambivalence a step further in her musing on the issue of representation; that is, whether what she perceived as the privileging of content about Europe at the expense of Africa in the curriculum was "motivated somehow racially." In fact, Eurocentrism within the curriculum was also named during a focus group conversation at School A; after agreeing that there was great value in learning about diverse cultures, David mused that it was also important "to level the playing field, because we learn so much about Europeans, and how their traditions are, and what they do, but they don't really teach you about other cultures."

Building on this, several students commented that teachers appeared even more hesitant to address issues of race in relational contexts, even in the face of discriminatory behavior. In sharing a striking incident when a classmate trivialized an example of her Indian culture, Misha lamented a lack of support from teachers, lamenting their unwillingness to "stand up for me":

There's this one boy in our last class. He put on some like racist Indian music. And he like started dancing to this, like, he's like American, like he's White and stuff. And I was like "that's not okay—that's racist." And he was like, "girl, how is this racist?" I'm like "that is racist" . . . And like the teachers don't do anything about it. Like, I wish they could just like stand up for me.

The varying levels of ambivalence, silence, or failure to "stand up" around issues of race and ethnicity that were conveyed by the students above exist alongside appraisals of teacher behaviors as maladaptive by a small number of students in Schools A and B, where Black and Latinx students constituted the largest majority. Specifically, four students—all male—commented that either they themselves or others in their circle were treated differently as males of color in ways that they perceived as unfair or overtly racialized. Alfonse, who is Puerto Rican, reveled in speaking about the characteristics of his favorite history teacher as supportive and thoughtful, and in so doing, provided a counterexample of another teacher who referred to him and his peer group as "thugs":

So he [favorite history teacher] treats us in a good way, when [another teacher] said, "Oh, they're thugs, these boys." So look, it was, like, a way difference, like, why are you calling us thugs? They [other teachers] call us "young men" when you're calling us a "thug." And it doesn't look right on us.

Another of these four students, Alfredo, explicitly noted that while some teachers in his school did not care where students were from and "liked everybody," there were some that "might be racist," as evidenced when they "scream at Black kids more than White kids." Evano described an example of differential treatment by teachers in the form of classroom interactions that favor White and female students, respectively:

Well, like sometimes they [teachers] will, like, pick their—sometimes they'll pick their favorites. . . . So like, if it's a White teacher, prolly they'll pick their white favorites, and stuff. Yeah. Yeah, that happens. Like, they always, like, talk to that kid, or that girl . . . they always will, like, you know, when they know the answer, they could be the last one in the class raising their hand, and they'll pick on that person.

Interestingly, however, there were several occasions where students were equivocal in their responses about teachers' racialized treatment. For example, Andre appeared conflicted in his assessment of whether his race-ethnicity played a role in his getting "in trouble with teachers" or whether this was just an "excuse":

Sometimes I used to think that it [racially-based teacher treatment] was like that but it was really never like that—it's never really—I used to try to find an excuse of reasons that I got in trouble with teachers. . . . I have thought that, like, you know, even now I still, even that like I still think it's because of that but I don't—I don't—I don't know why like, maybe I'll say it like at that moment and I'll think later like, "Why would I say something like that?"

As illustrated in this theme, students' narratives provide evidence that teachers are implicated in the process of helping students navigate the complexities of the racial-ethnic climate in school in ways that, first and foremost, do not inflict harm upon them. Indeed, teachers have the potential to serve as invaluable sources of support and affirmation as adolescents begin to articulate their own and others' racial realities and grapple with some of the contradictory understandings around its salience in school spaces that were reflected in many of the comments above.

"Every Person Matters in this School, and They Treat All the Kids Fairly"

The benefits of school racial-ethnic diversity appeared to have an important contingency for students: that one's racial-ethnic positionality did not lead to differential treatment from teachers or peers. This sentiment was most richly illustrated by students' elaborations on the two-part interview question of whether race-ethnicity was important in school, and whether race-ethnicity mattered. Although the question as it was presented was not intended to make a distinction between the adjectives "important" and "matter," it was clear from analyses that students did, in fact, interpret them differently in terms of their implications. Put another way, although students' responses to this question, and throughout their narratives, acknowledged the many ways that race-ethnicity was *important* in school, they were clear that it did not—or should not—*matter* in how they were perceived or treated by others. It is important to point out that such an assertion stands in direct contrast to the examples of racialized treatment that were shared by students in the previous theme, and that will appear in subsequent themes. Rather than ignore or elide such contradictions, they are acknowledged as findings in themselves throughout this book, as they reflect the complexity and nuance that characterize students' interpretations of their experiences with race in school.

Toward this end, it is indeed the case that a majority of students in all schools described their school's racial-ethnic climate as positive, where student treatment was equal, and where they could expect that they wouldn't be treated differently because of their race or ethnicity. In his articulation of this sentiment, Eli describes equal or "same" treatment across ethnicity-race as "regular" treatment at School C:

> Because everyone gets treated like regularly—if they're like Black, or like Asian, or Hispanic, or White. They all get treated the same . . . Because they—I don't see a difference between—like race or ethnicity. Because everybody gets treated the same, so.

After acknowledging that race-ethnicity was a dimension upon which same-race people could "connect," Amura also implies that students experience equal treatment from teachers across race in School D, when she notes that teachers don't care about race-ethnicity "because there's no—there hasn't been a time when a teacher has called out or like favorited anyone, ever."

As evidenced in these comments, being treated "the same" was used by many students as a powerful rationale for why race-ethnicity did not matter in school. Among other things, this attests to the salience of the social context in adolescence and the ways that students are careful observers of the interactions in their environment. Their sentiments are consistent with prior research that has found that higher levels of racial-ethnic diversity in middle school are positively related to students' perceptions of teachers' fair and equal treatment of all ethnic groups.[18] Applied to the findings generated here, although this is heartening in that it might suggest a generalized sense of belonging among students across schools, it also reflects the limitations in students' understanding of the distinction between an environment that promotes equality (i.e., sameness) and one that promotes equity (i.e., fairness), the implications of which will be discussed in chapter 5.

As illustrated by Eli and Amura's representative quotations above, more students leaned into the concept of equality when using it as a justification for why race-ethnicity did not matter in school. Yet, several students did include the concept of fairness in their descriptions of equal treatment, suggesting the potential for students to appreciate the ways that accommodating individual differences (racial, cultural, or otherwise) can work in the service of equity and affirmation. For example, when being asked about what she liked best about School B and what the interview team should know about it, Kara responded that "every person matters in this school, and they treat all the kids fairly." Dev also mentions fairness in his assessment of whether teachers in School A felt students' race-ethnicity was important, although we again see evidence of the prominence that equality or being treated "exact" has in students' understandings and expectations for how they will be treated at school:

> I mean, like, we're all like treated, like equally. Like, it doesn't matter if you're like Black or White. You do like, the same thing. I mean like, the teachers don't care, like, what race you are. They just teach you exact, like fairly for everyone.

As evidenced in the examples above, teachers were often the implied or explicit point of reference when students discussed the ways that race-ethnicity did not influence their school experiences. The few students who did comment that ethnicity-race was important to teachers perceived that to be rooted in curiosity or attempts to learn more about them, but were still careful to clarify that it did not influence how they were treated, as Nita's comment illustrates:

> I think teachers like find it interesting to like, sort of learn about the different ethnicities and differences in cultures, but I wouldn't say that it impacts any way that they treat certain races or anything like that.

Interestingly, Evano linked equitable treatment to what appeared to be his own understanding of one of the mandates of public schooling. In response to a question regarding whether he felt students' ethnicity or race influenced teachers' treatment of students, he noted:

> No, I don't think they [teachers] really care, because you know, they teach in a public school, and public is for everyone—every single race.

A final example from students that reflected their perception that race-ethnicity was not associated with unequal treatment in school was their comments regarding friendships and the peer context. Specifically, many students across all schools noted that they did not select their friendships based on race, and their vivid descriptions of the diversity among their peer and friend groups often emerged spontaneously to attest to the insignificance of race-ethnicity in their interactions. This is illustrated by Joseph's comment, in which equal treatment is implied in his description of peers not being "block[ed] out" because of race-ethnicity:

> Um, we don't really like—we don't like block someone out because of ethnicity. But we—we're like all friends no matter what. So, yeah, race or ethnicity isn't really like important.

Students in all schools were clear that cross-ethnic friendships were common, describing the peer groups that interviewers might see as "all mixed," and that individuals' racial or cultural backgrounds did not matter because "we're like brothers," as Colon described. From their view, this meant that personal and behavioral characteristics were more important influences on their interactions. In fact, for a small number of students, race-ethnicity was subordinate to what they believed were universal aspects of being "a human being," as noted by Andre:

No. I'm fine. I'm a human being. It's just like . . . It's like M&Ms, there's just so many different ones, so what's the difference between one and the other? Nothing . . . I think about, I'm, I don't see what's different from me and the next person next to me. . . . there's nothing different between us, you know? We're all human beings. It's really just how we are and how we act and sort of like what, how we are.

The following striking comment by Max resonates with Andre's, especially in the way both students clearly articulate a color-blind ideology, whereby race-ethnicity is purported to have no bearing on one's interactions, experiences, or opportunities. As well, we again see a focus on the aforementioned concept of equality in Max's response, phrased in terms of students being on the "same level":

Everybody's in the same . . . everybody's in the same level. It's the same level as any. Like every race is the same. There's no barrier against any Hispanics, Blacks, Whites, Asians . . . because all of us came from the same place. We came from evolution over ape, but we just got different skin color. We talk different, we look different, it doesn't matter.

Thus, it seems clear from the narratives that were presented in this section that perceptions of equal treatment across race-ethnicity are a key aspect of students' feelings of acceptance within the school environment. This expectation holds significance for students of color in the context of our nation's complex history with racism and interracial conflict and tensions. Their narratives in this section not only reflect a compelling mix of increased perspective-taking, generosity, and goodwill but also reflect something that is notably absent: a discourse on the schools' attempts to legitimize race-ethnicity as a source of strength and pride. As the next theme will illustrate, while students do not want to be treated differently because of their race or ethnicity, they do consider these to be core dimensions of self, and they appreciate when this is validated. Holding both truths in mind is part of our work with young people who are engaged in the processes of identity construction in earnest during the adolescent period.

"You Carry It Around Wherever You Go"

Ethnic pride was evident in students' narratives across all schools. Although students were clear that factors such as gender, religion, being part of the LGBTQ+ community, or personality were important characteristics, race-ethnicity was a prominent dimension of their cognitive constructions of self and identity, often communicated succinctly as something they were just "proud to be" by many students. Being asked directly about this (i.e., "so you identified as [race-ethnicity] at the beginning of our conversation. Is being [race-ethnicity] important to you? Why or why not?") helped students to clarify their thinking about what their race and ethnicity meant to them as a dimension of identity, resulting in rich and varied descriptions.

First, many students described their race-ethnicity as a generalized, yet core, dimension of self, as articulated by Suna's initial response to our question: "Well, I think it's [race-ethnicity] just like a part like of you, and you like carry it around wherever you go." Put another way, students saw race-ethnicity as an important aspect of self that couldn't be changed, because "it's part of you," as Kara explained. This centering of race-ethnicity was also illustrated succinctly by Abel; in response to the question of whether and how being African was important to him, Abel names it as core to his identity, or "what makes me, me":

> It's [being African] a part of where my family's from and it's a place where I have a bunch of family, and I follow the culture over there. And like, that's what makes me, me—that's what I feel makes me. I mean, your identity's the most important thing . . . it's just like the way you view yourself, and how some people view you.

As suggested in Abel's response above, a majority of students discussed ERI as fused with essential aspects of both one's symbolic and material culture or cultural practices. Students frequently described their ERI as linked to their religion, specific traditions/observances, or as akin to family, geography, or heritage. In particular, language, or being bilingual/multilingual, was a salient dimension of ERI for students, and one many discussed with immediacy. After noting that his ethnicity was important because "my whole family is from South America, and I grew up basically eating the foods that are from South America," Eli clarified, "but it's the speaking Spanish at home with my mom, too." Similarly, Cam responded to the question of whether and how being Chinese was important to him with, "well, I speak Chinese at home." In Schools A and B, where there were more recent immigrant students, bilingualism appeared to have a stronger presence; that is, students discussed the ways that being native Spanish speakers framed their identity-based experiences in school in more detail. For example, Alfredo elaborated on the primacy of language multiple times, linking a lack of English fluency with a reduced sense of belonging within the school. Yet, being a native Spanish speaker was also integral to his Puerto Rican identity—something that cannot be extracted from "the way you are, or from where you are":

> Nobody can change the way you are, or from where you are. If you wanna speak Spanish, you can speak Spanish, but nobody needs to force you to speak English. In the classroom, in ELL, we always speak Spanish.

Rosa also described speaking Spanish as a distinguishing aspect of her Dominican heritage, commenting with pride on the pragmatic and stylistic features of what she described as "Dominican Spanish," and why many of her School B peers were drawn to it:

> Dominicans, like us, we have like a type of language that is like really, people like . . . I don't know how to say it. Como que llama a la gente [like it calls to people].

Several students in School A also described the ways that being bilingual Spanish speakers afforded them skills and resources that they were proud of. In response to questions regarding the importance of being Puerto Rican, Evano and Alfonse immediately mentioned language, each commenting that their ability to communicate with different groups of people was something that allowed them to be "helpful" in school.

Finally, ERI was also valued as a source of connection by students. As noted earlier, although students readily conveyed that cross-racial-ethnic friendships were important, many students explained that they were able to connect with others from the same racial-ethnic background in ways that were particularly meaningful and that they could relate to them more easily. The following quote from Nita is illustrative, as she articulates the ways in which she "values her culture" in herself:

> I really value my culture in myself. Before the pandemic, I did like, a lot of um cultural-related activities. And a lot of my friends are also Indian. And it's [being Indian] is also a way that we connect over and talk about things.

Vivian described being "a little closer" to her Chinese friends, and being able to communicate more easily with them:

> I'll talk to other Chinese kids about, like, Chinese stuff—there are a lot of, uh, other kids that are my race. Generally, my Chinese friends I'm a little closer to because, uh, I guess it's easier to communicate with them, or for my parents to communicate with them.

Similarly, Jinda described this in terms of "having more things to talk about" with other Indian-American students. She went on to speak more broadly about the challenges inherent in communicating with those outside her racial-ethnic group about material aspects of her culture, noting "it's kind of hard to explain, like, my race to them, because sometimes they don't understand . . . and sometimes, I don't have words for what it [particular food] is."

ERI as a source of within-group kinship and respect for one another also emerged in student focus groups. For example, during a focus group at School B, Yolanda noted that being Puerto Rican was important because "we [Puerto Rican students] should treat each other like we're family, because we're like from the same place." In a focus group at School A, this in-group connection was described in terms of the sense of psychological support and comfort that having same racial-ethnic peers offered. Specifically, Anton and Enzo reflected on what it would be like as Puerto Rican students in a majority-white school. Their exchange below illustrates the feelings of comfort they derive from being in the presence of same-ethnic peers, alternately described as "mates" and "family":

Enzo: If there was a school with different people than us [Puerto Ricans], I would love to go, but I'm just going to say that sometimes it might be too overwhelming . . . you might just want to keep staying with your friends because you think they're family, because you think they came from the same country, so you want to stay with them . . . you can forget about everything else, and you just want to stick with your, your mates.

Anton: They feel family with others.

Interviewer: Family with people . . . who are Puerto Rican, like them?

Anton: Definitely.

Despite the ways that ERI was a prominent manifestation of the salience of race and ethnicity in students' conceptions of self and in their relations with others, there was nuance that did exist in the narratives of some students in this area. That is, for some, affirming their ethnic-racial identity without equivocation was difficult, and students appeared hesitant to reflect pride in their racial-ethnic heritage without qualifying it. For example, several students were careful to note that having racial-ethnic pride didn't make one "better" than anyone else, as illustrated by Anton, despite his earlier focus group comment regarding the way same-ethnic peers feel like "family" with each other:

You should never find a reason to make or try to be more than anybody else, and especially for like ethnicity or race. You should never be able to be able to do anything like that or say "I'm better than you because of that" . . . But like at the same time you want to be proud of who you are and how you are, but you don't want to do it so that you make other people feel bad or tear somebody down.

Jaden's comment is also illustrative, and contains similar equivocation; when asked to clarify anything that was important about being Dominican, he shifted between noting his ethnicity as special, but only because "every race is special":

> Well, it [being Dominican] means having a large community and, I don't really think about it as being like really special. It's special, but, like, every race is special. We have our own cultures, our own, like, we might be alike, but we do things different that make us what we are.

For some students, it was important that they did not elevate their ERI above other aspects of their identity, such as when Vivian concluded her description of the many valued aspects of being Chinese with the following caveat:

> And I wouldn't say that being Chinese is really important—I don't know if I gave off that impression earlier. But it's a part of my identity, just like the other stuff that I like to do. I wouldn't say there's anything that mainly defines me.

By far, however, the tensions associated with the emergence of a positive ERI were revealed in the narratives of students who identified as biracial, all of whom were from School C. Specifically, three out of four students who identified as biracial (Mata, Nala, and Zandra)—regardless of ethnic-racial heritage—spoke of tensions that lay at the intersection of identity, belonging, and affirmation. These students described feeling like they didn't fully fit in with either of their racial heritages because of limited participation in or information about their respective ethnic-racial traditions or history. For example, Zandra noted, "I don't know my history . . . so I don't really have that deep a connection to it. . . . I would like to have more of a connection to it—I just don't know how." Similarly, students viewed having two racial positionalities as something that made authentic connections and mutual understanding with others more difficult; they perceived members of the same ethnicity-race as able to "understand each other more . . . and all communicate with each other," as noted by Nala in her description of feeling "left out" in class after revealing that she celebrated two ethno-religious holidays (Diwali and Hanukkah).

Students also spoke powerfully of their biracial identity not being legitimized by others, describing interactions where they felt pressured to choose or provide evidence as to which race they "really" were. In the following compelling quote, Nala describes feeling frustrated, undermined, and criticized by what she perceives as an inability by others to accept her being "more than one" race:

> If you were asked—a lot of people say, "Where are you from?" if you have maybe a different colored skin, or you—they heard your mom has an accent or something like, that . . . And they only remember one of those. But they kind

of forget that I'm more than one. And it can—it can be frustrating sometimes because like, you're more than something, and someone's kind of like, undermining you a little bit. It kind of feels like, criticism, kind of. Sometimes, it feels like they—they don't want to believe it.

Like Nala's comment above that "they don't want to believe it," biracial identity was also described as being obscured or rendered insignificant in the social environment under certain conditions. For example, both Mata and Zandra identified themselves as White-presenting. Mata's comment that "I don't think it's [being biracial] something people pay attention to . . . because I look White, so people just assume I'm White" illustrates the way that phenotypic presentation—here, phenotypic proximity to whiteness—can dramatically mediate biracial individuals' interactions. Framed more critically, Mata's comment is an example of the way that biracial identity can be easily subsumed by the normativity of whiteness, in school or otherwise.

"If We Face the Same Hate as Each Other, We Can Relate"

As noted in the previous sections, although students readily conveyed to us that they appreciated the many benefits of having cross-ethnic-racial friendships, many students across all schools shared with us that they were able to connect with others from the same racial-ethnic background in ways that were particularly meaningful and that they could relate to them more easily, especially in the face of racialized behaviors or treatment. In the following segment, Misha discusses the protective benefits of same-race peer groups. Specifically, in discussing the ways that race-ethnicity mattered in School D, she shares her experience of fitting in with peers who "are not like White" as a place where she "won't get teased" because of her race-ethnicity:

> It's [same-race peer groups] a good thing because like I've seen like other kids at lunch like all White, all White and talking. And like, there's like a group that's all Asian. But like with people who are not like, White, there's like the girl from United Arab Emirates . . . and I feel like she's not, she's not really like American, so, I kind of fit in. Both of us [fit in]. Because there I won't get teased.

It is noteworthy that Misha suggests that she "fits in" more with one of her Arab peers who she considers "not really like American," despite the fact that she was also born in the United States. Jonah takes this a step further, illustrating the emotional salience of same -racial-ethnic peers as a source of advocacy both within and outside of school in the face of "hate":

> I can relate with other Asian Americans . . . like the recent Stop Asian Hate crimes, I can protest with them . . . sometimes, like we say, if we face the same hate as each other, we can relate.

Jonah's comment regarding racial solidarity via protest is the only comment of its kind; that is, no other student referenced opportunities to engage in organized protest (racial or otherwise). In fact, during a focus group at School A, when asked about whether there were ways that kids could come together to advocate or "petition" to change practices that they perceived as unfair, focus group participants were adamant that this wouldn't work, because "the teachers have more power," and "we're gonna get in trouble." Yet, as the conversation evolved, participants were able to envision ways that this might happen; for example, if things were "well-organized and well-presented," and "kids could agree, and teachers could agree" on important issues, change might be possible.

Jonah's explicit reference to Asian "hate," which occurred in the context of increased anti-Asian rhetoric and violence in the wake of the COVID-19 pandemic, is an example of the way young people are aware of and impacted by racism in the larger society. Although no other students noted explicitly that they faced "hate" in school, many examples of differential, racialized treatment by peers and teachers were woven throughout students' narratives. That is, despite the assurances that race-ethnicity did not elicit differential treatment in school that are evidenced in previous themes, participants across all schools provided numerous examples of the ways that race-ethnicity could function as a source of discomfort—even if it was not characterized or named as hate.

First, students often discussed making or hearing jokes about race-ethnicity (either their own or others). Although these were often described as playful and not intended to harm, several students also expressed confusion or uncertainty about whether certain jokes or comments were "racial" or not. For example, Nala expressed the sentiment below following the question of whether issues of race-ethnicity came up often in classes at School C:

> People make jokes about it [race-ethnicity]. So, if someone was like, to talk about someone as of a different race because they were like trying to explain the situation, someone would come up and be like "oh, are you being racist?" Even though they're just trying to explain something . . . so it's like mentioned, and they know you're not being racist, but they make jokes about it, and that's not funny.

The following comment by Kara is similar in that it reflects the tension between what she refers to as "playful" banter and "really rude" comments that can emerge between different Latinx groups in School B:

> Sometimes a lot of the Dominicans like you know, they just wanna like say some stuff. About Puerto Ricans. Yeah like mostly, mostly Dominicans but like

sometimes some like other . . . kids. Just like, "Oh, we're better." "We do this, you that" and you argue about this. [Laughs]. It's just playful. Unless like they say like the most really, really, rude things.

There were several examples where students' racialized discomfort was more clearly expressed, most commonly in confronting racial-ethnic stereotypes, which were evidenced by both teachers and peers. For example, Dev, who had completed his early school years in his native country of India, reported that a former teacher had teased with sarcasm that, of course he "wouldn't know how to use a computer." David spoke candidly about his own role as part of a diverse school environment in the context of stereotypes within the peer context at School B:

Personally with me, it [being West African] means that I can basically show people that stereotypes aren't true. When I told people I was African, they'd ask me if I'd ever seen a lion, or ever ridden a rhino or ridiculous questions like that . . . basically, I told them [peers] that in Africa, we have cities, airplanes, like we can be just as modern as Europe and America, that we're not just a bunch of people living in straw huts walking around with spears and all that stuff.

Mona elaborated on the way that elements of her Indian culture, such as food, marked her race-ethnicity as different, despite the relatively large number of East Asian/Indian students at School D, in what surely was an uncomfortable exchange:

Um, one thing that kind of bothers me about it [being Indian] is like I love the food that we eat, it's like—I think it's delicious, but at school people are like kinda—someone said like, "That's gross." And then, some girl said, "Just because the food she eats is gross doesn't mean she's gross."

Mona went on to describe an example of feeling stereotyped by her (presumed) preference in food choices:

And then someone asked me what my favorite food was, I said cheesecake, 'cause that's my favorite food. And then, they'd go, "Aren't you like Indian or something? Shouldn't you like spicey food?" Which I do, but it was just really stereotypical.

Racialized stereotypes were also gendered on some occasions. Of the five male students who identified as Puerto Rican at Schools A and B, three spontaneously articulated stereotypes that map onto extant cultural stereotypes in the United States that associate being Black or Latino, and male, with dangerousness and threat. Such stereotypes appeared to inform their personal evaluations of their ethnicity (i.e., private regard), as well as their perceptions of how others viewed them (i.e., public regard).[19] Alfonse, who had a very dark phenotypic complexion, offered the following striking example:

> My math teacher—he might think—well people say I got that face of looking like a criminal, or got, like I did something bad. But . . . my teacher will be like "people probably say that because they don't really know you. They think you might do that because you're that person, you look like it. But really, on the inside, you're just different."

In the segment above, several phrases are telling. First, Alfonse's mention of "criminal" might suggest that he is aware of society's attributions of what a "criminal" should look like (i.e., darker skin tone or "face"). Second, although it is couched in a supportive comment ("on the inside, you're just different"), the teacher actually affirms this perception, noting that others might assume him likely to engage in bad behavior because "you look like it [a criminal]." Similarly, Evano clearly names the perception that Puerto Ricans will "kill someone" as a prominent stereotype among his peers, while also noting that "not a lot of White people will kill":

> Like they [peers] would think . . . I don't know 'cause like, there's like a stereotype of, like, all Puerto Ricans—like, you'll see them—they'll always kill someone or something . . . not a lot of White people will kill but, like, most Puerto Ricans and Blacks do. They'll treat you a little different 'cause of it.

Not surprisingly, language emerged as a potential source of racialized discomfort for some students. In School B, both Rosa and Colon—both of whom had been attending school in the United States for less than five years and were the least fluent English speakers among study participants—identified a lack of proficiency with English as a distinct vulnerability in school, particularly among their peers. Specifically, not speaking English well was described as a source of bullying or teasing by Rosa:

> Like because basically people just come to be bullying people . . . because of their language . . . they try to hurt people . . . cause like how they speak English. Like most of the people in here . . . if you be speaking English, like trying to speak English and you don't speak it correctly, then people bully you.

Colon echoed Rosa's observation in his explanation that bullying in school was mostly based on speaking English with an "accent," such that "when they [peers] hear your accent, they will start making fun of it." In short, being a bilingual speaker with an "accent" served to racialize students within the middle school peer context, often marking them as the racial-ethnic "other." It is noteworthy that this occurred at School B, where there were large numbers of immigrant and native Spanish speakers. Such issues of hypervisibility are centered in the final theme.

"It Can't Really Be Forgotten and You Can't be Really Unnoticeable"

The examples of racialized stereotypes shared by students in the above section—such as Alfonse's description of looking like a "criminal" in School A, and Mona's description of reactions to her Indian food in School D—are striking illustrations of the way that students of color must navigate a kind of unsolicited hypervisibility due to their race-ethnicity in school settings, where whiteness and Eurocentrism permeate school norms, practices, and expectations, irrespective of the demographic profile of the school. In both examples, hypervisibility occurs because one's physical appearance or behaviors confirm extant stereotypes that are fueled by whiteness: that Black or Brown males are "criminal" or that Indian food is "gross." In Schools A and B, language—specifically, speaking Spanish in the school environment—often rendered students hypervisible. Although students in both schools recognized the adaptive features and communicative benefits of speaking Spanish, they also cautioned that it contributed to a separation between them and their English-speaking peers, where speaking Spanish with friends fostered suspicion and uncertainty among non–Spanish-speaking peers. Such uncertainty often fueled the kind of negative reactions (i.e., teasing and bullying) to the use of Spanish that were evidenced in the examples offered by Colon and Rosa in the previous theme.

But hypervisibility can also manifest in more nuanced, yet no less pervasive ways for students. For example, many students of color do not have the same level of choice as White students in acknowledging their race-ethnicity because they present outside a normative white phenotype. Reis, who identified as biracial, commented that this racial-ethnic hypervisibility came up early in the school year at School C; his rather contradictory account regarding the way his ethnicity is read by others (i.e., it is noticed, but only superficially) is interesting:

> I think, like, everyone respects my ethnicity, but they don't really ask questions. They just, like, respect it. People just know. Like they can see it when they look at me and then, I also just tell people, I guess. Like on the first day of school. People will ask and stuff.

Reis' reflection also calls attention to the ways that hypervisibility is mediated by school contextual factors; that is, by virtue of the large number of

White students at School C, Reis' race-ethnicity is immediately visible as "different"—something "people ask about" right away. Although Reis frames his experience positively, it is reasonable to assume that students' psychological experience of racial-ethnicity hypervisibility could be influenced by whether they are part of the racial-ethnic school majority or minority. We see evidence for this in Schools A and B, where there were many Latinx students enrolled. For example, several Latinx students in both schools named the school's racial-ethnic demographic as the foremost reason for why their ethnicity-race was important in school. While on the surface this might reflect rather concrete thinking, whereby the simple fact that "most of the kids here are Hispanic," as Kara noted, seemed to constitute the salience of race, the following comment by Catia might suggest that there are more substantive benefits to being part of the majority group:

> Yeah I do think it's (Latinx) important because—'cause we're like a race that's like really common now and it can't be really forgotten and you can't be really unnoticeable, you're always there and it's always mentioned.

In Catia's response, the adaptive value of being part of a Latinx majority in school is the antithesis of being invisible; that is, her use of the words "forgotten," "unnoticeable," and being "always there" illustrate the complexities of being seen and acknowledged (or not) in a group setting.

Such complexity was also illustrated by students who were not part of their school's racial-ethnic majority. In School C, Abdul also addresses the concept of hypervisibility when he refers to the potential "outcast" status that can occur when ethnicity-race is legitimized by others in school:

> I feel like they [people in school] don't care [about ethnicity-race], but I'm fine with that because it's just uh, yet again, it's like being framed as an outcast. And sometimes people treasure it, sometimes people don't, some people just feel neutral. And I prefer the neutral side because then you know that they don't think poorly of you or greatly of you.

In this segment, Abdul reflects a preference for color-blindness or "neutrality" around race-ethnicity among his peers. Being part of a smaller Asian subgroup (Pakistani) in the school environment may have contributed to Abdul's assertion that taking a racially "neutral side" might reduce the vulnerability of being seen as a racial-ethnic outcast. In fact, we see this more clearly in a description by Abel. As one of the very few Black students in School C, Abel illustrates such vulnerability when he articulates a heightened feeling of scrutiny—akin to hypervisibility-in response to teachers' questions about his ethnic heritage:

> I mean, sometimes it [discussing ethnicity-race] might get personal and some people don't want to . . . and even though some people might want their teacher

to know about them, when the time's right, there might be some spacings in class where you just like-oh, I'm- I am Sudanese, this is what I do. . . . And if you don't want—if the teacher's asking questions, and if it starts to get too much, that's when I'm like—it's like I don't really wanna go into that much about it.

In considering the issue of hypervisibility for students of color more broadly in the context of hegemonic whiteness, it is important to also consider its alternate dimension: invisibility, or not feeling "seen." Invisibility as a feature of students' experience was not evidenced in the narratives of students from Schools A and B, but did emerge in Schools C and D, although somewhat infrequently. For example, although Ria commented early in her conversation that a focus on inclusivity was the best thing about School C, she quickly described her view of its limitations:

I feel like some small issues are always overlooked at times, like how people feel when comparing others, or like as a minority group . . . as much as we talk about like including people, sometimes, honestly, I feel like I'm different, and like, people of specific races would like, only hang out with people who look like them.

Although Ria does not make specific mention of feeling invisible per se, her use of the term "overlooked" might carry this connotation. In School D, despite the large number of pan-Asian students in the school community, several Asian students described individual behaviors or school practices that carried the potential to render them (and their race-ethnicity, in particular) invisible. Hope shared an observation of the way this could occur in response to unintentional behaviors among teachers, as she asserts the importance of teachers learning and saying her name correctly:

Um . . . well, I have like a teacher who can't tell Asian girls apart . . . which is kind of frustrating because they can tell other kids apart that are the same race. . . . Um, they just look in my general direction with like other kids and they just like try to guess. . . . I know they're trying because my teacher, like, said my name right several times recently, but in the past, she couldn't really remember.

In a similar frame, Anwar lamented that while the school named or acknowledged the celebration of some ethno-religious holidays, his own was often left out:

Sometimes I see other holidays for, like, Hannukah and stuff like that but I've never seen . . . there are Indian holidays in the calendar and stuff but they've never been celebrated here. . . . Like, Chinese New Year, they mention it. There's an Indian holiday called Diwali—they don't mention it.

The aspects of their school experience that Ria, Hope, and Anwar share above are small but impactful examples of the myriad ways that students of color, as well as their respective cultural practices, can be delegitimized and rendered invisible in school—even if that is not the intention. Taken together, the collective narrative told by students in this final thematic category is consistent with research studies that have examined the ways that people of color can experience both hypervisibility and invisibility simultaneously in historically white spaces.[20]

CONCLUSION

Several conclusions can be drawn from the thematic categories that emerged from the narratives of diverse, early adolescent students of color that were presented in this chapter:

- Students of color are sensitized to issues of race in the school environment; although they appreciate the benefits of being part of a racially and ethnically diverse community, they grapple with contradictory understandings about its salience.
- Students of color are actively engaged in the construction of their ethnic-racial identity in ways that reflect both pride and ambivalence.
- Students can locate and identify the presence of racialized stereotypes in the school environment and in their interactions with both teachers and peers.
- Students observe and notice what teachers do and *don't* do, regarding issues of race, diversity, inclusivity, and "standing up" for equity.
- Students are uniquely positioned with regard to hegemonic whiteness in schools and must negotiate issues of visibility and invisibility in varied and nuanced ways.

If White teachers and educators aim to effectively teach and build authentic relationships with students of color, they must first aim to *know* them. Among other things, this means that they can neither disregard the kinds of experiences with race in school that were reflected in students' narratives here, nor underestimate the impact such experiences have on their school lives or emerging sense of self. In describing their experiences, it is noteworthy that the role of White students was named on only a few occasions, and students were not pressed to do so during interviews. Notwithstanding this, an underlying argument made throughout this book is that White adolescents do not stand outside the racial-ethnic climate of the school. Rather, they contribute actively to it in ways that uphold the normativity of whiteness. This will be illustrated in the narratives of White student participants, whose perspectives are the focus of the next chapter.

Chapter 3

The Salience of Race and Identity in Middle School

"There's Just Nothing Really There" for White Students

Interviewer: When we started talking, you identified as White American. Is this important to you?

Student: Not really. I mean, I mean, I guess there's just nothing really there. I don't know. There's no—nothing I really follow, nothing I can really stand for in that, so, yeah. (Brit, White American, eighth-grade student)

The salience of race in the consciousness of White individuals is tenuous and often ambivalent. Following logically from the argument made in chapter 1, despite complexities in the way that White racial categories have shifted throughout history and continue to the present day (i.e., which groups should be considered White[1]), the ideological power of whiteness is intractable, with enormous pull. That is, by virtue of its assumed normativity, the salience and impact of being White are rendered invisible; that is, most White people think of themselves first as individuals, without a meaningful white identity.[2] This is no less true for White adolescents, as reflected in Brit's comment that "there's just nothing really there" regarding the importance of her identification as a White American.

Can we take Brit's comment at face value, however? If you reflect carefully on her sentiment, what does it suggest? What information does she have, and what is lacking? When considered in the context of self, identity, and agency, is her sentiment adaptive or growth-promotive? Is there anything that *is* there? Is white identity something that adolescents like Brit can begin to "stand for," and if so, how, and in what ways? Indeed, questions like these take on great significance when considered in the context of recent sociopolitical events. For example, increased awareness and acknowledgment of systemic racial oppression at the national level were spurred by the events of 2020; specifically, in the massive wave of protests across the country and worldwide in response to the police killing of George Floyd amidst the ravages of the COVID-19 pandemic, as noted in chapter 1. At the time of this writing, historic tensions between Israel and Palestine that are deeply rooted (but certainly not limited) to issues of homeland, sovereignty, ethnicity, identity, and self-determination have erupted into what many historians and scholars have considered unprecedented levels of violence and civilian deaths across the region. These events are juxtaposed with a rise in white nationalist, alt-right groups over the past several years, including the use of explicit propaganda in the United States that warns against "white replacement" by people and immigrants of color, under the guise of what is presented as American "patriotism."[3] In this context, interrogating the power of whiteness and its implications for white identity is even more imperative—especially during pivotal periods of growth and learning for adolescent youth.

In this chapter, the ways that White students perceive the significance of race in their school lives, interactions, and identity are presented and discussed. Specifically, the voices of 15 student participants who identified as White across both research studies will be featured. In doing so, it is important to acknowledge that White students are a relatively small group when considered in relation to the number of students of color who participated in the projects across all schools. On the surface, this is an obvious reason that the story around race and identity that emerges from White students is less elaborate and detailed than the one that was told by students of color in the last chapter. Yet, even if the number of White student participants had been notably higher, the essence of the story likely would not have changed. That is, one premise of this chapter is that the lack of clarity around race and identity among White adolescents is an important finding in and of itself because it provides insights into the necessary precursors of White anti-racist advocacy in young people.

A second premise that undergirds the choice to include the perspectives of White adolescents as part of an argument for the case of race in school—however underdeveloped such perspectives might be—is that examining the trajectory of racial understanding and ethnic-racial identity development among White youth acknowledges that race shapes the development of *all* people, not just people of color, in varied and intersectional ways. As argued by authors Öslem Sensoy and Robin DiAngelo throughout their book, *Is Everyone Really Equal? An Introduction to Key Concepts in Social Justice Education*, it is incumbent upon everyone—especially those with racial privilege—to address racial inequity.[4] As such, White people—including White youth—play a key role in both the maintenance of race-based oppression, as well as the struggle and fight to upend it. Identifying the antecedents of critical racial consciousness and subsequent advocacy in White adolescent students—explored in this chapter through students' narratives—pushes back against the trend to consider and study race with primarily Black and Brown students.

Hence, there is both urgency and possibility regarding the development of an anti-racist identity among White adolescents in school-based contexts, where students are immersed in negotiating aspects of their identity, participate in varied learning and critical thinking opportunities, and engage in a variety of interpersonal encounters with peers and adults. Whether schools consider—or feel they even can consider—such an initiative as part of their DEI efforts is certainly an open question. Although school district mission statements highlight a partisan divide over DEI content in K–12 education,[5] this book is meant to inspire teachers, educators, and school leaders to consider such statements with a deeper acknowledgment of what might be missing or not named; that is, that even amidst controversy, many DEI initiatives are often devoid of a focus on white identity and anti-racism among White students, focusing instead on inclusion and understanding of the racialized (i.e., non-White) other. The myriad complexities inherent in such considerations will be addressed in subsequent, later chapters.

To provide evidence for the two premises discussed above regarding a focus on race and White youth and to contextualize the findings that will be presented from White student participants, a brief overview of what is known about White adolescents' understanding of race and ethnic-racial identity, as well as their engagement in anti-racist actions, is presented in the next section, based on recent developmental studies. This is followed by a discussion of a conceptual model for the development of anti-racist behaviors in White adolescents that provides insights into the requisite cognitive, psychological, and behavioral correlates of anti-racism in adolescents that are necessary for such exciting changes to occur.

White Adolescents' Perspectives on Race: What Do Recent Studies Tell Us?

Although the theoretical and empirical work on children and adolescents' understanding, attitudes, and experiences with race has historically been centered on youth of color, there is an increasing awareness that it is just as important (if not more so in some ways) to understand the ways that these processes unfold for White youth. Such a shift in focus has gradually emerged in the developmental literature in the past decade. Stated most broadly, this body of research and scholarship supports the contention that White adolescents think about race much less often than students of color do, with regard to the ways that it bears upon their sense of identity (i.e., the importance and meaning of being white) and daily lives, as well as its salience within the larger society. Although early adolescence confers the necessary sociocognitive skills for racial perspective-taking, it stands to reason that White youth will move through this process more slowly, as they are not prompted by race-relevant experiences in their daily lives that impel them to grapple with such issues.[6] As well, the normativity of whiteness in society confirms being white as the neutral, homogenous standard. As recipients of this dominant socialization, White adolescents come to see themselves as "raceless," where ethnicity, not race, are more salient constructs—something that is not inherently bad, but reflective of a more limited understanding of systemic racial privilege.[7] As a result, racism becomes defined only as individual acts of meanness by a few "bad" people, framed within a "good/bad binary," where being not racist/racist are distinct and mutually exclusive.[8] As a member of the racially dominant group, positioning oneself on the "not racist" side (e.g., because one does not use in racist epithets, or because one is a "good" person) absolves one (adolescent or otherwise) of the responsibility to develop a critical understanding of race and racism, and undermines the will and agency to speak and act against it.

Within this context, developmental studies have examined sources of continuity and variability in White adolescents' understanding of race and racial identity on several dimensions. To begin, a logical question is how, and in what ways, White children's understanding of race will progress and deepen based on their cognitive growth; that is, as a by-product of maturation. A recent longitudinal study published in 2021 by researchers Ursula Moffit, Leonandra Onnie Rogers, and Kara Dastrup that included White children and early adolescents (ages 8–14) regarding their understandings of their own white identity provides important insights into this question.[9] The authors used a seminal model of white racial identity development, the White Racial Identity Development (WRID) model, developed by renowned scholar of race Janet Helms, to analyze White students' responses to semistructured interview questions at two different time periods (in middle childhood and early adolescence, respectively) regarding their meaning-making on racial (not ethnic) identity, as well as their subjective experiences on race-related issues. This model proposes two broad phases of white identity development, each of which contain three schemas, or psychological states of being. Phase 1 schema, characterized by a less sophisticated, yet more conflict-ridden, understanding of race, begins with an obliviousness to race and denial of the salience of being White (Contact), to grudging acknowledgment of racism and subsequent defensiveness (Disintegration) to a tentative embracing of the inequitable status quo (Reintegration). Phase

2, marked by deeper reflection, begins with recognizing racism and can include attempts to "rescue" people of color (pseudo-independent), to an active exploration of the systemic nature of racism (immersion/emersion), to a more nuanced and intersectional understanding of the role of whiteness in maintaining racial oppression that is tantamount to a healthy white identity (Autonomy).

Consistent with earlier studies with White adolescents, the researchers found that regardless of age, participants viewed their racial identity as relatively unimportant, with the majority of participants' statements coded in Phase 1 schemas at both time periods. At the same time, there was a shift toward the more meaningful reflection on whiteness and resistance to the status quo characteristic of Phase 2 schema during early adolescence (Time 2), as compared to interviews conducted when students were in middle childhood (Time 1). However, most responses at Time 2 reflected superficial engagement with race among students; while racial inequity was acknowledged, adolescents consistently downplayed its significance and distanced themselves from whiteness, as illustrated by comments such as "you're just a person, so as long as you're a good person, then you're fine." Although the fact that Phase 2 reasoning was more prevalent at Time 2 speaks to the early adolescent period as one of potential growth and learning, there was great variability in students' responses, indicating that sociocognitive development alone cannot account for more complex reasoning around race for White students.

Other important dimensions upon which the salience of race has been examined in White adolescents are the valence (i.e., positive or negative attributions) and centrality (i.e., how central or important) of race and ethnicity as aspects of identity, and the ways these factors might influence their peer interactions. This is particularly relevant in racial-ethnically diverse school settings, where interracial group contact can be experienced and observed. In a recent study published in 2023[10] with White high school students, Megan Satterthwaite-Freiman and colleagues found that an awareness of white privilege and its associated tensions (negative valence of ERI) and less ERI centrality predicted higher levels of intergroup contact among students. To clarify further, students who reported higher levels of ERI centrality—which might be akin to a strong sense of pride in being White—reported less intergroup contact and more avoidance of interracial interactions than those with lower levels of ERI centrality.

Yet, context is important. An earlier study by Jennifer Grossman and Linda Charmaraman published in 2009[11] also examined the role of school composition on White high school students' explanations of the salience of race as a dimension of identity, as well as the meanings they attributed to their racial identity. Participants were drawn from three high schools; two schools were comprised majority of Black and Brown students, with White students as a racial minority, and one where White students comprised the racial majority (84%). Interestingly, and consistent with other research, the reported salience of ERI was low among White participants across all schools, suggesting that simply being around students of color does not inevitably facilitate deeper reflection among White students. A thematic analysis of students' open-ended responses to the question "how important to you is race/ethnicity in describing who you are?" revealed that White students' views across schools were most commonly reflected by two themes: Racial Disengagement, which reflected color-blind and individualist ideologies (e.g., "a person's skin doesn't make a person"), and Positive Regard, which more commonly reflected ethnic, not racial, pride among students (e.g., "being Jewish is a big part of my identity—it connects me with a large group of people who share ancestral history").

Interestingly, school composition accounted for the most variability in students' expressions in the Positive Regard theme; specifically, aspects of (ethnic) Positive Regard were most frequently expressed in the white-minority schools, suggesting that racial-ethnic consciousness was primed in settings where there were more students of color. While this might implicate the peer group as a potential source of growth and learning about race-related issues, findings on the role of peers on White adolescents' attitudes in this area are mixed. For example, some recent studies have found that opportunities for intergroup contact are not associated with more cross-race friendships or race-based conversations among White students,[12] or that the benefits of cross-race friendships for White students are minimized if significant adults (i.e., parents or teachers) do not at least indirectly socialize youth with positive attitudes toward racially and ethnically minoritized youth.[13] These findings lend credence to the abovementioned suggestion that the mere presence of racial-ethnic diversity does not inevitably lead to deeper reflection on the salience of race for White students.

What are the relations between White adolescents' acknowledgment of ERI, white privilege, and systemic forms of societal inequity, and the extent to which they engage in anti-racist actions? This is a logical and important question. In the research literature, the link between youths' understanding of inequity—racial or otherwise—and the impetus to address it has often been studied through the lens of critical consciousness. Initially conceptualized by Freire, a central tenet of critical consciousness is that individuals who have experienced oppression become liberated through a critical analysis of systemic inequality, which leads to critical action aimed at social change.[14] Although individuals or groups with privileged status were not centered in Freire's conceptualization, both he and recent scholars have argued that the development of critical consciousness is essential for socially privileged groups as well; in Freire's words, liberation must come from "the oppressed themselves, and from those who are truly in solidarity with them."[15]

Building upon the work and theorizing of Freire, researchers in psychology have operationalized critical consciousness as having three components: critical reflection, critical motivation/efficacy, and critical action.[16] Although the former two dimensions (especially critical reflection) have been more widely studied across racial groups in adolescence, critical action (i.e., active efforts toward equity and justice) has been studied much less, especially among White youth. As it regards the adolescent period, critical action can take the form of interpersonal acts (e.g., calling out a friend for using a racial slur), school organizing, protesting, digital or social media advocacy, or school and community engagement, to name several examples.

Two recent studies published in 2022 shed a bit of light on this area. Focusing on racial advocacy, Amy Heberle and colleagues examined connections between several forms of critical action (interpersonal, communal, and political) and psychological well-being, and how these relations were influenced by parental and community anti-racism, among Black and White adolescents aged 13–17 years.[17] First, it was the case that White youth engaged in lower levels of all three forms of critical action than Black youth. Parental support had an impact on all youth actions in the political domain (such as attending a protest or preparing an action project), but not on interpersonal or communal domains. For all youth, engagement in interpersonal actions were associated with more depressive symptoms, reflecting the inherent tensions involved in anti-racism within relational contexts, as well as the need for youth support and processing during this time in development. In this regard, both parental and community support for anti-racism were protective factors (associated with well-being) for Black students, but only parental—not community—support was protective for White students. The authors hypothesized that White youth, for whom racism does not pose a direct threat, may not experience an unsupportive community as a threat, or alternately as a source of inspiration, when engaged in anti-racist behaviors and actions.

Using longitudinal data from the Maryland Adolescent Development in Context Study (MADICS), Brandon Dull and colleagues also examined contextual influences on White adolescents' critical action around race and inequity in middle and late adolescence,[18] reasoning that youth do not develop their ideas around race in a vacuum. The researchers used a technique called mixture modeling to capture the various socializing influences that shape how youth make sense of race at ages 16–17. Specifically, with this analytic techniques, typologies, or profiles of students' racial contexts were constructed, based on measures of parent (racial attitudes and conversation), peer (peer conversations about race), and school-based (school diversity and curriculum) influences, each of which are key in adolescence. The profiles generated were then used to predict critical action (political involvement, protesting, participating in civil rights groups or initiatives) approximately two years later, at ages 18–19.

The study findings revealed three distinct profiles of youth's racial contexts: *Low Race Engagement* (63%), characterized by low racial socialization and engagement, and negative parental attitudes toward Black Americans; *Race Conscious* (20%), characterized by more diverse racial-ethnic curriculum and school population, and higher engagement in race-based conversations with parents and peers; and *Race Silent* (17%), characterized by an avoidance of conversation about race, color-blind attitudes among parents, and lower cross-racial friendships. First, it is notable that the majority of students' profiles fell into the *Low Race Engagement* category; this is consistent with several of the studies reviewed here that reflect the ambivalence toward race-related issues among White adolescents that was suggested at the opening of this chapter.

Yet, the associations that were found among the three profiles and students' critical actions hold both excitement and hope regarding the development of anti-racism among White youth. Importantly, being in the *Race Conscious* profile was associated with significantly more reported critical action, as compared to the other two profiles. This finding provides insight into why some White adolescents lean into anti-racist actions, and others do not, while debunking two widely held misconceptions: that simply being a "good person" is all that is required to act against racism, and that color-blindness serves this goal. Rather, a critical consciousness around the salience of race among White adolescents—one that is not inevitable, but that must be nurtured within the contexts that were considered in the study—is a necessary precursor for their anti-racist actions.

The brief literature on White adolescents' engagement with race and identity reviewed in this section provides evidence of its evolving and contextual nature during this developmental period. As well, many of the study findings reflect the ways that adolescents' knowledge and ideas are tethered to individualistic and meritocratic ideologies that uphold deep racial disparities in society, along with the invisibility of whiteness. This is not meant to suggest that White adolescents are uncaring, deficient, or inherently racist, or that they intend to inflict harm upon their peers of color. Rather, it underscores the fact that by virtue of their socialization in a society that is stratified by race and undergirded by white supremacy, they will internalize systemic racial messages that inform their sense of white identity.[19] As teachers, educators, and mentors, as we seek to build our knowledge about the racial positionality, growth, and potential advocacy of White adolescents in the quest for a more racially just society, how do we bring disparate, albeit related, research findings like the ones reviewed here together—especially as it regards the ways we might support students? Do we focus first on students' reflections on and learning about race, or capitalize on both naturally occurring and structured opportunities to engage? What roles do certain experiences, contexts, and emotions play in White adolescents' motivation to participate in race-based conversation and action? The conceptual model presented next provides a compelling, useful, and highly relevant framework with which to consider these questions.

An Integrative Model for the Development of Anti-racist Behavior in White Adolescents

In the social sciences, the role of a conceptual model is to explicate human phenomena and interactions, based on extant theory, research, and observations. Many times, theoretical models attempt to explicate varying dimensions or aspects of a construct and the ways in which such dimensions relate to one another in both linear (i.e., *a* leads to *b*) and bidirectional (i.e., *a* and *b* influence each other) ways. Put simply, conceptual or theoretical models provide a framework for interpreting what we see in the world. Within disciplines or settings that are highly applied—that is, those where people are engaged in real-life activities or endeavors (like education and schooling), a good conceptual model can help us to identify the processes by which a desired outcome might occur, and/or the conditions that are necessary for this to happen. For phenomena that are particularly complex in that they are simultaneously influenced by multiple domains of development (e.g., the way our emotions influence our cognition or social interactions) *and* have historical, ideological, and cultural significance, a contextual model provides us with a "roadmap" of sorts for navigating this complexity—especially in cases where there is more limited knowledge about the construct to begin with. The development of racial consciousness, action, and advocacy in White adolescents is one such example.

In this regard, scholars Genevieve Alice Woolverton and Amy Marks have made an excellent contribution that is worthy of recognition, study, and application. In their 2022 article in the widely respected *Journal of Adolescent Research*, the authors present what they describe as an integrative model for the development of anti-racism in White adolescents.[20] They correctly note that no theoretical models currently exist that attempt to do so, despite an increased focus on the need for White people—including adolescents—to engage in the work of anti-racism in meaningful ways, as opposed to viewing this as the sole work of people of color. As well, the authors point out that qualitative studies highlight that youth of color often perceive a lack of allyship and urgency among their White peers to stand in solidarity with them against racism. It is often the case that ideas about race solidify in adolescence. Although learning about race and anti-racism should be considered lifelong endeavors, the fact that the adolescent period is a developmentally sensitive "window" where youth are particularly well-suited to grapple with complex issues around race with a fresh sense of curiosity, creativity, and emerging autonomy supports the authors' contention for the need for a model that focuses specifically on these years.

Broadly described, the integrative model melds developmental, psychological, and contextual factors that contribute to the readiness and eventual enactment of anti-racism in White youth. To do this, the model synthesizes core ideas and research from four theoretical frames that provide complementary insights into the development of anti-racist interpersonal behavior in White adolescents, all of which have been alluded to or discussed in this book: critical consciousness, color consciousness, anti-racism (i.e., Bonnett's web of resistance), and critical race theory. The model deconstructs White adolescents' growth and understanding of racism into a tripartite framework, comprised cognitive, psychological, and behavioral components. Hence, a strength of the model is that it can account for the multifaceted nature of both racism and anti-racism, highlighting their cognitive and psychological underpinnings. For example, cognitive judgments, such as negative bias or stereotype, are mediated by affective, psychological experiences, such as fear, anger, or guilt, which might lead to behavioral expressions of racism, such as discrimination or hate speech. Alternately, as a White person, learning new informational schemas about racism is also influenced by affective states like guilt, but under certain conditions, may also be accompanied by more adaptive emotions, like empathy and sense of agency, that can lead to anti-racist behaviors.

Figure 3.1 (as it appears in publication) provides a visual representation of the integrative model. Specifically, as depicted in the model, the seeds of anti-racism in White adolescents begin with prerequisite or "predictor" cognitive factors, such as learning about white identity and racism, respectively. These are mediated by psychological factors such as guilt, tolerance for negative emotions, and anger toward injustice; collectively, these serve to build White adolescents' stamina for staying engaged in racial issues, despite the ease with which they can easily disengage, due to white privilege. As a result, behaviors associated with anti-racism, such as the ability to name, critique, and act against it, are more likely to occur.

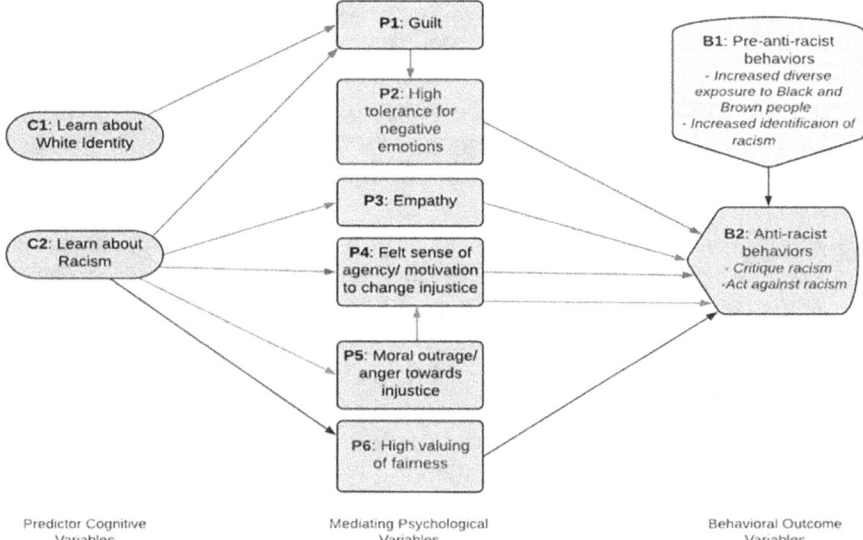

Figure 3.1. An Integrative Model for the Development of Anti-racist Behavior in White Youth. Red indicates cognitive variables, orange indicates psychological variables, and blue indicates behavioral variables. *Woolverton, G. A., & Marks, A. K. (2022). An integrative model for the development of anti-racist behavior in white adolescents.* Journal of Adoloescent Research, *1–33.* https://doi.org/10.1177/07435584221091492.

Woolverton and Marks position their integrative model not as prescriptive, but one that is meant to generate future research and theorizing in this area. As well, they acknowledge that its implications for practice are preliminary; that is, the authors' recommendations for how to engage White adolescents in each component of the model (e.g., teaching mindfulness-based skills to tolerate negative emotions as they regard racial phenomena) have not yet been widely studied. Despite its evolving nature, the argument being made here is that because the relations among its tripartite components are empirically supported, the model serves as a powerful tool to inform efforts to skillfully intervene with adolescents to foster anti-racism, and helps us to understand the possible reasons why our collective efforts may fall short. To be clear, guiding White adolescents in their engagement with each component of the model with intentionality is essential, as are authentic opportunities for them to experience what the model specifies as "pre-anti-racist" behaviors, such as cross-racial interactions and the ability to identify racism when it occurs. In this regard, it is critical to stress that the processes involved in reaching the behavioral outcomes of anti-racism that are depicted are neither inevitable nor assured; that is, as documented in the literature, emotions such as guilt, anger, and fear can effectively stagnate and block further growth and learning about race and racism, *unless* additional supports, such as structured conversations, empathy-building, or opportunities for personal reflection are provided. The potential for teachers and educators to create, facilitate, and monitor such opportunities is an exciting and fruitful one—albeit the challenges in doing so—that will be addressed in subsequent chapters.

Indeed, Woolverton and Marks' model provides cohesion and insight into the research studies reviewed earlier in this chapter, especially when we consider themes like low engagement with race, and more limited salience of white identity among youth. In the final section of this chapter, we turn to the voices of the White students who participated in our two projects. Indeed, while it will be easy to locate their stories within both the research studies and the integrative model, their narratives lend additional depth, nuance, and contextual specificity to these contributions. Consistent with the presentation of themes from students of color in chapter 2, each thematic category that was generated through analyses is again illustrated with a student quotation. For ease, White student participants and demographic characteristics are presented in table 3.1 below. Of note, all but one of the White students were participants in Study 2 (i.e., Schools C and D), so the findings should be interpreted with this in mind.

Table 3.1. Demographic Characteristics of Project Participants Who Identified as White (*n* = 15)

Name (Pseudonym)	Age	Grade	Gender	Race-Ethnicity	Place of Birth
School A					
Joel	12	7	Male	White	US
School C					
Lila	12	6	Female	White	US
Solomon	13	8	Male	White	US
Trey	13	7	Male	White	US
Aidan	12	6	Male (for now)	White	US
Sue	12	6	Female	White	US
School D					
Agatha	11	6	Female	White	France
Ivan	12	6	Male	White	US
Clara	13	7	Female	White	US
Geoff	14	8	Male	White	US
Gia	13	8	Female	White	China
April	12	6	Female	White and Jewish	US
Natalia	13	7	Female	White	US
Aline	13	7	Female	White	US
Brit	13	8	Nonbinary/they	White American	US

HOW, AND IN WHAT WAYS, ARE RACE, ETHNICITY, SCHOOL DIVERSITY, AND IDENTITY SALIENT TO WHITE STUDENTS IN MIDDLE SCHOOL?

"I Can Broaden My Circle of Understanding"

Approximately half of all White students characterized race-ethnicity as important in school because school diversity yielded important opportunities for learning. Students described this in terms of learning about other people, cultures, and cultural practices, such as holidays, religious traditions, or material artifacts. In the majority of examples, students did not make reference to this happening primarily within the classroom, via formal instruction or classroom content; rather, similar to what was expressed by students of color, diverse friends and the peer group provided the context for this. According to students, this often happened spontaneously, through everyday school interactions, such as when Sue explained that the opportunity for cross-racial interactions at her school could occur "at random," throughout the day, as when "sometimes, they'll be someone at my table, and I don't know anything about their race or ethnicity. And so, I can learn about it." Several students noted that being part of a racial-ethnically diverse school provided a context for them to learn about racial, ethnic, and gender-affirming language, or the "right terms to use," as Sue later described it.

In addition to acquiring more information about racial-ethnic differences, students also referenced other cognitive benefits of being part of a diverse school environment, especially as it regarded their perspective-taking abilities. For example, Trey spoke of being able to interact with different cultural groups in school as "kinda cool," because it helped him to understand how "they see the world differently." Similarly, April referred to the way her "circle of understanding" was influenced by meeting ethnically diverse people:

> For me, meeting different people with different ethnicities [is important] because that way I can broaden my circle of understanding. So I can understand them better.

In fact, in the same interview segment, April names ethnic diversity as the best thing about her school, describing the school environment as a "welcoming" space that affords her the opportunity for a larger network of friends:

> The best thing about my school is that there's a lot of different ethnicities that are welcome in the same, in the same space, and um, actually most of my friends are from a different ethnicity. So, I like making friends from different ethnicities because it, I guess widens my circle of friends, because then they know other

friends who know other friends, and it's just much easier for me to have more friends.

Hence, the value of school racial and ethnic diversity as a valuable source of growth and learning was undoubtedly a prominent theme across all study participants, regardless of race. However, one aspect of this that appeared only in the narratives of White students was the way that such learning could function as a source of discomfort or offense; that is, although it is reasonable to conclude that students of color appreciated the sensitivity of cross-racial interactions, there were no caveats expressed in their descriptions of its value that would presumably outweigh its benefits for learning. In contrast, although explicitly addressed by only five White students, there were inherent tensions embedded in what Trey characterized as the "difficult topic" of race—especially as it regarded issues of identity and emotions, as described by some participants. In the segment below, Lila vividly illustrates the unease and uncertainty around explicit conversations around religion (which she brings up spontaneously) and race that exist among both students *and* teachers, where "feelings [could] get hurt," or things could "go wrong," causing things to "escalate":

> I think it would be great to like talk about where you're from and like what you believe in. But like we're not allowed to talk about our religion . . . but like the teacher, they're like sensitive to stuff like that, cause they are trying not to, they're trying to do the right thing and I don't want to be discriminatory—somebody's feelings to get hurt. Cause that could really easily escalate . . . but like, it could also be like somebody could be like curious and ask a question about like their race, and they could take it the wrong way . . . there's like a ton of reasons it could go wrong, but I think it should be talked about, and we shouldn't like *not* talk about it because something that might happen that might be like uncomfortable.

Using more concrete terms, Sue references the way that using incorrect language or terminology around race and ethnicity can contribute to an "awkward" situation. According to her, although race and ethnicity were rarely brought up in any class, it was "kinda" introduced in her English class:

> Right now, in my English class, we're reading a book about 1960s, and how there was a lot of separation, and I like how they're kinda introducing it. Because it's awkward if you're talking about something, and but you don't know, like, the right terms to use, and stuff like that.

In a comment that makes a distinction between the messages received by her school and the larger society (i.e., media), Brit also identifies the presence of negative sentiments about learning from and interacting with racial-ethnically diverse "other" people:

> I do not have any problem with it [interacting with racial-ethnically diverse groups]. I love learning about people's cultures, and I just love getting to know different people. I've heard so many like—no people in this school—but I've heard like, on the news it's been like oh, you cannot like, be friends with these like, people from other—who are other races or ethnicities because like, it's bad and like, well why is it bad? Like, it's great to like, like, meet all these different people.

What is noteworthy in each of the examples above is the way that students express a desire to persist, stay engaged, or commit to learning about race through diverse interactions, despite the challenges that might come from this, from their perspectives. Indeed, Brit's question of "why is it bad?" to embrace racial-ethnic diversity and interactions is one that White adolescents will likely grapple with, due to their inevitable consumption of explicit and implicit messages that inform their sense of white identity as superior or ideal.[21] They need and deserve support and reassurance to help them to understand such racialized complexities.

"They Choose All Kids"

Despite their ability to identify sources of value in racial-ethnic diversity, an area in which students clearly felt that race and ethnicity did not matter regarded what they perceived as "equal treatment" in the school environment; 10 out of 15 students commented explicitly on the presumption of equal treatment across race, often justifying their perceptions with generalized statements such as "everybody is just treated the same." According to students, ethnicity-race influenced neither how they were treated by teachers, nor peers. Since this theme was also present in the narratives of students of color, there may be some developmental continuity in adolescents' sense of what constitutes "fairness" at this age, irrespective of race. To clarify, as discussed in the last chapter, a fair school is one where students expect to be treated the same and given equal opportunities; the nuances that might exist in the delivery of differential treatment to students according to factors such as race-ethnicity, ability, gender, or the like may not be appreciated by students in early adolescence, and may need explicit clarification. We see this in Joel's response to the question of whether things like race or ethnicity were important in school, where he asserts the importance of "all kids" being chosen:

> They [teachers] don't really care about race, like, they don't choose anyone because of their race . . . it's [race] not really important. Because if you only

choose on certain people because of their race, then it's not fair to the other kids, so the teachers don't really do that. They choose all kids.

In justifying their perceptions of equal treatment, Natalia was the only student to use racial or cultural identity affirmation by the school as evidence; she noted that in School D "everyone's treated the same and everyone's valued for who they are—like most holidays for each culture are observed" (a perception that was refuted by one of her peers, Anwar, in the last chapter). Rather, aside from more generalized assertions of equal treatment, several students made a link to student behaviors; specifically, that one's behaviors or actions determined how you would be treated by teachers in school, especially as it regarded consequences. For example, Trey shared that he felt that "punishments are equal across like no matter what race you identify with, or gender." Ivan elaborated on this; in clarifying "the person and your behavior" as determining factors with regard to student treatment, he moves on to equivocate the experiences of "Black" and "White" students in a statement that shows clear awareness of the potential salience of race, in his assurance that there are "no racist comments" in school:

> We are all treated the same. It depends on the person and your behavior. But there are no racist comments. Some people are treated differently, but like, it's not because they are Black, but because of their behaviors and actions, not what they look like. Some Black kids get in trouble, and some don't, and some White kids get in trouble, and some don't.

Like Ivan's mention of "racist comments," in pondering the ways that equal treatment was evidenced in school, several students used similar, race-based counterexamples (i.e., the absence of racialized treatment) to make their point, which attests to their ability to conceptualize and notice race and racism in early adolescence. Brit makes explicit reference to this, commenting that, in her experience, "I have never seen anyone, um, really be I guess, *discriminated* against because of their race or anything. What I've seen is that most people are treated the same." Although the majority of students did not implicate race in this way within this category, it is still important to highlight, since many White adolescents struggle to differentiate naming acts of racism with being or endorsing racism, especially if they hold color-blind attitudes.[22] As illustrated in the following segment, in response to the question of whether race or ethnicity were important in school, Clara noted that "they aren't really important, but they're not ignored, either." She went on to clarify that while people often spoke about "where they are from," they were never treated differently, and certainly never "targeted" or "separated" because of that:

I mean, people talk about where they're from and stuff, but they don't treat people differently, like . . . if someone is like from a certain place and we're like learning about that, like we might ask questions to them. But like, we don't target them or anything. They don't like separate people based on like activities and stuff based on like race and ethnicity.

Clara addresses equal treatment by both teachers and peers in the above segment in her use of different pronouns; while it seems clear that "they" refers to teachers who have the power to "separate" students, her use of "we" in her explanation that *"we* don't target *them"* is more interesting, especially considering that she is a White person. Similarly, the following example may be evidence of Solomon's implicit awareness (not necessarily endorsement) of racial (white) superiority, in explaining his perception that although teachers care about people's identities, they don't think of a "White person as better than a Black person":

They [teachers] don't like think of people that different. Like, they don't think like, "Oh, he's White, he's better than, oh, than a Black person." But they don't think of it like that. They're just like, "All right. Well, like, I'm there to like support you." It's, it's— race doesn't really ever come into play.

In sum, White students perceived the climate of their schools as one that was fair for all students and characterized by equal treatment, regardless of race or ethnicity. Notwithstanding this, the next thematic category provides more nuanced insights into the perception expressed by many students that "race doesn't really ever come into play," as phrased by Solomon above. As students' narratives attest, the story is a bit more complicated.

"There's a Lot of Awareness of Race—I Wouldn't Say a Lot, Lot, Lot, but It Comes Up"

The thematic quotation above, contributed by Geoff, is emblematic of some of the complexity, contradiction, and hesitancy around calibrating the salience and impact of race in the school environment among White student participants. First, Geoff's perception that "there's a lot of awareness of race" among his peers refutes key elements of a color-blindness. Although it could be argued that students' perceptions of equal treatment across race is a dimension of color-blindness, only two White students explicitly used or promoted color-blind tropes that are central to this ideology, such as not "noticing" race, the salience of one "human race," or that all races are "the same." For example, Ivan's succinct comment that "we are all equal" is an example of this. This was a surprising finding, considering the pervasiveness of color-blindness among the White populace in the United States,[23] but one that may reflect the sociopolitical context (i.e., societal racial consciousness) in which Study 2 was conducted.

Instead, the nuances in students' assessments of the salience of race were most strikingly illustrated in the ways they discussed their friendships and peer interactions. Similar to what was reported by students of color, White students readily assured us that they enjoyed being in an environment where they could have cross-racial friendships. For most students, this was described as something that was devoid of tensions and not very noteworthy, as illustrated briefly in the following responses across schools, each of which occurred in respective conversations regarding the ways that race and ethnicity were important (or not) in their school interactions:

> We [peers] all just get along. It's like everyone like mixed together . . . it's [race] not really a thing. Everyone just accepts each other. (Joel, School A)

> When I do hang out with people who are different than me, because it's like obvious in how we live or what we believe, sometimes we talk about it. But like sometimes we don't. (Lila, School C)

> It [having diverse friendships] feels the same as meeting kids from my same, like, ethnic and racial group. (Agatha, School D)

In each of the example above, students simultaneously value having cross-racial friendships, but consider them rather unremarkable. On the other hand, Brit and April spoke more pointedly about seeking out cross-racial friendships more intentionally, and the ways this conferred specific benefits. The segment below builds upon Brit's earlier reflection on the benefits of learning from people outside one's own racial-ethnic group, despite her perception of the societal message that having racially diverse friendships was "wrong":

> One of my friends, um, my best friends, are like um, the ones, my best friends, they're all, we're all different races and it's—there's nothing wrong with it. I don't know why there should ever be a problem with it.

Similarly, although her language is a bit circular, April describes the way she views the tendency among some of her peers to stick to their racial-ethnic in-group as "shameful," and indicative of them wanting to have friends that are "copies" of themselves, from her view:

> If [peers] are not treated the same as people who would be the same race or ethnicity as they are, well, shame on them. Because they just wanna be friends with who they are as well. They wanna be, they wanna be friends with copies of them. The benefits of [cross-racial friendships] is because [student name], she's my best friend. She's on the robotics team. And because of her I think

I'm going to join her team this year. And I'm going to be like the only White person on that team, and I'm proud of it. I'm like, oh, okay, I was smart enough to join that team.

Across all students, April's comment is one of the most open and explicit in how it conveys a willingness to connect with racial-ethnically diverse peers. It also illustrates the way that diverse peers can serve as a gateway to new experiences and learning for students. However, we also see evidence of April's internalization of racial stereotypes regarding which students are "smart enough" to be on the robotics team—students who she later identified as pan-Asian. Although April does not acknowledge this as a stereotype in the example above, students' recognition of racial-ethnic stereotypes or racialized language or behaviors was a final dimension upon which their awareness of race in the environment was reflected. Although this was also the case for students of color, as evidenced in the previous chapter, White students' reflections in this area were different in both scope and content; that is, as suggested in Geoff's thematic quote, White students have some "awareness" of race, but "not a lot" of it, especially as it regards being the recipient of a racialized comment or action. Put another way, several White students (six in total) discussed racialized language or behaviors as something they had observed within the peer group, but had not personally experienced, in contrast to the larger percentage of students of color who reported personal experiences with racism by both teachers and peers. Ivan and Sue were the most direct in their reflections on examples of racist behaviors at school; while Ivan readily acknowledged "some people are racist . . . and they even make jokes about gay people," he assured the interviewer that "it's a minority of kids who do it." In the exchange below, Sue identifies some students being "ignored" or "not as part of the community" using race-neutral language, which the interviewer attempts to clarify:

Interviewer: So what about students—is race or ethnicity a thing for students? Do you see it come up?

Sue: A couple times. Like, someone will come over, and people will kinda just ignore them. Or not technically ignoring them, they just won't be as part of the community, I guess, and like the conversation, so.

Interviewer: Okay. And so you're thinking, hmmm, is something going on here? Do you think those being excluded are those kids who aren't White, or have you not noticed a difference there?

Sue: Yeah. It usually is kids who aren't White.

More often, however, students (the remaining four) spoke about racialized stereotypes in the form of teasing or jokes that "we know [are not] being rude, it's just jokes, it's just stereotypes," as Joel described, that were not meant to be hurtful. In a way that was strikingly similar to some reports from students of color, several students observed that some of their peers often made jokes about their own racial-ethnic group, but that such comments were often hard to interpret. Geoff reflects this uncertainty in the compelling segment below; while he acknowledges the presence of "weird, racist jokes," he also shows hesitancy or what might appear to be resistance to legitimizing whether they were "racial" or not:

> There's a lot of weird, racist jokes. I'm not sure if whether that's just like, jokes, or if they mean it's actually important. There are lots of ways to interpret jokes, and I don't know why we're in the era of interpreting jokes. Sometimes I, I . . . some of them make jokes, like, "is that racially motivated?" It's like, no—you're just being a jerk.

Hence, it appears that White students' "awareness" of race, as Geoff phrased it in this thematic category, emerges primarily within the peer context, where it "comes up" during what might be ongoing, intimate, conversations that occur throughout the school day among peers, when adults (i.e., teachers) are not present. Although this might be expected (and often welcomed) in adolescence, due to youths' increased need for personal space and autonomy, it also leaves White youth without adult mentors who can help them grapple with some of the questions and ambiguity around racial phenomena that were expressed by students in this section. This ambiguity—namely, the ambiguity of being White—was very prominent in students' narratives around their ERI, a subject to which we now turn.

"Being [White], You Don't Have . . . Really Important Culture"

All students in the study were asked to identify both their race and/or ethnicity in their own words at the beginning of their interview. As conversations progressed, interviewers referred back to the way students identified when asking about their ERI, and the ways it might be important; for example, "when we first started talking, you identified as [race-ethnicity]. Is that an important thing for you? Is it important in this school?" As might be expected in early adolescence, many White students described their race-ethnicity as a generalized dimension of self—one of many characteristics that made up who they were. Developmentally, this is not inconsistent with the way students of color often discussed the salience of their race-ethnicity in chapter 2, or in other published works by our research team.[24] Indeed, young adolescents are actively engaged in the normative developmental task of fusing different aspects of identity (e.g., gender, religion, vocation) into a more integrated and stable sense of self, as well as considering—or reconsidering—what these different aspects mean in relation to their place in society.

However, consistent with the research studies reviewed at the beginning of this chapter, the *centrality* and *importance* of race-ethnicity as a dimension of identity was markedly different for White students. In stark contrast to the way students of color described race-ethnicity as something they "[carried] around wherever [they] go," race and ethnicity were described as more unremarkable characteristics of self by White students—factors that didn't "really come into play that much," as noted by Solomon. For example, in response to the direct question of whether and how being a White ethnic (if ethnicity was named) was important, several students answered succinctly, as Natalia did: "I don't think being White really matters. I was born this way." Ivan's response to the question was also brief and includes the perception of equality that was centered in the previous theme: "No—there's no talk of that here. We're all equal."

Hence, the significance and meaning of being White was elusive to students, marked by its inaccessibility; that is, students had a harder time articulating why, or in what ways, it might be important or might matter. On the one hand, students viewed this in terms of their ongoing interactions at school—interactions that did not, in their assessment, appear to be influenced at all by white ethnic identity. Because of this, race didn't appear to make a "difference" in their school lives, as the following similar comments by Clara and Gia, respectively, reflect:

> I mean, it's [being White and Irish] not like super important to me, it doesn't make a huge difference for me. I mean, it doesn't make much of a difference. They like people don't really pay attention to that, usually.
>
> Race, I don't think it really matters to me. Um, gender, it also doesn't matter. I don't really see any difference with anyone if they're a different gender or a different race.

In both comments above, we see that being White is perceived as something that people "don't pay attention to," as Clara noted. Several students framed this in terms of their inability to name concrete aspects of being White, not only as exemplified in the segment opening this chapter from Brit but also as this was viewed in relation to other racial-ethnic groups; that is, race and ethnicity had meaning for "other groups," but not those within the racial category of white. In the following comment, Agatha directly addresses what she feels is a lack of "culture" in her racial (Caucasian, as she named it) and ethnic (French) background, especially when compared to the "culture" and "tradition" that exist for other racial-ethnic groups (which the interviewer did not ask her to clarify):

> Um, well I guess being um, Caucasian and French, you don't have, like, a lot of, like culture, really important culture . . . I guess there's other, like ethnicities where, like, cultures have more tradition.

The limited salience of ERI as rooted in a lack of connection and access to racial, ethnic, and cultural history or traditions is also illustrated in the interaction between Geoff and the interviewer in the exchange below:

> *Interviewer:* So, when we first started, you had talked about being White and European. Is that important to you?
>
> *Geoff:* Uh, absolutely, pretty much not? Um I honestly don't try to actively sort of avoid thinking about like that, because I . . . don't think it's that important to who I am or who other people are that much. I think it's more important their personalities and hobbies and all that. I mean, especially ethnicity. Because it's like, I'm—it's like many generations of Americans, of many people born in America as my ancestors. And then when you get really far back, you're really branching into 30 different places in Europe. But, none of those cultures are really, like, present. So, it's not that important.

While Geoff's reflection clarifies the way that he sees his diverse ethnic background as both diffuse and inaccessible, this was not the case for some students. Specifically, several students either self-identified with ethnic or ethno-religious heritage, rather than race, or identified as both (e.g., White and Jewish), but clearly connected more with ethnicity. On the one hand, this illustrates the complexity of both race and ethnicity as distinct constructs, and the ways they are often conflated in research and practice (i.e., not just among adolescents). In terms of the ways that ethnicity was described as meaningful by students, this often centered on familial history or stories, or cultural artifacts, as Sue, who identified simply as Italian, described:

> It's [being Italian] important, just because my grandmother, immigrated here, so I'm like, we have a funny story in our family where one of my ancestors . . . they changed his last name to [name]. So like, our family and our house—you could clearly tell we were Italian if you went in. Like, we have some like paintings that my grandfather did, and like, a bunch of Italian things in there.

Jewish identity was prominent for several students, who also drew upon aspects of symbolic, material culture as what made "being Jewish" important; although Solomon commented that his ethno-religious identity—Jewish—did not "come into play much" at school, he noted that it was inherently important because "I have like a Star of David that my grandparents gave me." April, who identified as both Jewish and White, reflects her awareness of anti-Semitism—described in her words as "bullying"—in her description of why being Jewish is a particularly important aspect of her identity:

> Being Ashkenazi Jew is kind of important to me, because I want to show people that I am not afraid to be bullied because of my culture, and that I will stand up if I am bullied for my culture. And it's an important part of me because it's important for me to have a Bat Mitzvah, it's important for me to show that I am who I am. And I'm not gonna change my culture because of that.

As Sue, Solomon, and April's examples illustrate, the reasons White students might identify more closely with ethnicity, as opposed to race, can be influenced by factors such as cultural history (including historic oppression), family context, or familial traditions. From a more critical perspective—especially as it regards the development of an anti-racist consciousness and anti-racist actions as delineated in Woolverton and Marks' integrative model, although connection and pride in ethnic heritage are valuable and most worthy of celebration, for White people, including White adolescents, ethnic identification that is devoid of the acknowledgment of race as a meaningful category can serve to distance oneself from whiteness and its implications.

In this regard, as discussed throughout this book, the historic role of whiteness (of which white identity is a part) in perpetuating racism, as well as the role that racial dominance plays in blocking the salience of being White for students, was more directly acknowledged by only two students. In response to the question of the importance of her white identity, Aline quickly shifts the topic to racism; from her response, it seems that she is struggling to understand the relation between white identity (an individual construct) and racism (a systemic construct), something she comments that has been "talked about," but that students don't really "learn about":

> Ummm . . . I don't know if it [being White] is important. I mean, we've talked about, like racism. Like we don't really learn about it. There's just like times, I guess, like during World Geo, maybe. Like when we talk about, like we've talked about like the Holocaust in English. But I don't really feel like we have any big units on it.

In response to the same question by the interviewer, Trey seems to have a bit more information. Specifically, Trey's response reflects some understanding of the role that being a member of the dominant racial group—both in society and at school, as he notes—renders one's positionality and its impact (what Trey refers to as "the pressure") invisible:

> It [being White] doesn't feel important to me, and I think um, part of that is being the dominant race, in many ways. That becomes like—you aren't as aware of your position and you don't feel the pressure of, um, like if you were Black, if you identified as Black, you might feel a stronger, like feeling of that because you realize you're other than White, which is more of the dominant race here. And definitely the majority here.

The fact that only a few White students—Trey being foremost among them as featured above—articulated an understanding of elements of systemic racism, along with the way that white identity itself is both a "product and ingredient" of this, as characterized by Woolverton and Marks,[25] suggests a few things. First, it is likely the case that these are difficult concepts for early adolescents to grasp, especially without intentional study, reflection, and guided support. Second, is also likely that schools and teachers do not feel informed, confident, or inspired to provide such support, especially in our present moment, and hence, either do not address elements of systemic racism, or do so in a cursory way. Our findings from both White students and students of color provide strong evidence of the latter possibility, as suggested by the many comments that reflected students' perceptions of brief or limited content around race-related issues in their classes, such as Aline's comment above that "we don't have any big units on it [racism]." Although specific strategies for engaging adolescents in the study of race, ethnicity, identity, and racism (as well as other forms of oppression) in developmentally appropriate ways will be discussed in chapter 5, an initial starting point must be that White adolescents must come to see themselves as integral and relevant to these conversations and to see race as something that matters for *them*. As will be shown in the last theme below, several White students articulated the benefits of learning about race and ethnicity as learning about *other* people, but not about themselves.

"We'll Talk About Identity . . . and How Other People Might Identify"

While the content of White students' perceptions of the salience of race, ethnicity, and identity are captured in the previous thematic categories, a close examination of the *way* some students responded to questions around the relevance of these constructs revealed something important; specifically, the way that being White served as the reference point upon which being "different" was defined, or upon which "differences" could be celebrated. Put another way, racial or ethnic diversity was something that White students could benefit from, yet were not themselves a part of. Brit's response to the interviewer's question of whether differences in people's race or ethnicity were acknowledged or celebrated at School D is illustrative:

> Oh yeah, definitely. Definitely. So um, at this school, I, we celebrated, um, Black History Month. And there was a . . . it was upstairs and it was like a little thing celebrating all of these, um, Black Amer— like these Black people in history, and it was pretty cool . . . and they do a bunch of stuff like that, and they celebrated Chinese New Year, where they did a week, or was it, it was either one, or Lunar New Year. Where they did, like, a week where you can go to like, answer all these questions about the culture and stuff. And it was pretty cool.

In this quotation, Brit automatically interprets "difference" as something that applies to people/groups of color—something she views positively and notes as "pretty cool." Although it is fair to say that Brit is responding to the question according to the opportunities that the school provides, the immediacy of her response might suggest she has come to expect this pattern; that is, that celebrations of "difference" are celebrations of people who aren't White, thereby positioning White people and white history as the default group, not worthy of examination or celebration.

This positioning of oneself as "outside" issues around racial and ethnic diversity was also seen in the narratives of several other students, via the use of two discursive strategies: the use of the term "other" as an adjective, and the use of the pronoun "they," both of which appeared to be used to refer to students of color. In the following segment, we see the way Trey first characterizes being White as *unimportant* in school and immediately shifts the conversation to aspects of identity and difference, something he considers to be about "other" people. Soon after, he considers race and ethnicity as an *important* part of "who you are," while immediately shifting back to a focus on "other" people:

> *Interviewer:* Do you think race and ethnicity are important in this school? Like, for you, is being White important in school?
>
> *Trey:* I can't think of a way it'd be important. I mean, we'll talk about identity and um different, how other people might identify.
>
> *Interviewer:* Do you think teachers and adults at this school care about kids' ethnicity or race, or does it not matter so much?
>
> *Trey:* I think adults understand that it's an important part of who you are. Um, like so you understand other peoples' cultures and where they're coming from, un, um, to help everyone make sure they're being inclusive and not discriminating against others for, because they're different.

In Trey's response, we again see the way being White is removed as a category of identity that has relevance, the way that it does for "other" people—people or groups Trey does not explicitly name, but characterizes as "different." Similarly, the segment by April that was illustrated in the first thematic category regarding her assessment of the benefits of having diverse friendships contains a similar focus on learning about people other than herself:

> I do [like meeting friends of different ethnicities], because for me, meeting different people with different ethnicities are better because that way I can broaden my circle of like, understanding. So I can understand them better.

We can see the potential for reflective learning that is embedded in April's comment; that is, the process of deepening her understanding of other people that comes from being part of a diverse environment also brings with it opportunities to learn more about herself as a White person with an ethnic, Jewish heritage. The fact that April does not articulate this possibility is significant and predictable due to the way whiteness is normalized in both school and the larger society.

Hence, although the particular discourse strategies used to convey the irrelevance of whiteness in relation to racial and ethnic diversity and identity as presented above were not found in a majority of White students' transcripts, they are lifted out and featured here because of their strong implications for theory and practice around the promotion of an anti-racist consciousness necessary for racial advocacy among White adolescents. An understanding that all people—not just "other" people—have both a personal identity and multiple, overlapping social identities (such as race/being white) that influence one's perspective, experiences, and ways of being in the world is a critical prerequisite for these things to happen. White students need time, space, and support to make these kinds of connections.[26]

CONCLUSION

The thematic categories that were generated from the narratives of White student participants as presented in this chapter suggest that their perceptions of the salience of ethnicity-race in their school environment and identity constructions are largely unsophisticated, uncritical, and contradictory, yet also infused with curiosity, thoughtfulness, openness, and possibility. Specifically:

- White students recognized the value and richness of a racial and ethnically diverse environment and saw it as an opportunity for learning about other people, other racial, ethnic, or cultural groups, and other perspectives.

- White students acknowledged that conversations around race, ethnicity, and identity could be "difficult" ones, where things can easily "go wrong."
- White students perceive their school environment as inclusive, evidenced by what they perceived as equal treatment of students across race and ethnicity.
- White students are not color-blind; they understand that race and ethnicity are salient constructs in society and can function as sources of discrimination and oppression, but since their cross-racial interactions at school were often viewed as positive, they struggled to identify whether certain comments or behaviors were "racial" or not.
- Overall, the salience of race as a dimension of identity was low for White students; that is, being white did not hold significant cultural meaning for them, nor did they view it as something they—or other people—really thought about, cared about, or "noticed."
- Whiteness, or being white, was often cast as the default reference point upon which "difference" was defined or considered by students.

The summative points above fit within and lend specificity to the cognitive, psychological, and pre-anti-racist components of anti-racist behavior in White adolescents that are delineated in Woolverton and Marks' integrative model; for example, learning about white identity and racism (cognitive), tolerance for negative emotions and valuing of fairness (psychological), and exposure to Black and Brown people (pre-anti-racist behaviors). Indeed, early adolescents have the capacity to engage in the quest for racial equity, but our findings suggest that they find it hard to see themselves as implicated in the journey.

Hence, it is essential that educators and schools consider the role and potential that White young people must play in the promotion of racial and ethnic justice in both their schools and communities and commit to guiding them in this endeavor. The findings in this chapter provide insights into both where White adolescent students are in the process, as well as exciting possibilities for where they can be expected to go. Before they can support students in this work; however, educators must begin with themselves. In a democratic society, public schools are uniquely positioned—although not uniformly supported—to create sustained models of equity for all students to thrive. For U.S. schools to fulfill this potential, White teachers must move from a place of racial complacency, to one of honesty, radical reflection, and critical multicultural praxis—even amidst—perhaps especially amidst—the polarizing discourse around race that is often promulgated by those outside the field of education. Engaging in such praxis with intention, commitment, creativity, and renewed vigor is the subject of the next chapter.

Chapter 4

Starting with Our (White) Selves
Teachers, Teaching, and Race in Middle School

Interviewer: What are things you really like about your teachers?

Maybe they, um, raised awareness about things that's going on. Like, they talk about with us instead of just pretending like it's not going on. Um, like the war [Ukraine] that's been going on. Our teachers have like—yeah, have talked about it, and it was, like, pretty good to just talk about it. Instead of ignoring it, you know? (Agatha, White, sixth-grade student)

Teachers, like, they respect you, I guess. Most of the classrooms they've got like, "I'm an ally," for sexual orientation and stuff. They'll be there for you. Like, no matter what sexual orientation or race you are. I see posters in most of the classrooms, they'll say "I'm an ally" and they've got like a rainbow flag thing. (Hope, Chinese, sixth-grade student)

Sixth-grade students Agatha and Hope put a lot on the table in their responses to the question of what they really liked about their teachers, as illustrated in the opening segments above. Indeed, few would argue against the belief that an important role of a teacher is to provide students with "raised awareness" about the world in which they are part, as Agatha notes. Yet, it is likely more complicated than that, since this belief begs the question: awareness about what? The subject of war? What it means to be an ally? One's sexuality? Race? Broadly viewed, these and other presumably "divisive" topics might be among those targeted by the many "divisive concepts laws" that have been enacted since 2021 in states like New Hampshire, Oklahoma, South Dakota, Florida, and Arizona, to name only a few across the country.[1] Although the definition of what constitutes "divisive" can be traced back to Trump's Executive Order 13950 (which was repealed by Biden in 2020), much of the language of the order, considered by many to be vague, erudite, and confusing, has been incorporated into state legislation applying to public schools.[2] This sets up a context in which educators' right to free expression and obligation to engage students in critical thinking about important issues is threatened, especially in K–12 settings, where teachers' claims on academic freedom are less robust than they are in higher education.[3]

But despite the content and scope of various legislative or executive actions, issues such as the ones named by students above are still omnipresent in the lives of young people. Legislating, restricting, or banning "controversial" issues from school curricula does not magically remove them from students' consciousness, especially during the adolescent period, when students are capable of higher-level thinking and reasoning. Such issues are certainly on the minds of Agatha and Hope, as we see above. If topics like war, sexuality, or race can emerge spontaneously during interview conversations with people that students do not know well, as was the case here, it seems reasonable to surmise that students might raise such topics even more frequently with a trusted teacher or mentor. As teachers, how will we facilitate and respond to such conversations in sensitive and developmentally appropriate ways?

This chapter will address the inherent complexities that exist for teachers as they attempt to integrate social justice content around race, identity, and systemic oppression and privilege into the curriculum in ways that are relevant, informed, and courageous. In recent decades, scholars of educational policy have noted that the imposition of increasingly bureaucratic, private-sector logics (e.g., competition, high-stakes testing, narrow assessment, efficiency) on public schooling writ large poses a threat to teachers' sense of agency and efficacy.[4] Despite this, the vast majority of teachers remain steadfast, determined, and committed professionals.[5] The fundamental and ethical role that teachers play in nurturing an educated, informed, and empathic citizenry must be respected and honored. Indeed, this kind of pedagogy lies at the core of what renowned educator, writer, and activist bell hooks referred to as democratic education, where school classrooms are part of real life and real issues, and where learning is co-constructed through authentic teacher-student interactions.[6] A central tenet of this book is that supporting students in the development of critical consciousness, racial awareness, and racial allyship is tantamount to democratic education, and that all teachers take part in this initiative, regardless of their racial background. After all, we bring all of who we are to this work. Creating and enacting a vision of racial equity and justice takes collaboration among people with diverse social identities—racial or otherwise.

When it comes to the work that goes on with youth in schools, however, such a vision, and however laudable and aspirational, isn't as egalitarian as it sounds. This is especially the case when one considers the lack of diversity within the teaching profession in the United States. As noted in the opening chapter, the vast majority of public and private school teachers in K–12 classrooms in the United States are racially White and female. Specifically, according to the 2020–2021 National Teacher and Principals Survey, a nationally representative sample survey of U.S. public and private K–12 schools, principals, and teachers that is disseminated by the National Center for Education Statistics (NCES), roughly 80% of public school teachers identified as non-Hispanic White, 9% as Hispanic, 6% as non-Hispanic Black, 2% as non-Hispanic Asian, and 2% as non-Hispanic, multiracial.[7] Roughly three-quarters of both public and private K–12 school teachers identified as female (77% and 75%, respectively).[8] Racial demographics in school leadership shows a similar profile, with 77% and 83% of school principals identifying as White in public and private schools, respectively.

It is critical to acknowledge the implications of the racial-ethnic profile of teachers in the United States; that is, while access to a racially and culturally diverse teacher workforce is beneficial for all students, research continues to show that educational outcomes for children improve if their teachers are from the same racial background.[9] Herein lies a sobering issue: despite their dramatically increasing prevalence in U.S. classrooms across the nation, children of color are far less likely than White students to have a teacher or school principal who looks like them, if they ever have this opportunity at all.[10]

This demographic imperative is one of the more practical reasons that this chapter will focus primarily on White teachers. Their dominant presence in students' classrooms makes this a logical choice, especially in a book that seeks to make a case for teaching about race in schools. But the impact of such dominance does not only derive its power from numbers; that is, the fact that the sheer number of White people in the teaching field contributes to the racialization of schools is not simply the result of their holding the numerical majority.[11] Such dominance derives its power because of the historical, ideological, institutional, and cultural significance of whiteness and its pervasive impact, on both individual and systemic levels.[12]

Hence, the development of racial consciousness among adolescents in classrooms that seek to be culturally responsive means that White teachers must continuously interrogate their whiteness and its relationship to teaching; that is, how it may show up in their attitudes, instruction, and interactions with students—especially students of color.[13] Stated more powerfully, they must become aware of the way whiteness can be weaponized, even in school spaces, regardless of the presumed imperative to educate all children.[14] In doing so, White teachers must grapple with their racial identity in a new way, with the goal of developing a healthy, positive, anti-racist white identity and consciousness that supports culturally responsive practices.[15] Viewed within a humanizing pedagogy that is aligned with the concept democratic education, this is an awesome responsibility, but one that we—White teachers—must take on with intentionality, vigor, and determination. It requires us to think more deeply about what teaching is at its best, and why we are called to do it.[16] White racial positionality is not irrelevant to either question simply because "we love and care for children." Rather, understanding its relevance is tantamount to the kind of love and care that we give.

WHITE RACIAL POSITIONALITY, WHITE TEACHERS, AND RADICAL REFLECTION

The reader will notice that the possessive adjective "our" is used in the chapter title, as in "our (White) selves." Doing this indicates the insertion of a first-person point of view that will appear in this and subsequent chapters. More specifically, in writing about the inherent complexities that exist for White teachers in teaching about race and racial phenomena with young people, I locate and identify myself as a member of this group. As a White teacher and professor, it feels most authentic to address the concepts around whiteness that will be addressed in this chapter as a *person* who continues to grapple with the ways such phenomena appear in my own thinking, work, and relationships, not just as an *author* who maintains an academic distance. Hence, my use of first-person prose in sections of this chapter is meant to convey transparency, humility, and solidarity with others who aim to do this work with intention, at the same time it acknowledges that I, myself, am still engaged in the ongoing journey of figuring out what being a White racial ally means in educational spaces, in my writing, and in my own life. As such, the imagined audience for this chapter, in particular, is other White readers and educators who are engaged in this struggle.

I refer again to the writing of bell hooks, who noted that racialized oppression is perpetuated by, among many things, the belief that White people are inherently racist.[17] That is, we cannot simply believe that people "just are the way they are." For racial equity to occur, we must believe that oppressive beliefs and values can be positively transformed in people. My many years in both K–12 and higher education have shown me that this is true. The inspiration for this chapter derives from the following set of related beliefs: that there are many White teachers across the nation who acknowledge the legacy of systemic racism and inequity in our schools and on the lives of students. Perhaps they have come to see the ways they have been complicit in maintaining inequitable school practices. Perhaps they know they have fallen short, yet want to use their own spheres of influence—however contested—to do more, and to do better for their students, colleagues, and school communities. I am one of these teachers. As White teachers, we *can* do better, but we need to know where to start, and we need to identify reasons to continue our efforts that go far beyond a desire be a "good teacher" for all children and youth. Indeed, such sentiments, however well-intentioned, often redirect White teachers' energy toward denying racism, rather than confronting it.[18] And of course, it must be stated that the choice to engage meaningfully in this work as a White teacher is itself a manifestation of white privilege; that is, if we choose *not* to engage, we will *still* be affirmed, feel a sense of place, and perhaps continue to advance in our teaching careers—at least in many school contexts and communities.

Instead, in my view, as White teachers, we must develop and nurture a passion and commitment to racial justice and the elimination of systemic inequity that will serve as a touchstone for all that we do in schools and with students—even when, *especially* when, the inevitable pull of whiteness to maintain the (white) status quo takes hold. By virtue of our pedagogical training, concrete activities designed to promote specified objectives or learning outcomes are often what we look to first. However, a commitment to racial justice does not happen via a set of curricular lessons, steps, or strategies. Rather, it occurs at the level of ideology or beliefs and includes "soul-searching" work[19] that is of a particular kind for White people. As it regards White teachers, in an article published in the journal *Education & Urban Society*,[20] I have referred to such soul-searching as *radical reflection*. My contextual use and application of this term (which may have been used in other contexts) was inspired by an article by Jeffrey Duncan-Andrade's published in 2009 in the *Harvard Educational Review*. Duncan-Andrade appeals to educators to nurture and hold fast to a radical sense of hope for the future—in both themselves as teachers and with urban youth—especially in politically fraught, under-resourced, and contested school spaces.[21]

Like Duncan-Andrade, I realize that pairing the adjective "radical" with anything to do with teachers may be destabilizing, but it is intentionally meant to be so. That is, although practice-oriented reflection among teachers (e.g., ongoing assessment of pedagogical strategies or effectiveness) is considered a hallmark of effective practice that is likely enacted on a regular basis, I argue that it is very often not sufficiently radical, especially as it regards the role of whiteness in teachers' consciousness, pedagogy, and interactions with students, colleagues, and families. If we ever want change to happen, *we* (White teachers) need to change our thinking about race, whiteness, and education in radical ways.[22] Hence, I conceptualize radical reflection as having to engage the topics of whiteness, privilege, and institutional racism in schools, as well as a willingness to consider and push past the widely held belief that the delivery of a set of "culture free" skills and practices to all students is a characteristic to effective classroom pedagogy and relationship-building with cultural and racially diverse students.[23]

Radically reflective practices have the potential to move White teachers from complacency to an active journey toward a more affirming teacher pedagogy. Yet, I believe the power and potential of radical reflection must be anchored in a coherent framework around addressing issues of diversity, equity, and inclusion that has historical and contemporary meaning in school contexts. Multicultural education (MCE) is such a framework—one that schools, teachers, and teacher-training programs are familiar with and embrace as a means of addressing the needs of diverse children, but that often falls far short of its intended goals for a fundamental reason: it is conceptualized and implemented in a decidedly uncritical fashion, and is not oriented toward equity.[24] As such, it does not provide a space for radical reflection among teachers to be nurtured in community with each other in schools.

In the next section, to contextualize the notion of radical reflection, I first problematize contemporary, oft-used notions of MCE in schools, despite its original goals and intent. Following this, I argue that a critical multiculturalism and praxis that moves beyond a spurious acknowledgment of cultural traditions, toward a commitment to equity in school systems and practices is necessary. The term "praxis" refers to actions or practices that are intentionally informed by theory, contain a moral commitment to others, and are oriented toward the long-term interests of society.[25] In this way, critical multiculturalism serves as the theoretical grounding for promoting radical reflection and consciousness-raising among teachers in diverse school settings, providing the impetus for action. As we will see, however, the enactment of critical multiculturalism and radical reflection are not linear processes—that is, one need not come before the other—but mutually constitutive ones that provide sustenance for us—White teachers—to work and stay engaged in the teaching of race-related concepts in bold, creative, and contextually relevant ways.

The Equity-Oriented Roots of MCE: How Schools Have Digressed

The roots of MCE can be found in the civil rights movements of historically oppressed groups; specifically, the social activism of African Americans and other groups of color in response to discriminatory institutional practices in the 1960s.[26] This paved the way for advocacy among other groups who had experienced historic oppression such as women, people with disabilities, LGBTQ+ folks, and the elderly. Although these advocacy efforts shined a light on systemic inequities in areas such as hiring, representation, and civil liberties across institutional contexts, the ways that such inequities were present in educational institutions were a particular area of focus, which was among the most hostile to the goal of racial equity.[27]

In response to demands from activists, community leaders, and families that educational settings be more attuned and committed to the racial and linguistic diversity in our country, in the decades following the 1960s, schools and educational settings eagerly sought to broaden their institutional and curricular focus to be more representative of multiracial and ethnic groups.[28] Notwithstanding these positive changes, education scholar James Banks cautioned against viewing MCE as solely as the "addition" of content related to various racial-ethnic groups (i.e., groups of color), which can provide a justification for it to be relegated to the margins of the curriculum, or outside the purview of "core" subject areas like math and science.[29] Referring to this practice as mere "content integration," Banks developed a more comprehensive conceptualization of MCE that included four additional, equity-oriented dimensions: knowledge construction (e.g., how knowledge is produced, and by whom), prejudice reduction, an equity pedagogy, and an empowering school culture and structure. Further, Banks conceptualized the school as an integrated social system that included such things as school policies and procedures, staff and teacher attitudes and beliefs, teaching styles, languages/dialects used, and assessment procedures. To implement MCE in a meaningful way, these school dimensions must be examined, evaluated, and ultimately transformed. In these ways, MCE becomes systemically embedded in school practices, in the service of more equitable outcomes.

Despite the way that Banks attempted to reconnect MCE with the focus on systemic oppression and struggle for equity-based change that characterized its origins, such a focus did not sustain itself within educational spaces—an observation that still holds true today.[30] In an article published in 2000 in the magazine *Rethinking Schools*, Christine Sleeter and Peter McLaren draw attention to something quite fundamental, and that certainly is still relevant more than 20 years later: the way that the terminology or nomenclature used to describe phenomena—educational or otherwise—reflects both our ideas about it, as well as our subsequent responses or actions (or lack thereof) in response to it.[31] In particular, the authors point out that the early and more frequent use of the term "multiethnic education" in the 1970s by scholars of education, which positioned the categories of race and ethnicity as focal points, was replaced with the term "multicultural education," which was broadened to include other dimensions of diversity, such as gender or ability. Despite its utility in addressing intersectional dimensions of difference, this more expansive conceptualization and terminology also served another goal: to obtain the buy-in of White educators. More specifically, the authors note that the term "culture" was adopted because it was more palatable to White educator audiences.[32]

Incidentally, I have experienced a similar set of differential reactions to the terms "race" and "culture" firsthand, in the reactions (from mostly White people) to a particular undergraduate course that I teach. The formal course title is The Psychology of Race. Upon hearing that I teach a course with this title, there are usually two characteristic responses: halting and uncertain (e.g., "oh, that's . . . interesting"), or incredulous (e.g., "oh wow—I could never do that"). As an informal experiment of sorts, on many occasions, I have inserted the word "culture" into my description of the course, explaining that I teach a course on "race and culture." This description almost always elicits more enthusiastic (e.g., "oh what a great course") or curious (e.g., "what kinds of things do you talk about?") responses from folks. Clearly, the mere presence of the word "culture" is less threatening, acting as a buffer of sorts to the more emotionally charged naming of race—again, especially among White people in my personal circle.

Herein lies a core issue in the way MCE is still most often conceptualized by schools and teachers: an overemphasis on nebulous, ill-defined, and often essentialized notions of "culture," as opposed to a focus on educational systems and practices that create and perpetuate injustices across intersectional categories—race and ethnicity being among them.[33] As well, our essentialized perceptions of different racial-ethnic groups—that is, our belief in group-based characteristics or traits that are inherently stable, consistent, and predictable—are not neutral. Rather, they are constructed, supported, and promoted in the context of white hegemony; that is, being racially White is both normalized and idealized. As such, groups of color are viewed as inferior (e.g., Black and Brown groups), or legitimized to the extent that they uphold the notion of the United States as a meritocracy that is devoid of racism. Indeed, a striking example of the latter is seen in the "model minority" image of Asian Americans.[34]

In a similar frame, Stephen May and Christine Sleeter vividly describe this core issue as the "affirmational and politically muted discourses of 'culture' and 'cultural recognition'" that constitute what they and others characterize as *liberal multicultural* initiatives in schools—initiatives that are focused on helping racial and ethnically diverse students to get along and understand each other better, through targeted curricular activities.[35] In practice, such an approach commonly manifests as a celebration of difference, which often consists of sharing cultural practices, traditions, foods, or perspectives—the celebratory approach to MCE that was briefly described in chapter 1. This culture-based approach is framed within what Sensoy and DiAngelo aptly describe as "the ideology of individualism, applied to each unique ethnic group," but is devoid of an examination of unequal power and status between such groups.[36]

It is important to state that some educational, social, and relational benefits to a liberal approach to MCE are possible. After all, learning about cultural traditions, practices, and histories that are different from one's own has the potential to reduce ethnocentrism, increase one's knowledge base, increase critical thinking and perspective-taking, and facilitate empathy and respect—all of which are highly adaptive during the adolescent period. Within the curriculum, ethnic studies courses might also contribute to these outcomes. Over and above the sheer excitement of getting to know new people, intergroup contact theories developed and tested within the field of social psychology suggest that contact between members of different social groups can reduce prejudice, diminish stereotypes, and improve intergroup relations.[37]

Yet, if only it were that easy. It is not an overstatement to say that while the above benefits are laudable, they are neither inevitable, nor easily reached. To be clear, simply bringing diverse individuals or students together does not ensure that pluralistic attitudes will emerge, especially in the context of whiteness that begets the unequal status that exists between racial-cultural groups; in fact, both the quality and frequency of cross-cultural interactions are often limited by such factors. The mistrust, confusion, unease, and in some cases, contempt, for racial or culturally different groups that can and does often emerge is a cost of racism for all of us—including adolescents—although such costs are not experienced in the same way across individuals and groups. To reap any benefits of liberal multiculturalism as it serves the promotion of a more inclusive and respectful school climate, intentional, skilled, and informed support and intervention from teachers and adults—nurtured through radical reflection—are necessary elements.

But there is something even more important to consider when we consider the potential merits of liberal multiculturalism. If our goal is educational equity and the eradication of unjust practices in schools, this approach falls even further short. Education scholar, author, and founder of the Equity Literacy Institute Paul Gorski notes that common manifestations of a liberal MCE such as cultural celebrations, or cultural arts and crafts, "are not about equity because they are no threat to equity—no threat to racism or xenophobia or heterosexism."[38] From this view, as compelling as it is to learn about different racial, ethnic, and cultural traditions or identities as a school community, this is not adequate preparation for recognizing and responding to the ways that oppressive systems and beliefs are embedded in the practices of the school. Although there are obvious contextual differences in the needs and initiatives of schools across the nation, whiteness gives currency to the following systemic, equity-oriented (and far from extensive) questions that might easily be overlooked when there is a myopic focus on a celebratory approach to MCE:

- What discourses around achievement are promoted in school?
- What is the traditional and established curriculum that is taught? What topics or areas are *not* taught or addressed?
- Which students are able to participate in special programming, enrichment, or after-school activities?
- What are the demographics of students in advanced or honors classes, and in special education?
- What forms of family engagement are legitimized by the school?
- Whose voices are at the table when planning school events?
- Which students are expected to excel, or to fail?
- Which holidays or traditions are legitimized by the school calendar?
- What beliefs and practices exist around language diversity; specifically, regarding languages other than "standard" English?

Hence, a liberal notion of MCE in school may appear as racially and culturally inclusive on the surface, yet is not radically reflective, insofar as it does not interrogate systems of inequity. In so doing, it masks the ways that students from historically marginalized groups may experience educational injustice. That's where *critical* multiculturalism comes in.

The Equity-Oriented Roots of MCE: Critical Multiculturalism as the Way Back

In their book, *Critical Multiculturalism: Theory and Praxis,*[39] coeditors May and Sleeter provide a comprehensive discussion of the theoretical underpinnings of this approach to multiculturalism, which legitimizes its equity-oriented roots. As well, this approach adds necessary conceptual depth to the depoliticized focus of liberal MCE, which ignores the ways that different racial and cultural groups are positioned unequally, with differential access to resources. Rather than a focus on reified and individualistic notions of culture and cultural "exchange" that typify the way that liberal MCE has evolved in educational spaces, critical multiculturalism seeks to problematize and actively challenge racism—as well as other forms of injustice—by situating inequality within societal-level relations; specifically, by examining the inequitable distribution of resources and power. Furthermore, the widely held presumption that laws, institutions, and practices in the United States are racially and culturally neutral—that is, that they are accessible to and serve racial and cultural groups equally and objectively—would be critically questioned and contested within a critical multicultural perspective, holding that such claims of neutrality serve to both mask and reinforce systems of historic privilege.[40]

Broadly viewed, the authors note that critical multiculturalism is grounded in two theoretical traditions that have been discussed in this book, in previous chapters: critical race theory and critical pedagogy. In both traditions, the term "critical" has a particular meaning outside of its vernacular usage (i.e., to criticize or find fault). Specifically, critical theories seek to examine social phenomena within their historical, ideological, and cultural contexts, especially as it regards the influence of power (and who holds it), toward the betterment of society.[41] The way we think about knowledge and its transmission in schools serves as a compelling example. Critical theory challenges the belief that there is an "objective" knowledge that exists, or that "pure" knowledge is obtained through a rational, value-neutral process that is removed from any political agenda.[42] Instead, knowledge is exposed as socially constructed, dramatically influenced by the ideologies, values, and perspectives of those who produce and control it. Hence, in educational settings, using a critical perspective, the following questions around knowledge (content or otherwise) or claims presumed to be "objective" might be asked: Whose objectivity or rationality are such conclusions based upon? In what context was such knowledge developed? Whose interests (which groups) are served by such knowledge, who is invested in it? Whose voices have been included, and excluded? Finally, how does one's positionality as a teacher influence what they know, what they teach, and how they teach?

These elements of criticality are embodied in both critical race theory, which was discussed more fully in chapter 1, as well as critical pedagogy. The essence of critical pedagogy is perhaps most eloquently expressed by Freire in his classic text, *Pedagogy of the Oppressed*, which is fundamentally concerned with the processes by which individuals and groups, particularly those for whom social agency and opportunity have been denied, come to a critical awareness of societal oppression, through revolutionary educational practices.[43] Specifically, Freire critiqued what he called the "banking concept of education," in which students, presumed as lacking insight and thought to be "inferior," passively receive knowledge that is "deposited" by teachers, who consider themselves more knowledgeable, and the sole authority.[44] Such a mechanistic pedagogy undermines students' ability to develop the critical consciousness, or conscientização, needed to work toward societal transformation. Instead, it renders them apathetic, willing to accept and "adapt" to inequitable circumstances, and is essentially a practice of domination, not freedom.[45] If critical consciousness and equitable relations and practices are goals, students must instead be invited to become co-investigators in dialogue with the teacher through what Freire called a problem-posing pedagogy. In this dynamic process, "students, as they are increasingly posed with problems relating to themselves in the world and with the world, will feel increasingly challenged and obliged to respond to that challenge."[46] Thus, student voice and dialogue are essential and exciting, and aspects of critical pedagogy, which is inherently humanizing.

We can now see the way that the *critical* in critical multiculturalism is not incidental, but has intentional meaning that is drawn from the larger body of critical theorizing and scholarship. As applied to schools, such an approach would engage students in critical reflection and analysis of historic systems of inequality—including those that exist in education—as well as their own positionality regarding such systems; that is, how their personal and social identities interact and frame their experiences, beliefs, and responses.[47] Although critical multiculturalism can (and should) address multiple dimensions of oppression (e.g., gender, religion), not just racial oppression, the latter *is* often the focus, especially when applied to education, due to the historic racial inequities in school policies, practices, and outcomes.[48]

Hence, as it regards the focus of this book, a critical multicultural approach in the classroom would be one that is explicitly and unapologetically antiracist. Specifically, it engages teachers and students together in learning to identify, name, and challenge the ideologies, norms, patterns, and traditions that keep racism in place.[49] It is important to stress that within a supportive and loving classroom environment, such investigations hold the potential to bring racial, ethnic, and culturally diverse students together in solidarity, not drive them apart, through a deeper understanding that reality, and hence, their lives, are susceptible to transformation, as Freire envisioned.[50]

Yet, when we consider the objectives of a critical multicultural approach as outlined above, we can see why this approach has gained less traction in schools. First, its central tenets run counter to those upon which schools were derived; as noted in chapter 1, historic, institutionalized school practices and curricula are based upon the ideologies of meritocracy, individualism (i.e., individual effort), and equal opportunity characteristic of Western liberalism, especially in capitalist societies.[51] As a result, teachers and administrators lack both the knowledge and motivation to move from a cursory (or even celebratory at best) acknowledgment of differences, to a focus on how such differences manifest as inequity for historically marginalized groups. Relatedly, within the liberal paradigm, critical multiculturalism often appears too destabilizing (yes, radical again), with the potential to disrupt presumably "objective," and "tried and true" methods.[52] Such methods and practices become internalized as our cultural scripts about effective schooling and often have an emotional, nostalgic salience. In fact, May and Sleeter contend that the less likely so-called multicultural practices are to disrupt inequity or the racialized status quo, "the more likely they are to be taken up in schools!"[53] Once again, although the authors made this bold claim several decades ago, it is still highly relevant today, especially in the face of conservative attacks and rhetoric around EDI content and initiatives in school—racial or otherwise.

As noted earlier, the enactment of critical multiculturalism cannot be easily packaged or mastered in a set of standard curricular lesson plans. Consistent with this, despite the transformative potential of critical multiculturalism, May and Sleeter note that schools and teachers lack accessible examples of its enactment; that is, what can a critical multicultural approach or strategy actually look like in classroom practice?[54] This is a considerable weakness in the literature, especially when considered alongside the ideological and practical challenges for schools noted above. Similarly, reviews of the White teacher identity literatures in the past decade have also noted that although gains have been made in understanding the construct and evolution of teachers' racialized identities, as well as the interplay between racial identity, hegemonic ideology, and interracial alliances, studies continue to point to the difficulty of integrating theory to practice for teachers.[55] In effect, this amounts to a lack of direction around ways to address very complex ideas around race, identity, and racism with students. Toward this end, chapter 5 is dedicated to making such a link between theory and practice, and will present concrete ideas, strategies, possibilities, and examples of critical multicultural praxis around race with adolescents in the classroom.

But a prerequisite—indeed, the premise of this chapter—is that we begin with ourselves, and our own understanding. As White teachers, how do we start? I argue that we begin with what I have identified as focal points of radical reflection that are needed to achieve or enact such a praxis. In developing these foci, I am mindful of a caveat offered by scholar of whiteness studies, Zeus Leonardo, that the racial advocacy work White people do "should be guided by non-White discourse."[56] That is, while White people need to take responsibility for educating themselves about the complexities of race, the insights of people of color can help them to "get in touch" with its critical elements, as Gloria Yamato articulated in her compelling essay, "Something about the Subject Makes it Hard to Name."[57]

Based on my ever-expanding knowledge and ongoing growth as an antiracist educator that has been inspired by powerful insights from colleagues and scholars of color, I consider the following topics of radical reflection, framed broadly, as essential to White teachers' ability to employ a critical multiculturalism to their work: the institutional nature of race, the construct and enactment of whiteness, cultural neutrality, and white emotionality. Each is discussed in terms of its implications for teacher pedagogy, classrooms, and schools.

THE PRACTICE OF RADICAL REFLECTION: ESSENTIAL TOPICS FOR WHITE TEACHERS

Analysis of the Institutional Nature of Racism

> Teachers need more professional development for understanding inequality in order to confront it. (Bettina Love)[58]

Although Love's quote considers inequality in broad terms, we can easily apply it to the topic of race. As outlined in the first chapter of this book, both the construct and definition of racism in U.S. society, as it is commonly understood by most White people, is incomplete, uninformed, and deeply flawed. Specifically, sociologist Eduardo Bonilla-Silva implicates color-blindness as the dominant racial ideology that most Whites subscribe to, whereby contemporary racial inequality is explained as the outcome of nonracial dynamics; in particular, that individual hard work determines success, irrespective of one's racial positionality.[59] In this way, with color-blindness framed as an adaptive feature and a testament to our presumably "equal opportunity" society, the idea of racism becomes merely incidental, reduced to individual acts of prejudice or meanness that only "bad" individuals would engage in.[60] Put simply, the structural dynamics of inequality—racial or otherwise—are masked, in favor of a myopic, yet very familiar, focus on the individual, or one's individual efforts.

Because teachers often enter the profession with a personal and often idealized imperative to nurture the individual abilities and potential of *all* students, embrace and teach *all* children, and to treat *all* students equally, I argue that they are particularly susceptible to holding the abovementioned ideologies regarding the dynamics of race and inequality, and that these ideas are readily internalized as a guide to instructional best practices. Specifically, the idea of color-blindness serves as a duplicitous strategy for seeing and treating each child as their own individual, with a unique constellation of traits, characteristics, learning styles, and interests that are unmoored from culture, race, and ethnicity. Indeed, both pre-service and practicing K–12 teachers that I have observed and worked closely with in my career have often asserted that "they don't see color" in their classrooms—a statement that can be considered patently false and dishonest, since we know that even infants are capable of noticing phenotypic differences across racially different individuals.[61] Such a sentiment among teachers is likely intended to serve as evidence of their ability to deliver fair and unbiased treatment to their students, and of their love for all children.

But love in the context of teaching requires *seeing* students for who and what they are. Especially in adolescence, attempting to ignore or look past a students' culture, race, or ethnicity de-legitimizes its salience as a dimension of self, the nature of which will vary both across and within cultural and racial groups. It squanders the opportunity to leverage cultural and racial heritage as a source of affirmation, strength, and empathy among students. Love in this context also requires an acknowledgment of the well-documented evidence from empirical studies in teacher education that now spans many decades that show that White teachers at all levels of preparation frequently hold deficit-oriented views of students of color, especially Black, Brown, and Indigenous students, and especially in urban school contexts.[62] Needless to say, such practices are anything but loving, and anything but color-blind.

The long-held (and not completely incorrect) belief that supporting children's best individual efforts at persistence and hard work in school has been newly recast in recent years. Inspired by scholar Angela Duckworth's widely popular book, *Grit: The Power of Passion and Perseverance*, a focus on a specific blend of noncognitive (i.e., intelligence or memory) attributes, such as perseverance, sustained effort, and passion toward one's long-term goals—what Duckworth calls "grit"—is often considered a hallmark of school achievement and success among both educators and families. Duckworth rightly qualifies the fact that grit is not an immovable trait that students either have or do not have, but something that can be developed and nurtured by caring adults, which explains its obvious appeal and relevance to teachers.

Yet the appeal and utility of grit as a construct is grounded in something deeper, in my view; that it is, it fits well within the ideology of individualism. Although I do not deny that the features of grit are positive, hopeful, and potentially adaptive in some contexts, and when held in balance, I agree with scholars such as Paul Gorski who call for criticality and caution around its conceptualization and application.[63] Specifically, a focus on grit can quickly devolve into blaming students themselves for not putting forth enough individual effort, not being sufficiently focused, or at worst, being "lazy"—an adjective that easily maps on to extant stereotypes about the "work ethic" of some racial minority groups. In effect, striving to promote grit "reinvests" in meritocratic notions of achievement and success. As Gorski notes in a recent piece entitled "Embracing a Structural View of Poverty and Education: Ditching Deficit Ideology and Quitting Grit," it becomes problematic when we attempt to "fix" students who have experienced historic marginalization with grit, rather than attempt to address or fix the conditions that lead to such inequities. Moreover, the conceptualization of grit elides the fact that students who experience systemic racial or other oppression often persist and succeed in school *despite* the challenges they experience, making them among the "grittiest" of students.[64]

Let us return now to the quotation from Bettina Love presented at the beginning of this section: for teachers, an understanding of inequity is a prerequisite for confronting it. What is notably absent from each of the commonly held views and strategies that I have presented above is an understanding of the structural nature of racial inequity, and how this is relevant to schools. To be more clear, knowledge about the ways that unequal, racialized systems of power, access, and opportunity are historically embedded in our education system in ways that systematically benefit White students and disenfranchise students of color is typically lacking among White teachers.[65] To enact a critical multicultural praxis, a fundamental understanding of these intersecting "rules of the game" is necessary.

White teachers' firm grasp of the institutional nature of racism is paramount to their ability to identify, name, and challenge inequitable school practices and policies as they play out within the landscape of schools and in their own classroom pedagogy and relationships with students. It guards against a reliance on racialized notions of individual grit or potential, as well as pedagogical scripts that are presumed to be racially or culturally neutral, which will be discussed in a section below. This level of understanding is neither assured or inevitable; however; by virtue of their racial privilege, White teachers must learn about systemic racial inequity "second hand," and usually not through their own lived experience.[66] Hence, it must be sought with intentionality and openness, with the expectation that it will be a lifelong endeavor that is difficult, yet exceedingly rewarding. Teachers must commit to this dimension of radically reflective growth and understanding not in isolation, but through collaborative, multiracial alliances that are actively sought out, as they pursue an understanding of race, diversity, and inequity that extends beyond a superficial level.

Interrogation of Whiteness

> Beyond learnt vocabulary, theories, and pedagogical strategies, the question that needs to be self-asked and continually self-answered by White teachers is "am I emotionally committed to being a culturally responsive teacher even if it means learning about how I am repressing my understanding of race and whiteness merely because it makes me feel uncomfortable?" (Cheryl Matias)[67]

In chapter 1, whiteness was defined briefly as a sort of collective consciousness and way of being and interacting in the world that allows white supremacy to survive and thrive. Described by W.E.B. Du Bois as a powerful "dictum" akin to a "new religion of whiteness" that emerged in the nineteenth and twentieth centuries in the United States and globally,[68] whiteness doesn't refer to biology or racial categorization, especially since the definition of

White people has and continues to shift over time. Instead, it exists as a social construct, historically derived from the (racialized) organization of society;[69] a pervasive and potent ideological "container" from which our worldview and meaning-making around race are drawn. To concretize this a bit more, we can think of whiteness as a set of cognitions, perceptions, responses, claims, and action patterns that are transmitted and shared through hegemonic means among White *people* in a broad sense, not White *individuals*; that is, most White people are never directly taught how to behave, communicate, think, or act according to white cultural standards. In this way, whiteness is also marked by its invisibility—hidden from our consciousness through its tacit promotion, secured in place by dominant narratives of meritocracy, individualism, freedom, and equal opportunity.

By virtue of our collective socialization in a white supremacist society, while the construct of whiteness is not new to many people of color,[70] learning to locate and understand its impact holds powerful significance for White people, since they are the ones who receive racialized benefits from the system, and hence, will be inevitably drawn to maintain it. If we seek to disrupt the power of whiteness in the service of racial justice, we must become more astute in identifying the ways we enact it across different settings, not the least of which are schools and classrooms. As scholar and educator Cheryl Matias' quote above vividly notes, for White teachers, uncovering the ways that whiteness has become buried in our consciousness is emotional and difficult, but essential to the work of becoming a racially and culturally competent educator.

In his book *Race, Whiteness, and Education*,[71] scholar and author Zeus Leonardo theorizes the deep complexities and contradictions of whiteness for White people, which can be experienced in different ways, ranging from protestations of racial ignorance, strong investment, or critical analysis of its oppressive features. While acknowledging extant arguments regarding whether White people can ever truly divest themselves of the "false and oppressive" nature of whiteness, as it has been characterized by historian David Roediger, Leonardo argues that a critical pedagogy must forge a "third space" for White people who seek to become racially just educators, where they are "neither enemy nor ally but a concrete subject of struggle."[72] Hence, for White teachers, to disrupt whiteness is not to disavow oneself as a White person, or from white culture. Instead, it refers to a process of interrogating the places where whiteness as a depraved construct lives in us, and how it inevitably frames everything we know and do in the classroom. Through this radically reflective process in which the self is positioned as "the object of study," Leonardo's third space can be realized as a place of hope and possibility, where the meaning of white identity is reimagined, and an anti-racist teaching ethic can be nurtured.[73]

Yet entering such a space is riddled with emotional challenges that are often unexpected among White teachers, who often lack the stamina to navigate the complexities inherent in seeing oneself as a racialized being.[74] In fact, several scholars have examined the impact of unexamined whiteness among White teachers in the classroom. In an article that calls upon White teachers to "check" themselves before they "wreck" both themselves, and especially, their urban students of color, Cheryl Matias uses counter-stories and teacher narratives that emerged in her work as a teacher educator to illustrate the ways that White pre-service and practicing teachers reflect their deep investment in whiteness, even as they express a desire to become culturally competent practitioners.[75] For example, teachers often approached their work with a strong "savior" mentality, casting themselves as the all-knowing, superior and well-meaning "authorities" who would not "give up" on urban students of color. In teachers' attempts to become more culturally responsive, the consistent focus was on the desire to master presumably concrete strategies or "checklists" to understand the racial "other"—their students—rather than consider their own positionality as White people as part of the equation. On occasions where these sorts of views were challenged or problematized, teachers co-opted the dialogue or space in ways that manifested their deep investment in whiteness by expressing feelings of outrage, shock, defensiveness, and victimization. Put another way, their powerful emotions were directed toward the goal of (white) self-preservation, rather than the educational and systemic injustices that many of the students in their classrooms had experienced.

The abovementioned examples illustrate the myriad ways that whiteness can become weaponized in educational contexts. In a broad sense, whiteness as weaponized refers to a demonstrated sense of entitlement, anger, need for retaliation, and white fragility that emerges in the face of a perceived racialized threat, behavior, or encounter.[76] In classrooms, it often manifests when White teachers perceive challenges to their own power and control; studies show that it emerges frequently in response to the behaviors of Black youth, in particular, which are often read by White educators as defiant, disrespectful, or challenging.[77]

Whiteness as weaponized can also happen at the school level in contextually relevant ways, as scholar Marcus Bell illustrates in his book, *Whiteness Interrupted: White Teachers and Racial Identity in Predominately Black Schools*.[78] In a fascinating examination of the meaning of white racial identity (i.e., what it means to be white) among 32 White teachers teaching in a predominately Black school district, Bell found that teachers constructed a narrative of white victimization around their experiences and interactions in such spaces, where Black students were perceived as having racial advantages and privileges. In this context, where race was made salient on a daily basis in ways participants were unaccustomed to, they perceived aspects of their white identity as stigmatized, maligned, and subject to "reverse discrimination."

Unexamined whiteness among teachers can also be mobilized as a strategy for maintaining the racially inequitable status quo in schools, and for indoctrinating students with the dominant color-blind, meritocratic ideologies upon which U.S. schools are founded. In her book *Reading, Writing, and Racism: Disrupting Whiteness in Teacher Education and in the Classroom*, pre-service teacher supervisor and educator Bree Picower uses multiple sources of data collected over many years, including an in-depth analysis of case study material from four White teachers, to illustrate the ways teachers use what she terms "Curricular Tools of Whiteness" to preserve white supremacist ideas, whereby whiteness is positioned as "good, superior, and ever present."[79] For example, the curricular tool "White Out" avoids teaching U.S. history accurately, such as avoiding the presentation of White people as perpetrators of violence, while erasing of the experiences of people of color. The tool "All Things Being Equal" masks the role of power in the maintenance of inequity, by creating a false equivalency among racial groups, where all perspectives are valid, emanating from a presumably neutral, even, playing field. As Picower notes, although these and other Tools of Whiteness are enacted both consciously and unconsciously, a lack of self-reflection creates the conditions for both.

Hence, the interrogation of whiteness among teachers serves as a prerequisite for a critical multicultural praxis that is explicitly anti-racist. It also guards against the perpetuation of racialized harm upon students of color, or racialized ignorance, in the case of White students. On an individual level, it is an opportunity for teachers to develop a healthy white identity, not in the sense of white nationalism or white pride, but in the context and service of racial justice and cross-racial allyship. For White teachers (and White people!), becoming informed of the trajectory of white racial identity development as it has been theorized and mapped by scholars like Janet Helms, whose seminal model of White Racial Identity Development (WRID) was presented in chapter 3, can help to illuminate and normalize this process, notwithstanding intersectional sources of variability that come into play. As well, as part of the process of exploring white identity, examining the way that the history of whiteness in the United States emerged in the context of Euroethnic assimilation and ethnocultural loss can be an affirming experience for White people—an opportunity to regain a sense of "rootedness" and "cultural grounding" in ethnic heritage that helps to clarify one's connection to whiteness.[80]

Examination of the Fallacy of Cultural Neutrality in Teaching

> Many educators still believe that good teaching transcends place, people, time, and context . . . individuals who subscribe to this belief fail to realize that their standards of "goodness" in teaching and learning are culturally determined and are not the same for all ethnic groups. (Geneva Gay)[81]

In all my years of teaching, I have never met a teacher for whom the idea of "good teaching," as Gay frames it in the segment above, was not highly relevant, as well as an inspiration for their work. Although most teachers would readily acknowledge that honing their pedagogical strategies in the classroom happens both in the moment (e.g., enacting or adjusting strategies as they unfold) and over time, rarely are critical questions that interrogate widely held conceptualizations of what constitutes "good teaching" ever posed. That is, what are the presumed core elements of good teaching? What are these expected to look like? Who defined these elements? What values and assumptions about children, learning, and the relationship between students and teachers are embedded in what good teaching looks like? To frame things more specifically, is being personable and establishing a strong rapport with students the key to good teaching? What are the observable characteristics in teachers that reflect such rapport, and based on whose assessment? Does a commitment and an attempt (however successful) to simply look at and treat each child as an "individual" get us out of the bind that these questions might pose, and hence, define good teaching? If this final question resonates with you as a way out of the complexity, consider the way it is powered by an embedded assumption—that respect for children's individuality is a universal value, as well as a pedagogically neutral one.

Yet, it is likely true that the question *does* resonate with so many of us, because the idea that "good teaching is transcendent," as discussed by Geneva Gay in the aforementioned book *Culturally Responsive Teaching*,[82] permeates the ethos of teaching. Stated another way, the attributes of good teaching are presumed to transcend factors like culture or race. Where does this idea come from? As a logical place to start, we might first reflect upon our pre-service teacher training; because these experiences are formative ones, they play an outsized role in the construction of our professional (teacher) identity. Although variable to some degree, such training is heavily biased toward mastering universally "good" teaching practices, at the expense of critical self-reflection around the contextual nature of teacher identity as it relates to sociocultural differences between students and teachers.[83] Indeed, the curricular content of most teacher education programs in the United States relies heavily on a set of carefully selected and sequenced teaching methods and courses that span curricular areas (e.g., reading/language arts, mathematics, science) across the K–12 years. Although there may be a sprinkling of coursework around "diversity" content such as multiculturalism, teaching English-language learners, or family engagement, it is often Eurocentric, infused with white sensibilities.[84] As well, teacher education is highly psychologized in U.S. institutions, drawing heavily on course content around child development, learning, and cognition, while minimizing courses in the field of anthropology, where the role of culture in learning would be more richly centered.[85]

In her book, Gay offers a compelling analysis of several paradoxical ideas that are inculcated in the standard training that teachers receive; namely, that the individuality and potential of each child—not their race, ethnicity, or gender, for example—is the rightful focus. Indeed, we can locate these ideas in the public outcry and legislative actions against the teaching of race or diversity content in school. However, as Gay clarifies, children's racial, ethnic, and cultural socialization *cannot* be severed from their individuality, and in fact, serve as "the filters through which one's individuality is made manifest."[86] Remaining willfully ignorant of the ways that such differences might present themselves in different cultural groups not only robs us of the opportunity to get to know our students and families better but also creates the conditions for fear, discomfort, and misunderstanding to fester, and for insults to occur. Moreover, when teachers ignore or invalidate such distinctions among groups, they are more likely to impose their own culturally based notions regarding a range of factors salient to the educational process (e.g., behavioral styles, social interactions, educational outcomes) on to them.[87]

In this context, I argue that an important outcome of radical reflection among White teachers who are engaged in the work of enacting a critical multicultural pedagogy is the recognition and insight that the practice of teaching, itself, is a cultural construction. That is, teaching is not a culturally neutral process. Put simply, within both United States and increasingly globalized contexts, both the content and form of what are often considered pedagogical "best practices" are derived from middle-class, White, Eurocentric interactional styles and expectations for student behaviors.[88] A vivid example of this is the conventional dialogic format between teachers and students in the context of instruction, characterized as a passive-receptive style.[89] The features of this communicative style are likely familiar to most educators: students are expected to respond only when called on by the teacher, respond one at a time, and closely tailor their responses to the teachers' questions in a linear fashion (i.e., without going "off topic"). Such passive-receptive responses are buttressed by nonverbal behaviors such as maintaining direct eye contact with the teacher and minimizing physical movement and emotions as students answer the teachers' questions. In contrast, the communicative style of many African American, Latinx, and Native Hawaiian students has been characterized as participatory-interactive, whereby speakers expect listeners to engage and co-construct the dialogue through vocalization and gesture, at the same time the speaker (i.e., the teacher) is talking.[90] Verbal assertiveness as students attempt to "gain the floor" as a manifestation of their high engagement is a distinctive feature of this style. Yet, because it violates the culturally informed expectations of most (White) teachers, students who communicate in this style are often viewed negatively, considered rude, and penalized for their engagement.

We can also think about the issue of cultural neutrality in terms of the school's manifest and latent curriculum. A school's manifest curriculum refers to those things we can see, such as materials, textbooks, curriculum guides, and representations in the environment (e.g., building names, bulletin boards).[91] By and large, Eurocentrism is historically and deeply embedded in all of these manifest aspects of school.[92] Yet, as many scholars have pointed out, aspects of a school's latent curriculum—what James Banks describes as "the one that no teacher explicitly teaches but that all children learn"[93]—is often more important than its manifest curriculum. While something like communication styles between students and teachers might be considered a part of both (since they can be observed, but are also internalized by students), a broad definition of the latent curriculum is that aspect of school culture that communicates its embedded ideologies and ideas about children and learning; this includes ideas about which groups are legitimized and valued across dimensions of difference, such as race, ethnicity, gender, ability, language, citizenship, religion, or sexuality. When we consider the ways that such factors are embedded within hierarchical systems of marginalization, we must ask ourselves a key question: Who benefits the most from a teacher's neutral stance on these dimensions of difference?

It is also important to consider the way teachers often *do* attempt to utilize the concept of culture in the classroom—which again, is often anything but neutral. In an article entitled "It's Not the Culture of Poverty, It's the Poverty of Culture," Gloria Ladson-Billings examines the way that White pre-service teachers employ culture as an explanation for children's behaviors, based on data from interviews, portfolios, and journal entries collected over many years.[94] She found that culture was often used in a nonspecific way as a "catchall" for difference. Most importantly, pre-service teachers most readily attributed behaviors they perceived as maladaptive as "cultural," especially when the students in question were non-White, not English-speaking, or not U.S. born. Moreover, in interviews, they described themselves as having "no culture," or "just regular," not appreciating the way that this invariably positions others (i.e., out-group members) as "irregular."

Hence, adopting a fallacious belief in culturally neutrality in the classroom has the net effect of maligning aspects of students' cultural identities and respective "ways of being" in the classroom, as well as invalidating the lived, often racialized experiences of students of color. As well, to the extent that it blocks teachers' ability to recognize themselves as cultural beings,[95] it subverts the potential for growth, deeper understanding, and advocacy among both teachers and students—especially in our present historical moment.

White Emotionalities: Grappling with Emotions Around Race

> In actuality, healing from racism is not just about what you know or what you do, but also about what you feel . . . when you start to check in with your emotions that come up when you really do this interrogation, you see that the feelings can go deep—really, really deep. (Anneliese Singh)[96]

The work of understanding the impact of race and whiteness in on our lives is not just intellectual—it is "deeply" emotional, as the quotation above vividly conveys. Although it is accurate to say that its influence is contextual, influenced by one's own familial history, contexts, interactions, and even personality, one's racial positionality is highly significant to the emotional valence that is brought to bear when grappling with race. As it regards White people, specifically, because they do not carry the emotional burden of living in a racialized society the way people of color do, they are often unprepared for the range and intensity of emotions that will arise as they seek to become more educated and informed about race, and as they work to become anti-racist allies.[97] This process is emotionally draining and psychologically taxing, requiring both stamina and vulnerability, both of which are undermined by white privilege (here, the ability to desist with little cost) and white supremacy, which by its very nature is ideologically inconsistent with an honest accounting of the way race frames one's life experiences and outcomes.

But how do these emotional reactions manifest for White people in real time? Succinctly, and notwithstanding the contextual differences noted earlier, when race enters the conversation or is made salient during intraracial, or especially cross-racial interactions or contexts, dispositions such as anxiety, discomfort, fury, or reticence often quickly ensue for White people. Writing from her perspective as a White person, Robin DiAngelo refers to these dispositions as *white fragility*, defined as the self-focused discomfort, defensiveness, and sense of outrage that is triggered in response to even a minimal amount of racial stress among White people.[98] Although these reactions do function as modes of resistance, DiAngelo refers to white fragility as a sort of reduced psychosocial stamina for race-based dialogue and engagement. As a broad-based construct that vividly captures the sense of disequilibrium felt by White people when race is "activated" or brought into the conversation, white fragility operates as a double-edged sword for White people, in that it reflects their expectations for racial comfort, while at the same time lowering their ability to tolerate racial stress. Such expectations are rooted in both racial insulation and racial dominance, both of which reinforce notions of whiteness as normative and superior. These expectations are also at play for teachers in terms of their professional work and interactions in schools and classrooms.

Hence, for teachers, white fragility can easily map on to the idealized, color-blind notions of caring for "all children" that were discussed earlier in this chapter. This is especially the case because teaching is hard, tiring, and often unsupported and contested work, leaving teachers vulnerable to viewing radical reflection about race and whiteness as an additional burden. As well, since we know that White teachers constitute the majority in U.S. schools, they enjoy an inherent sense of belonging and sense of "property rights"[99] in such spaces, which can block the potential for individual reflection around their teaching praxis. In this regard, Bettina Love contends that White teachers need anti-racist therapy and healing; that is, in their desire to become more culturally responsive and anti-racist, many White teachers "must first win the fight regarding racism within themselves."[100]

Although white fragility is often manifested in behaviors such as argumentation, silence, defensiveness, or withdrawal, the emotions of fear, guilt, and anger often underlie these behavioral maneuvers. In fact, in his book *The Heart of Whiteness: Confronting Race, Racism, and White Privilege,* author Robert Jensen boldly refers to these as the emotions of white supremacy.[101] As Jensen argues, we must consider White people's investment in white supremacy as fundamentally emotional—White people need to believe in the system in order to maintain it—and come to understand how these particular emotions serve this goal. For example, to acknowledge that some of what we have as White people is unearned, or that societal resources and access might become more equitable is disconcerting, and can elicit fear for those who have greatly benefitted from white supremacist beliefs and practices. Also significant, in Jensen's view, is the fear of facing the depravity of whiteness that lives in our hearts, and that this (e.g., superiority, racist thoughts, or ideas) will be revealed in our interactions with people of color. In many ways, these fears become more potent when considered in the context of the changing racial landscape in the United States, where demographic projections that people of color will soon constitute the majority pose an existential threat to many White people.[102]

The emotion of guilt is implicated in each of the above examples and in the commonly held sentiment among many White people that they feel guilty about things like slavery, racism, or inequitable schools. Here, guilt becomes conflated with sadness, which is a legitimate emotion in the face of historical injustice, but when constructed in such an abstract way, it serves to immobilize an individual from any action, and to avoid accountability.[103] The potential for anger among White people is also woven throughout all of these examples, each of which illustrates a real or perceived threat to the racial status quo that triggers feelings of racialized anger and resentment. In the classroom, these emotions might manifest in a variety of ways for White teachers: fear that unexamined racial biases or lack of understanding will be "unmasked" or seen (especially by students of color), guilt about the structural inequities experienced by historically marginalized students, or anger when supposedly color-blind, neutral teaching practices or responses are questioned or challenged by others (especially people of color).

Yet a commitment to feeling and grappling with the emotions that bubble up as White people and White teachers learn about racism and whiteness can lead to the kinds of adaptive emotional responses that can motivate our work for racial justice. That is, if we stay engaged and allow ourselves to sit with our powerful emotions, new insights and modes of operating emerge. For example, if we learn about the history of racism and whiteness, we come to a better understanding of our racialized fears, minimizing their power over us. If we hurt or offend someone, either by discriminating against them or committing a microaggression, allowing ourselves to feel guilt is an appropriate response, since it helps us to acknowledge our action and commit to do better. And finally, it is critical to point out that anger is an appropriate response to racial inequity, violence, and injustice—as White people, we *are* often complicit in maintaining inequitable systems, and we *should* feel outraged and angry about these things, not complacent and apathetic.

In many ways, grappling with our emotions around race is a process of honest psychological reconciliation—a belief in one's own ability to enter the fight against racial justice with imperfection, vulnerability, and humility. Such a perspective is the central thesis of social justice scholar and author Anneliese Singh. Drawing upon her training as a counseling psychologist who is of mixed race, her book *The Racial Healing Handbook: Practical Activities to Help you Challenge Privilege, Confront Systemic Racism, & Engage in Collective Healing* is a practical guide to understanding the ways race and racism affect all aspects of life, across cognitive, social, physiological/affective, and emotional domains.[104] Structured as a workbook of sorts, the book addresses topical areas of study and exploration such as the development of racial identity, internalized racism, racial consciousness in relationships and interactions, and the dimensions of racial allyship and advocacy, using a set of closed and open-ended writing prompts that support personal reflection and growth. In particular, Singh reveals the ways the powerful feelings and emotions that emerge when we implicate our own selves in the study of race relate to experiences of grief; that is, identifying and feeling the losses one has experienced as a result of racism and white supremacy is a process of grieving, with many emotional layers.[105]

Singh argues that grieving is necessary for healing from the wounds of racism.[106] Racial healing in this context is not meant to imply that there is a discrete end point in the pursuit of racial justice and allyship. Rather, it is an ongoing process of coming to understand one's role and agency in dismantling inequitable practices and systems, as well as the ability to navigate this with insight and humility. For White people, healing involves the ability to interrogate the ways that white supremacy and whiteness is embedded in our consciousness and our lives, and in marshaling the will and commitment to divest from it. It involves building the emotional stamina and resilience that is necessary to move from being simply nonracist and complacent, to anti-racist and activist, within our many shifting spheres of influence.

For White teachers, healing is learning to recognize ourselves as part of the landscape of our historically inequitable schools and reflecting upon the myriad ways this bears upon our educational praxis. It means constructing a newfound white teacher identity that is culturally responsive and explicitly anti-racist, as we aim to educate, love, and care for *all* children in our classrooms, but *especially* those for whom our schools were not (and still are not) designed to serve. Although this process of healing is deeply personal and reflective, it is nurtured and sustained through cross-racial alliances and community with others, both in and outside the school walls.

CONCLUSION

Although many would argue that the teaching profession garners less respect and status than some other vocations, it likely is the case that teachers *are* regarded as among the most nurturing, caring, and unselfish professionals. While I believe this sentiment to be true, these characteristics will not in themselves lead to a critical multicultural, anti-racist praxis, especially among White teachers. Indeed, a lack of humility can mask teachers' ability to see themselves—fundamentally good and caring people—as capable of holding racialized biases or prejudices against the children they serve, as well as the way the construct of whiteness subverts their best intentions.

As argued in this chapter, White teachers must begin with themselves, with a commitment to radically reflective practices that center on an understanding of systemic racism, whiteness, and the fallacy of cultural neutrality in teaching, as well as an awareness of the way dominant white racial emotionalities serve to neutralize their ability to effectively engage in the work of creating more culturally and racially equitable classrooms and schools. As curious, open, and highly engaged stakeholders, early adolescents can be part of this work during the middle school years, but teachers must first be ready to listen to them, to respond to them, and to guide them. White teachers who are committed to radical reflection and the enactment of a critical multicultural praxis are well positioned to engage with students around the teaching of race with confidence and insight, as well as honesty, humility, and vulnerability. Such exciting and humanizing pedagogical possibilities and strategies are the subject of the next chapter.

Chapter 5

Centering Race in Critical Multicultural Praxis

Pedagogical Possibilities and Classroom Strategies

I think people who are of *different* race are completely for it [conversations on race-ethnicity in school] . . . I think this is a pretty white community, so to speak. And I think it's like, normal, and I mean, it's [town name], so it's not really a big deal. . . . But I also feel like, those kinds of people who are of the same race, should also be open to other races. So, like, it's okay for it to be a completely white community, but you should also let other people come into that community. Welcome them. (Nala, biracial, seventh-grade student)

I think one of the teachers' main goals, even sometimes over teaching, is to make sure we belong. We're at our best so then we can learn our best at the same time. (Ria, Indian American, eighth-grade student)

On the morning that I was preparing the initial outline for this chapter, I came across an article published in *EdWeek* that discussed the "difficult, beautiful work" of teaching in the United States. It is likely that the myriad of daily tasks, roles, dispositions, and strategies for which these adjectives are meant to describe don't need to be clarified for those of us who spend much of our lives in classrooms. Indeed, Ria crystallizes the nature of our work in the quote above with such insight: to create opportunities for students to be at their best, so they can learn their best. What is more difficult and beautiful than that?

Although I suspect that the vocation of teaching has always been imbued with nuanced complexities, the contextual messages that are delivered about its worth and value are constantly changing, informed by historical and sociopolitical contexts. Of note, in our present moment, many perceive a growing public antagonism and mistrust toward the teaching profession and educational institutions writ large.[1] As I have argued in this book, such sentiments are particularly potent when it comes to the teaching of race, identity, and social justice content in schools. It is not an easy context within which to center race in a critical multicultural praxis; in fact, this particular topic is one powerful manifestation of what might feel most "difficult" in schools right now.

In pondering these issues, I often reflect on the book by Lisa Delpit that was referenced in chapter 1, *Teaching When the World is on Fire*, which is as much a testament to the indomitable hope and spirit of teachers as it is a reminder that our students—especially those with racially marginalized identities—need us to stay the course as we navigate the difficulties. We must recognize and believe in the potential for our classrooms to serve as affirming and transformative spaces and use this as sustenance to stay engaged. When we come right down to it, for so many of us, what makes the work "beautiful" is our students—students like Ria and Nala, who speak from different racial positionalities—but whose opening quotations draw our attention to the fact that race, belonging, and feeling "welcome" are integral to the teaching and learning process. Ria centers a sense of belonging in her perception of teachers' goals, characterizing it as equally, if not more important, than teaching. Although Nala's response also stresses the need to "welcome" "other people" in her (mostly white) school community, we also see her ability to recognize the ambivalence that exists around race-based conversations among White people, since she qualifies that those of a "different race" are "completely for it." Both perspectives are at once honest, insightful, and hopeful, and underscore the impactful role that teachers play in facilitating an inclusive school climate.

In her essay "Standing Up Against Hate," Mica Pollack[2] asserts that in our politically polarized nation, where unfettered social media content often replaces interactive discourse (especially for young people), schools may be the last place where youth can engage in critical analysis of new information and respectful dialogue with others about socially relevant issues, race being among them. It has long been acknowledged that schools are instrumental in the creation of an informed citizenry. Despite this, civic learning opportunities in subject areas such as government, history, or political science—where students might discuss current national and global events—are becoming increasingly limited.[3] Yet, the dynamic that develops between students and teachers bears upon how young people will enter the body politic; in a climate of trust, engagement, inclusivity, and interactive dialogue, students construct their concept of democratic citizenship.[4] In our racial, ethnic, and culturally diverse nation, color-blindness does not serve this goal. As teachers, educators, and school leaders, we must acknowledge that these factors (i.e., race, ethnicity, and culture) are intimately tied to one's citizenry, experiences, and opportunities, and commit to helping students understand the ways this is the case. Put simply, it is not enough for only "people of a different race" to be "for" conversations about race and ethnicity at school, as Nala described in the opening quotation. We *all* must be for it—especially if we identify as racially white, as I have argued in this book.

In this chapter, I provide a vision for what making a case for race in school can look like during the exciting developmental period of early adolescence. Specifically, I outline and discuss a set of pedagogical strategies and activities around a critical multicultural approach to learning about race, identity, and social justice content that teachers (especially White teachers) can consider, implement, and adapt in middle school classrooms. As a former K–12 teacher, supervisor of pre-service teachers, and current college professor, my process in formulating these practice ideas has been a consciously reflective one. Although I have been engaged in teaching, consulting, researching, and writing about race, equity, and inclusion content in higher education settings for many years now, I had to think differently about how this knowledge and applied expertise would map onto middle school curricula and contexts. Developmentally appropriate practice and relevance were key considerations in my thinking and reflection; that is, what might a collection of ideas and practices around the teaching of race, identity, and equity that are tailored to the unique developmental level and interests of early adolescents look like?

Although early adolescent students do not have the sole power to choose or dictate the curriculum, we know that starting with their experiences and listening to their voices is both informative and adaptive, to say the least. The studies described earlier in this book were based on the presumption that race, racial climate, identity, and inclusion were salient and meaningful to students, although not in uniform ways. I believe the findings support this; the richness of the data, reflected in both the breadth and depth of students' insights, provides evidence that such issues are relevant to them. They are open, curious, and sometimes confused, but are interested in learning more. They want to talk, and they appreciate when their perspectives are considered. Toward this end, the selection of activities and practice ideas that are presented in this chapter are grounded in the lived realities and perceptions of the middle school students who participated in both studies. As such, they can be linked back to the findings that were presented in chapters 2 and 3.

Lev Vygotsky's concept of the zone of proximal development (ZPD)[5] also provided a conceptual rationale for my strategy of starting with students. Vygotsky described the ZPD as the exciting space between a child's independent level of development or performance and their potential development; that is, what they can understand or accomplish with the assistance of a more skilled individual. In this way, the set of activities that will be provided here capitalizes and build upon what early adolescents *do* know and believe about issues of race, identity, and equity, and also what they *do not* know or are uncertain about—that is, they are meant to address areas where their knowledge might be lacking or incomplete. Hence, the role of teachers in creating a ZPD for students as they grapple with these issues in the classroom is at once innovative and essential, filled with potential. It is also both relational and humanizing and consistent with Vygotsky's belief that learning is a fundamentally social process—something that is co-constructed by individuals (here, teachers and students) in culturally mediated and relevant ways.[6]

There are several caveats to address before proceeding further. First, as noted above, the larger sociopolitical context of education in the United States is not irrelevant, and it affects teachers' perceptions of the feasibility of discussing topics such as race, identity, and culture. I acknowledge the weight of such challenges and that we do not bear it equally in terms of our respective privileges and circumstances. In the final, closing chapter of this book, I address this issue as it regards conservative rhetoric and current legislation around the teaching of presumably "divisive concepts" in schools, and the way it contributes to a culture of fear, anxiety, and defensiveness among teachers.

Second, I am also mindful of the reality of the organizational and curricular structure of most middle schools (especially public middle schools) in the United States, where students are often grouped according to team, ability, or multiage groupings, and move through relatively discrete curricular subject areas or separate classes, by following either a block or traditional schedule.[7] Within this structure, it is tempting to relegate topical content around race, culture, or identity only to particular classes such as social studies, government, history, or health, and to argue that such content has no relevance to the disciplines of math or science, for example. Although I acknowledge that this content may be integrated more seamlessly in some subject areas over others, it behooves us to consider James Banks' caution around such a narrow conceptualization of multicultural, antiracist education, which can become a legitimized form of resistance among schools and teachers.[8]

Collaborative forms of teaching have been embedded in middle schools in the United States for some time now.[9] In particular, interdisciplinary team teaching, where a group of teachers across subject areas share common students, schedules, and teaching responsibilities, is considered a best practice that affords the opportunity for a more cohesive experience and sense of connectedness among students and teachers.[10] This is actually an ideal structure within which schools can implement the kinds of topical activities presented here, once an authentic commitment to a critical multicultural, antiracist praxis is made within the school community. If this is not the context of the school in which you work, I encourage you to identify even just a few teachers who share this commitment as you consider the strategies presented in this chapter. Seek to collaborate with others who are willing to engage in creative brainstorming around ways to make their classrooms places where racial awareness, consciousness-raising, and activism among students are intentionally nurtured.

Third, although the strategies and practices are presented and discussed according to a broad framework that will be articulated below, they are not meant to be viewed as a rigid set of lesson plans or activities that must emerge in a particular sequence. Such a sequence might be ideal if it is possible—for example, understanding the salience of one's own racial positionality is thought by many scholars to be a prerequisite to understanding the nature of structural inequality,[11] but it is not completely necessary. Instead, the activities are meant to be used, modified, and applied in ways that are meaningful, relevant, and often emergent with regard to your particular school setting, content area, students, or community. Nor do I suggest that the set of activities presented is the *only* way to address topics of race, or the *correct* way to do so. My intention and hope are that you reflect upon, select, and implement the practices and strategies that feel like the best fit for you and your students, and that you adapt and build upon them in ways that only you can do, respective of the content that you teach.

SETTING THE STAGE FOR CENTERING RACE: PREPARING THE PSYCHOLOGICAL SPACE

One of the costs of racism for all of us is the collective sense of unease that emerges when issues of race, identity, and oppression are brought up, especially in mixed-race settings. This is no less true in the classroom, and I am explicit about this historic interactional dynamic with students. I have found that naming this tension at the outset clarifies for students that the unease they might feel is not unique to any of them as individuals or to our particular course—it is a result of our collective socialization in a race-conscious society that purports to be color-blind. In our present moment, to "normalize" the unease in this way with middle school students might also be very significant because it can provide them with some initial context for interpreting the powerful public backlash against conversations around race in school that they are undoubtedly hearing, but do not have a full understanding of.

When we talk about feelings of unease, we are talking about emotion, which always "sits in the room" with us, as I often tell students. The insights by Beverly Daniel Tatum[12] and Derald Wing Sue[13] regarding the need to understand and attend not just to individuals' intellectual knowledge, but to their affective, emotional responses to race-based content in the classroom have been invaluable to me as a social justice educator. Hence, while I acknowledge for students that learning and discussing these issues will elicit a range of emotions, such as shame, guilt, fear, joy, and hope, I also remind them that we are not having the *same* emotional experience. The reasons for this vary according to our history, family context, or level of knowledge, but our racial positionality is a prominent one; that is, in a general sense, students of color respond to the material as lived experience, while White students respond to the material secondarily, as an intellectual experience[14] (which does not mean they do not care or have good intentions).

Once again, acknowledging the emotional valence and impact of these issues during early adolescence is critical; in a developmental period of high emotionality and heightened sensitivity to environmental stimuli (such as perceived threat),[15] providing emotional support is even more essential. As articulated by Zaretta Hammond in her book *Culturally Responsive Teaching and the Brain: Promoting Authentic Engagement and Rigor Among Culturally and Linguistically Diverse Students*,[16] the ability to notice and attend to the ways students (especially those from historically marginalized backgrounds) might feel psychologically unsafe in the classroom—even when they cannot articulate these feelings themselves—is tantamount to culturally responsive teaching.

I have found that naming the discomfort that exists around issues of race, identity, and oppression, and legitimizing the role of emotion in both our individual and collective responses, accomplishes several things in setting the stage for conversations around race, and for preparing what I call the psychological space. Fundamentally, it reduces (although does not eliminate) the obstacle of race as a historically taboo topic—a characterization that is internalized by many students as far back as early childhood.[17] It acknowledges for students that they bring their whole selves into the conversation, and that they do so from different intersectional spaces. This facilitates empathy, both for themselves and for their peers, as well as perspective-taking.

An initial focus on the affective experience of learning about race is a relatable, meaningful starting point in preparing students to engage in these discussions. The following process-oriented strategies build upon this initial focus in ways that I have found to be essential and that we return to often. At the same time, they build a sense of trust and community within the class that is necessary for authentic engagement and learning of the material.

Leveraging a Diverse School Environment

Both students of color and White students across all schools that participated in the studies presented here recognized the value and richness of racial-ethnic diversity in school. They considered this an excellent opportunity to meet people who were "different" from them, broaden their perspectives, learn about new cultures and traditions, and prepare themselves for diverse interactions in the world. This is very consistent with developmental studies that have found that school racial-ethnic diversity has the potential to confer multiple psychosocial benefits for adolescent students, such as opportunities for cross-racial friendships, the promotion of positive intergroup attitudes, and the development of more complex social identities.[18]

It is certainly the case that public schools as separate institutions do not have control over the racial or ethnic demographic profile of their students (albeit the nuances that exist when we consider charter schools, for example), but they do have the ability to leverage such diversity as a source of authentic learning. Racial-ethnically diverse schools that adopt a color-blind approach in their interactions with students and throughout the curriculum (e.g., via Eurocentric content that is presented uncritically, or a lack of structured opportunities for students to engage and share in identity-based explorations) squander rich learning opportunities—ones that middle school students recognize are there, as our study participants did. In racially homogeneous schools, more (or perhaps a different kind of) intentionality, thought, and effort are required to provide such opportunities for learning—especially if the school population is majority white, where conversations around diversity, race, or equity are much less likely to emerge spontaneously.

Let's All Get Smarter

At the beginning of each semester, I ask college students to fill out a brief informational survey that includes several opportunities to share things about themselves that they want me to know. In my courses that address the psychology of race and systems of oppression and privilege, I ask students to write about what they are most nervous about in taking the course. The overwhelming majority note things such as "I will say the wrong thing," "I will show how much I don't know," or "I will unintentionally offend someone." These sentiments are also highly relevant during the early adolescent years, when students are easily aroused by the social environment. Indeed, young adolescents are self-conscious and very invested in how they appear in the eyes of others; they are aware of the sensitive and often emotionally charged nature of race-based conversations, where things "could really escalate," as Lila, one of the White study participants, noted.

In this regard, it is again important to normalize these fears, positioning them as another example of the lingering costs of racism for all of us. However, it is critical to point out to students that mistakes *will* happen and that many times, an insensitive or uninformed comment says less about them but more about our collective socialization around race, which often includes silencing, misinformation, or lack of direct experience. Put simply, I stress that mistakes are an opportunity for learning for all of us. Several years ago, at a training for higher education faculty, I recall a consultant reminding the (adult) audience not to "staple" a person to their mistakes, and to believe in the potential for colleagues to grow and change. I believe this metaphor also has great relevance in early adolescence, during a time when students are often quick to judge each other harshly and establish clear in-group/out-group boundaries. At the same time, they have a wonderful capacity to empathize with each other.

The abovementioned strategies help shift students' focus away from their individual attempts at "impression management" (a definite preoccupation during this developmental period) to the collective learning that is happening in the class. That is, it can be helpful to remind students that the goal of their work and conversation is that they all "get smarter" together.[19] At the same time, caution is warranted as "mistakes" are normalized. It is important to establish boundaries around what is acceptable speech in the classroom, even if that speech is considered "free speech," lest students attempt to use this (dominant) narrative as a justification to say anything they want. To be specific, I am clear with students that racial slurs or epithets, hate speech, or comments that demonize other people or groups—while free—have an impact on our classroom climate, and that they will not be tolerated. On the first day of one of my more recent courses, a student (a White student, I might add) asked me point-blank, in front of the class, whether I, as the instructor, "would address hurtful comments or microaggressions" if they were made by anyone in the class. She explained that this often did not happen in other courses she had taken. I responded that my practice was indeed to do so, in the most direct, informative, and supportive way possible. I asked the class whether they *wanted* me to address such comments (which I have found to be rare to nonexistent) in that way, and the number of heads that nodded in affirmation surprised me. Clearly, what was being communicated in this situation was students' need to feel protected from potential hurt or psychological harm, and this is no less relevant in the middle school classroom. In fact, perhaps it is more so, since we know that bullying in many forms often peaks during this developmental period.[20] This bears importantly upon the next process-oriented strategy.

Intention and Impact

Although the fact that there can be a discrepancy between one's personal intention (in speech, behavior, or otherwise) and its actual impact on others is one that most—including adolescents—would accept in theory, acknowledging this when it happens in the moment can be much more difficult. For example, in the face of realizing that a racialized, insensitive, or offensive comment has been made (especially if such a comment is pointed out by the recipient or another individual), a common response that often occurs is "but I didn't mean it that way," or, more strikingly, "you are being too sensitive."[21] Such responses—which shift the focus from the person who has been hurt or offended and back to the offender—not only reflect discomfort and defensiveness but also an unwillingness to take accountability for the error that was made. Although this dynamic can occur in many conversational contexts, it takes on additional salience when the content or comment at issue is perceived by the recipient to have racial significance, and is especially powerful if it occurs in the context of interracial dialogue, where historic differences in power and status are at play.

In her TEDx Talk entitled "No Way but Through,"[22] Melanie Domenech Rodríguez provides an insightful discussion around the importance of differentiating between intention and impact that can be used as a powerful teaching tool with middle school students. To illustrate this, she uses a personal story, drawing upon an incident when she herself was confronted by a friend about an offensive comment. Although she initially reacted negatively, she gradually was gradually able to listen, step back, and offer an apology. The example is compelling and one that students can easily relate to. In a fundamental way, considering the distinction between intention and impact strengthens students' perspective-taking abilities—understanding that although they might not have intended to commit an offense (i.e., a verbal microaggression), it still can have a felt, emotional impact on another person. At the same time, it builds empathy and understanding. It also legitimizes what I call "honest challenges" in the classroom—that it is acceptable to communicate with each other if we have been offended or hurt, and to expect listening, respect, and support in return (especially from the teacher). This helps us to be honest *with* each other, as well as accountable *to* each other for what we say and do. I remind students that I hold myself as their teacher to these same standards.

Rodríguez also asks us to consider the way that a comment such as "what you said really made an impact on me/made me uncomfortable" might be seen as an act of generosity—an occasion where an individual who has been hurt provides us with an opportunity for reflection and learning that would not occur if they had said nothing. This is also a critical point of reflection and learning for students. When we acknowledge that our words or actions can have an impact that we may not have intended, we are more ready (in the moment) to listen rather than react, to offer an apology, and to commit to doing better. Indeed, middle school students benefit from concrete scenarios and examples of how to navigate the kinds of interactional challenges that will undoubtedly emerge in discussions of race. As illustrated in Rodríguez's talk, there is "no way but through" these kinds of mistakes, and teachers play essential roles in helping them do so.

Distinguishing Between Opinions and Informed Knowledge

I have found Sensoy and DiAngelo's guidelines for how to engage constructively in social justice courses[23] to be helpful in my attempts to recognize and address some of the sources of difficulty that often emerge as we begin to delve into the kinds of topical content around race, identity, and inequity that are presented in the next section. In particular, two guidelines are highly relevant to early adolescent students who, on average, have less sophisticated cognitive abilities than later adolescent or young adult students, and who may experience what developmental psychologist David Elkind termed "adolescent egocentrism,"[24] or a difficulty decentering from their own perspective: clarifying the difference between opinion and informed knowledge, and distinguishing between personal anecdotes and historic patterns.

First, students must understand that we all have opinions, and that we have a right to them, but these are not the same as informed knowledge, which is the result of intentional study and practice. This may be a difficult concept for middle school students to grasp, especially when we think about the way a belief in the "primacy" of one's opinion is socialized. For example, Sensoy and DiAngelo discuss the way that U.S. society places a high value on opinions, reflected in cultural practices such as radio talk shows that solicit caller opinions, or reality television shows where viewers are allowed to cast their vote for their favorite performer, even without any expertise in the subject matter.[25] Obviously, the various forms of social media that middle school students widely engage in or are exposed to offer endless opportunities to offer an opinion on any number of issues, or to exert an opinion by "liking" or "tagging" other posts. Students often bring these expectations into the classroom space.

Yet, as the authors discuss, in academia and in school-based settings, opinion is the weakest form of intellectual engagement.[26] When material is challenging or does not resonate with our own experiences, or if we do not understand or agree with what is being presented to us, we often resort to opinions as the basis of our engagement. Doing so does not require us to engage deeply with new material—to question, expand upon, or interrogate the ways that new information might compare with one's existing knowledge—it simply reiterates what we already think. Since it is reasonable to assume that middle school students' understanding of issues around race, racism, and inequity may be limited, especially among White students, who may have less lived experience on these issues (as reflected by our White student participants), it is easy to see why distinguishing between opinions and informed knowledge is critical.

Hence, it is important to clarify for students that informed knowledge is based on an analysis and comparison of multiple sources—scholarly evidence, historical documents or primary sources, population reports or statistics, or secondary or tertiary (e.g., news) source material—and that this is different from opinion. Indeed, one's opinions, experiences, or personal testimony are considered part of the knowledge-building and sharing process, but only as they are considered in relation to multiple sources of information, documentation, and divergent perspectives. That is, opinions can and should be used as a point of entry in learning new material, as long as they remain open for examination.[27] This does not mean that we will all interpret information in the same way, but that the ability to develop an informed opinion and stance is always a foremost goal of classroom learning.

Second, as I have discussed throughout this book, an understanding of race and racism requires that we see and acknowledge historical societal patterns and the ways that racial privilege and oppression are built into societal institutions and practices. Although this is a major topic of conceptual learning for students that will be addressed later in this chapter, it is helpful to remind students at the outset that our goal as a class is to develop an understanding of phenomena that move beyond isolated anecdotes or stories. In the same way that students are vulnerable to weighing too heavily on their own opinions, so too are they vulnerable to using anecdotes—whether highly publicized or personal—to process or refute racial content.

As Sensoy and DiAngelo point out, since mainstream discourse and media seldom teach us how inequality (racial or otherwise) works, we often base our conclusions on anecdotal evidence.[28] Adolescents may be even more apt to do so than adults—again, due to their tendency to readily connect with salient concrete experiences or events, or to use their own point of view as the default. For example, when learning about the lack of racial representation in business or political leadership, students might use an example of a family member who has a boss who identifies as a person of color. Or they might point out that individuals like Barack Obama or Kamala Harris show that anyone can "make it," regardless of their race. In these or other similar scenarios, it is important to help students see the way that such anecdotes distort or outright ignore the broader picture, as well as the systemic patterns at play;[29] that is, that while there are always exceptions to any rule or pattern, such exceptions often prove the rule (here, that Barack Obama and Kamala Harris are the only people of color to have ever held the positions of president and vice president, respectively, throughout U.S. history). Reminding students at the outset that developing collective analytic skills to identify societal patterns of behavior is a big part of "getting smarter" as a class community can help to increase their motivation to stay engaged in race-based conversations.

Safe, Brave, and Accountable Spaces

The set of process-oriented, relational strategies presented in this section are meant to complement each other as they frame the psychological space for conversations around race. Although the teacher has a primary role in setting the emotional tone of the classroom and managing students' responses to the material, these strategies can go a long way in creating the kind of affirmational spaces for honest dialogue to occur. It is important to reflect upon the nature of these spaces with humility, however, especially if you identify as part of the dominant racial group. That is, although we as teachers may find the idea of creating a classroom where everyone feels "safe" to be intuitive and pleasing, it is important to remember that safety feels different for everyone, and that marginalized groups or students may never feel fully safe in classroom contexts where race is discussed (which does not mean we should not do so). Moreover, safety is often conflated with comfort for students in dominant groups, who often feel entitled to such comfort, as well as the expectation that students of color will constrain their comments and participation in ways that cater to white emotionalities.[30]

Acknowledging that discomfort is necessary for growth, some scholars have argued for an alternate conceptualization of the safe space as a brave space, an important linguistic shift that acknowledges that learning about race and other issues of injustice requires taking risks; for example, the willingness to reconsider old ways of seeing things in the face of new information, make oneself vulnerable by admitting a lack of knowledge, or make the choice to voice disagreement with a classmate's comment.[31] Taking such risks in dialogues focused on racial issues requires both bravery and courage among the entire classroom community in order to create a more honest and authentic interactional space. However, it is important to note that the notion of brave classrooms has also been challenged on several grounds; namely, that for historically marginalized groups (racial or otherwise), the ability to move about the world and to navigate inequitable systems and spaces is brave in and of itself. Put another way, bravery is enacted on a daily basis, necessary for survival. Further, minoritized individuals may risk violence of a psychic or physical nature if they "bravely" share their views in a public way.[32]

In these ways, global speaker and inclusion strategist Elise Ahenkorah suggests that the idea of creating an accountable space—in the classroom or otherwise—is inherently more affirming, especially for members of minoritized groups.[33] In dialogues around race and racism, an accountable space does not rest on false allusions of safety for all members or on privileged notions of bravery but on group members' willingness to take responsibility for their intentions, words, and actions.[34] In an accountable classroom space, students must listen to each other with respect and expect that they might be "called in" by others (including the teacher being called in) when necessary—to think about something more deeply, to reflect upon what might be an assumption or embedded bias, or certainly, when a hateful comment is articulated. When mistakes—which will happen—are made, they are owned and acknowledged, with an intent to do better. An accountable space is one where all students take responsibility for their own learning, and where members of racially (or other) privileged groups do not expect the minoritized group to take on the burden of "educating" others.

My intention in bringing these tensions forward is to challenge what I have found to be rather simplistic (if not well-intentioned) understandings within both K–12 and higher educational spaces regarding the constitution of a "safe" classroom space for all students; that is, that safe space has become a mantra of sorts. If delivered uncritically, our attempts to create a safe space can easily devolve into reinforcing interactional patterns that privilege the "comfort" of White students. It is not simply about choosing a different word for safety; how we name phenomena frames our thoughts around it, and hence, informs our subsequent actions. This insight itself is a powerful lesson. Hence, I have discussed the (varied) connotations of safe, brave, or accountable spaces directly with students, to encourage them to take collective ownership over the kind of classroom environment they want to create. Based on my own experiences, college students engage deeply, critically, and honestly in this conversation at the beginning of the term. In middle school, although such a conversation can thrive amidst students' emergent critical thinking and perspective-taking skills, more thought and attention might need to be placed on its delivery, considering students' different levels of knowledge. However, I am confident this conversation can be a fruitful one during this developmental period as well. After all, these are the kinds of accommodations teachers make every day, across the curriculum.

A FRAMEWORK FOR CENTERING CONVERSATIONS ON RACE: BYRD'S CYCLES OF DEVELOPMENT

In my attempt to bring a sense of cohesion to the many reflective, topical, interactive, and experiential activities that will be presented in the next section of this chapter, I found Christy Byrd's model of development for individuals as they engage in learning about social identities, diversity, and societal inequity to be a very useful organizing framework. Drawing upon interdisciplinary work in multicultural teacher education, educational psychology, and clinical and counseling psychology, Byrd proposes that the developmental cycle of learning about injustice unfolds according to two basic stages.[35] The first stage can be described as an understanding of the self in society; more specifically, competencies about personal and social identities, and the nature of structural inequality (e.g., how it functions). With this awareness, individuals move into the second stage, which focuses on the integration of knowledge about identity groups, their diverse histories, and the ways that identity-specific mechanisms (e.g., colonization, colorism, prominent stereotypes) frame their respective experiences. This kind of reflection, engagement, and learning are necessary for subsequent agency and action around social justice issues.

The model is meant to articulate general processes of learning about systemic privilege and oppression across categories of difference. As the studies presented in this book attest, race is a salient one during this developmental period. Further, although the model is not meant specifically for adolescents, it can be thoughtfully applied to this age group. In fact, the two progressive stages in Byrd's model are consonant with the Integrative Model for the Development of Anti-racist Behavior in White adolescents that was presented in chapter 3, which also posits that learning about identity and racism are necessary prerequisites for the development of critical racial consciousness, behavior, and action.

To be clear, in both models, situating oneself as an object of reflection and study is the place to begin. In my college-level courses, in order to minimize the kind of resistance that can emerge quickly when students must interact with individuals who they do not know well or have never met, I often adjust the framing of the course content, beginning first with a more systemic analysis of oppression, then moving to the kind of focus on individual, personal identity that both models suggest. However, due to the more emergent nature of abstract reasoning among early adolescents, along with their greater tendency to begin with their own (self-oriented) perspectives, as compared with later-aged college students, an initial focus on one's own personal and social identities, as both models suggest, is likely more adaptive.

A more comprehensive discussion of Byrd's model is beyond the scope of my purpose in this chapter (but I encourage readers to seek this piece out). Instead, I use the two stages outlined above to sequence and organize a set of critical multicultural praxis strategies, activities, and content lessons around key dimensions of learning about race, identity, racism, and inequality. To do this, I conceptualize each stage as understanding self in society (stage 1), and deepening awareness of the world and each other (stage 2). To attest to the relevance of the topics and activities that are included in each section, the voices and perspectives of our student research study participants are woven throughout.

Understanding Self in Society

Dimensions of Self and Identity: "What Makes Me, Me"

A way to start: The complexity of culture. Notwithstanding the ways that race and ethnicity were more salient dimensions of self and identity for students of color like Abel, who mused that his ethnicity was "what makes me, me," than for White students, students' overall narratives provided evidence that they appreciated the ways that their development—both the person they were, and who they were becoming—was a product of multiple influences: family, peers, teachers, traditions, extracurricular interests, religion, and past experiences, to name only a few. This developmentally emergent understanding of the self as embedded in context can be enhanced by a formal study of culture and its complexity. Although a formal definition of culture as the norms, values, practices, and meanings shared by a group of people located in place and time[36] can be offered as a starting point, working with students to concretize this—that is, to clarify the myriad ways that dimensions of culture are manifested—can be an enriching and exciting activity. As students begin to name prominent elements of culture, such as foods, language, music, holidays, or traditions, they begin to appreciate that these "material" aspects of culture also have a "symbolic" dimension; that is, embedded ideas, attitudes, rules, practices, and emotions associated with them, that we have to think a bit harder about to locate.

A very helpful visual representation of the dimensions of culture that is likely very well-suited for early adolescent students is the widely replicated (and easily found online across multiple sources) depiction of the iceberg of culture.[37] In this model, although the surface elements of culture that lay "above sea level," such as the ones named above, are readily seen and identified, a great majority of the way culture is embedded in our lives lies "below sea level" as deep culture. These refer to unspoken and unconscious "rules" of behavior, expectations, and ways of being that are implicitly understood within societal groups, such as conversational patterns, expressions of emotion, personal space, eye contact, or roles related to age, gender, family, class, or occupation. Ironically, those elements of culture that are well below the surface level carry a high level of emotional investment, even though they are not readily identified (because we internalize them as normative).

Conversations and activities using the iceberg of culture are bound only by your creativity and imagination as a teacher. They can be readily applied to virtually any context or curricular area; for example, students might create a cultural iceberg of their "school" at large, a sporting event, or a particular disciplinary occupation. They can analyze the dimensions of a construct like gender, for example, using this model; that is, what are the surface cultural elements of gender that we recognize? What are its deep cultural aspects? Where did they come from, and how did we learn them? Do our ideas on this vary, and if so, why? Have they changed over time?

After students have discussed and analyzed the dimensionality of culture in a broad sense, they become ready to consider its dynamic features with regard to their own lives and experiences. An activity that I have adapted and conducted with college students at the beginning of the term is called a cultural journey.[38] It consists of a reflective writing activity around several short prompts, all of which are designed to support students' understanding of themselves as cultural beings. Students complete these individually (and are allowed to skip any questions they do not want to answer), then come together to share them with each other. The conversations that ensue are never the same but always very rich and can take up entire class periods.

Below is a list of typical prompts that I have used in my classes. The prompts can certainly vary according to your curricular content or goals, but do make note of the ways they address varied dimensions of culture, self, and identity, as well as provide an initial scaffolding for more structural concepts such as historic privilege and oppression for students.

- When you think about your roots or ancestral heritage, what place(s) of origin do you identify as your own? Is this different for others in your family (however you define family)?
- Have you ever heard any stories about how your family/ancestors came to the place where you grew up/were raised? Do you have no access to or have never heard these stories or information? Why do you think this is?
- Are there any celebrations, ceremonies, rituals, foods, artifacts, or holidays that your family continues to celebrate that reflect your place of origin or some other aspect of your ethnocultural affiliation? What are they?
- Do you or does anyone in your family/family circle speak multiple languages? Are there similar or different feelings about this within your family/family circle?
- How/in what ways do you identify with the following, if at all?
  - Ethnicity (which ethnicity or ethnicities)?
  - Language
  - Gender
  - Race
  - Geography or country
  - SES (socioeconomic status/social class)
- When do you think you started to notice these factors?
- Do any of these factors make you feel like you fit in more? Do they make you feel like you fit in less?
- Can you think of one piece of advice or a prominent narrative within your family that has been promoted? What is it? Where do you think it came from?

A variation of this activity that allows students to integrate and bring cohesion to the myriad dimensions of culture that influence the self on their own terms is for them to compose "I AM . . ." poems. Once again, although the structure of this activity can be adapted in countless ways, the goal is to provide students with the opportunity to spontaneously identify aspects of their identity, clarify the varied meanings that these aspects have for them, and to reflect upon and articulate their own realities, hopes, and dreams.[39] The complexity and depth of students' poems will vary according to many factors, not the least of which are their preexisting knowledge (e.g., terminology) and developmental level (i.e., age), and accommodations can be made accordingly. Equally exciting is that this activity can move well outside the domain of written language, where students might be provided with alternative formats to convey "I AM" using artistic media (e.g., drawing, collage), technology, music, or movement.

This activity, along with the others presented in this section, aims to ease students into topical content and conversations around the socially constructed elements of self and identity (i.e., those categories that have social meaning and relevance) using the more nonthreatening, yet conceptually rich "meta" construct of culture. These activities also normalize being honest, empathic, and vulnerable in the classroom—dispositions that are necessary for students to engage authentically in emotionally challenging content.

"Zeroing in" on racial, ethnic, and "American" identity. It is probable and likely inevitable that categories of race, ethnicity, and Americanness will emerge as salient in discussions that are framed around the broader construct of culture. Even though culture is often immediately conflated with one's race or ethnic heritage in a one-dimensional way (and the aforementioned activities are designed to help students avoid doing so), it is undeniably true that both race and ethnicity are important elements of culture.

It is first important, however, to clarify the distinctions in the terms race (a socially constructed idea based on phenotypic characteristics),[40] ethnicity (socially constructed ties to shared ancestry, traditions, or geographic region),[41] and nationality (membership in a particular nation/country)[42] in a formal way, so students can appreciate such distinctions and their varied implications on people's lives. It is absolutely the case that such elements are often interrelated and hard to separate for many individuals regarding their cultural and identity beliefs.[43] In particular, content that helps students to understand that race is a social, not biological reality—despite visible (but unreliable) differences such as skin color or hair texture—that was constructed to establish, maintain, and reify hierarchies of privilege and power throughout (relatively recent) history[44] must ground the discussions around race and ethnicity that are to come.

Although it is upon teachers to seek out curricular content in this area as it applies to their particular courses and students, I consider the documentary series, *RACE: The Power of an Illusion*, to be an excellent teaching resource that can be used with this age group, in that it presents complex information around race in a way that is both thorough and informative, and that will support students as they grapple with what may likely be "contradictory" ideas. Specifically, in three parts, the series provides a historical analysis of the way race and racial categories emerged in colonial law and federal practices (e.g., the census), which provided the basis for legal racist exclusion (e.g., citizenship) and the provision of social, economic, and institutional privileges (e.g., housing) that were afforded to those legally classified as white.

With this foundational knowledge about the construct of race and its functional significance throughout history, a simple but profound question can lead students to a critical next level of analysis: What does being [race, ethnicity] mean to you, personally? Because our students are infinitely diverse along multiple criteria, there will be no single predictable, uniform response to this question. However, as we saw in both the developmental literature and findings from the studies presented in earlier chapters of this book, students of color, on average, can answer this question with more investment, specificity, and clarity than White students can, as Brit's vivid comment that "there's just nothing really there" around being white illustrates. Based on this, as well as on my own experiences leading cross-racial dialogues around race, it is reasonable to conclude that students of color may have already contributed the most to conversations of the sort described above; that is, they are often instrumental in moving dialogues around race forward. Hence, I consider these initial conversations about racial and ethnic identity ones in which students of color are afforded the privilege of listening, while White students now take the conversational lead in reflecting upon this critical question.

We know from studies that White students identify more readily with their ethnic identity, such as a German or Irish heritage, or as "just American," than with their racial identity as white.[45] The reasons for this can vary, but the presence of hegemonic whiteness in the United States that has been discussed in various sections of this book is likely a major one. Of course, it is certainly the case that *all* children should be affirmed in their ethnic heritage, and be given opportunities to explore this. However, because racial categories are the foundation upon which racial inequity and privilege are built, it is important that White students also learn to see and identify themselves as racially White people, especially when we consider their emergent and potential roles as antiracist allies. This, of course, is counter to the dominant, color-blind socialization that children likely receive throughout their childhood and schooling, especially among White students; that is, only your personhood, not your race, matters in life, and moreover, race is only relevant for people of color. With an eye toward breaking this cycle, I argue a dramatically different path in this book, and in this chapter in particular.

In many ways, prior study of the socially constructed nature of race, along with its evolution in U.S. (and global) history, can scaffold White students' exploration of white identity, especially as it shifts the focus from a presumed, personal attack on being white, to the meaning of being part of a (white) racial group, and what that means for future actions, interactions, and ways of being in the world (school, in this case). Even so, there will be tensions as White students grapple with the issue of having both a group-based racial identity (white) that has social relevance, and their own personal identity comprised of many characteristics, which may or may not include their racial (white) identity. This was certainly evident in the perspectives of our White student participants. It is not possible to avoid these tensions; instead, they must be normalized and used as sources of growth. Addressing them together as a classroom community of learners reduces their power, and at the same time, it builds students' stamina for engaging in such conversations.

In considering the numerous scholarly and popular sources, readings, films, and Internet material on the dynamics of whiteness, white identity, and white racial advocacy, I do not find the majority of them developmentally suitable for middle school students, although I am certain such materials must exist. Instead, I propose here that the aforementioned question, "What does being white [and ethnic] mean to you, personally?" can serve as a powerful organizer for students to acknowledge and explore white identity. Despite its simplicity, such a question engages students in important reflection across cognitive, emotional, and social domains, as they explore and consider what being white means, the emotions it elicits, and the ways it influences their social interactions, contexts, and lives. Once again, the direction and pedagogical format of such conversations can vary, but I suspect that the kinds of ancillary questions below might prove to be both illuminating and instructive for both early adolescent students and teachers:

- Why is it hard or confusing to talk about being white? What emotions do you feel when you are asked about it? Can you even describe what it is?
- In what ways is being white important in society? In what ways is it not important? Has this changed over time?
- In what ways is being white important in school? In what ways is it not important? Has this changed over time?
- What things are associated with being white? Are these things always true?
- Are there things that make you proud to be white? Are there things that make you not proud to be white?

Questions such as those listed above push students to reconsider the sentiment expressed by Natalia in our study, that "I don't think being white really matters. I was born this way," but to do so on their own terms. That is, the open-ended nature of the questions allows for a range of student responses in different areas and for students to control the direction of the conversation (which does not negate the role of skilled facilitation). However, a more pointed activity that illustrates the advantages of being white is for students to read the now classic paper "White Privilege: Unpacking the Invisible Knapsack"[46] by Peggy McIntosh. Although frequently assigned in college classrooms and widely adapted for organizational trainings in both the public and private sectors, its conversational prose and use of vivid examples of white privilege, such as "I can be pretty sure that if I ask to talk to 'the person in charge,' I will be facing a person of my race" makes it an effective article for early adolescent students, as long as there is scaffolding around it.

A compelling complementary topic that can enhance and enrich students' learning about racial and ethnic identity, as well as whiteness, is to engage students in conversations and activities around the idea of "being an American" as it is defined in the United States. Although this topic has relevance and can be examined across curricular areas (e.g., history, language arts/ literacy, political science), it can be fascinating to consider it in the context of identity-based discussions; specifically, how this can relate to feelings of belonging and acceptance among different groups. In thinking about the geopolitical boundaries of the United States, some scholars have used the term "imagined community" to describe the collective vision of who we are as a nation-state.[47] This community is "imagined" because we cannot possibly know everyone in our national community. Adolescent students are perceptive enough to know that our imagined community in the United States is racially, ethnically, and culturally diverse, due to both our history and our destiny as a nation of immigrants.

Yet, defining who is, can, and should be an American has been a recurring theme throughout our history.[48] Hence, although we may understand that the composition of America is culturally diverse on an intellectual level, we (including students) often have certain (and shifting) ideas about what being an "American" really means. Where do these ideas come from? Examining this with students from different racial, ethnic, or national (i.e., first or second-generation immigrant) perspectives is an enlightening and powerful exercise. That is, when we think of our "imagined community" in the United States, what does it look like? Which groups come to mind first? What language is spoken? What religion is practiced? Which holidays are widely observed—especially in schools? In discussing these questions, the ways that "American" is often conflated with whiteness and Eurocentrism will likely become illuminated. This helps students to understand why it is much easier for a White person to simply identify as "just American" than it is for a person of color to do so.

Biracial identity. In our study, as we "zeroed in" on questions around racial and ethnic identity with students, the added complexity of biracial identity was immediately clear to us in our conversations with students who self-identified this way. Because the number of biracial children in the United States is increasing and will continue to do so,[49] helping students to develop a healthy sense of being biracial or multiracial is both necessary and adaptive, especially in early adolescence. This goal takes on more weight when we consider the maladaptive beliefs around racial "mixing" and cross-racial relations that contributed to the implementation of racist, exclusionary policies (e.g., anti-miscegenation laws) in our nation's history. Although such ideas and laws are now obsolete, they likely contribute to persistent attitudes around biracial and multiracial individuals as inferior or defective that still exist today.[50]

In this regard, Nala's powerful sentiment of feeling "undermined" by others who appeared to be "critical" of her biracial identity well illustrates a phenomenon that has been well documented in the psychological literature: the way biracial individuals are often closely scrutinized by others—even at an early age—about which race they are. Relatedly, biracial individuals are often told that they "look" more like one race than the other. This kind of "racial patrolling"[51] contributes to a felt sense of pressure among children to choose or favor a singular dimension of their racial heritage(s), such that being biracial or multiracial becomes internalized as different, unnatural, or simply invisible, as Nala's later comment that people "don't want to believe it [biracial identity]" implies. As well, many biracial children must grapple with racialized tensions that can emerge within immediate or extended family members, such as issues of loyalty or betrayal, intrusive questioning, or overtly racist comments or behaviors.[52]

Mindful of these kinds of socialization experiences that might be unique to biracial children, middle school educators are well positioned to help students counter deficit-oriented associations with biracial identity and to help them feel less invisible in a variety of situations; for example, when they must select the category of "other" when demographic information regarding race is requested (e.g., job or college applications, the U.S. Census). This starts with affirming the ways that being biracial or multiracial is inherently a source of strength, richness, and resilience that might allow one to empathize and connect with others more readily, partake in different cultural traditions, or become more adept at "code-switching."

It is also critical to help young people assert their right to self-identify as biracial. In this regard, a very powerful activity for students (all students) to read, reflect upon, and discuss together is a piece by psychologist Maria Root entitled the "Bill of Rights for People of Mixed Heritage."[53] In this brief but now classic piece, Root celebrates the rich dimensionality of being mixed race by articulating a set of individual and collective "rights," all of which push back against deficit-based, societal expectations of what being mixed race means. For example, Root lists the following rights, along with several others not listed below, as ones that should be assured for mixed-race individuals:

- Not to justify my existence to this world.
- Not to keep the races separate within me.
- To identify myself differently from my brothers and sisters.
- To have loyalty and identification with more than one group of people.

The bullets listed above are only a few that are addressed in the book, and I encourage readers to seek it out. I view the curricular possibilities of using Root's piece with students as both varied and exciting.

At the same time, the process of navigating a biracial identity is a highly individual one that is profoundly influenced by factors such as family structure or family socialization, especially in childhood. Hence, acknowledging biracial identity as something that exists and flourishes along a dynamic "blended continuum"[54] is important. Adolescents should be supported in their agency to locate themselves along this continuum as they consider the ways that being biracial is meaningful to them. To clarify, they may feel comfortable with or connected to both racial identities (i.e., placing themselves in the middle of the continuum) or place more emphasis on a singular racial identity (i.e., placing themselves on either end of the continuum). It behooves us to remember, however, that this process is both fluid and contextual. For example, where biracial individuals locate themselves on the continuum might change in response to new learning, courses, experiences, or relationships. It is also highly context-specific, where a particular racial identity may be more salient in some settings over others. What is important is that the experience of being biracial or multiracial is acknowledged in conversations about identity in schools, and that they are facilitated with insight, sensitivity, and respect.

Challenging color-blindness. To engage in a historical, sociocultural, and identity-based analysis of the constructs of race and ethnicity means that students will be actively engaged in what has been called "color-talk,"[55] as opposed to color-blindness. Yet, the narratives of many of our student participants suggest that the ideology of color-blindness is inculcated in their beliefs, or at least is present in the language they use to describe their experiences, especially regarding their perceptions of equal treatment in school, as will be discussed below. But there were themes that did not fit with this. For example, students celebrated the presence of racial-ethnic diversity in school as a source of learning. They also identified many examples of racialized treatment, mostly among and against students of color. Both findings reject the notion of color-blindness as adaptive in school settings.

Put simply, the ideology of color-blindness—how it is defined, what it means, and when it is enacted—can be considered and interrogated with students. Because this ideology directly implicates race and racial difference at the same time it attempts to deny its salience, not addressing it with students can undermine attempts to have productive conversations around race, ethnicity, and identity. I offer the following questions that might guide discussions with students:

- What does it mean to be color-blind?
- When we are encouraged to be color-blind, what is the intended message or messages?
- Is it possible to really be color-blind? What does it mean if we are?
- Is there a time when being color-blind can be a good or helpful thing?
- Is there a time when being color-blind is a bad or unhelpful thing?
- Are there things in society, our community, or our school that we might miss seeing if we are color-blind?
- Are there things in each other that we might miss seeing if we are color-blind?
- Who might be most invested in people being color-blind?
- Are there groups who benefit from color-blindness? Are there groups who are harmed?

Indeed, these last two questions are critical ones, as students come to explore the relation and interactions between a personal identity (how one thinks about and labels themselves as important) and multiple social identities (one's understanding of themselves in relation to social categories and statuses).[56] Considering both are important because there can be dissonance between the two. Using the example of color-blindness, a Black or Asian student might articulate that their race (or race in general) doesn't matter and that it is not important to them. However, this individual perspective does not negate that race has social meaning (e.g., how one's race is viewed by others) and relevance (e.g., racial discrimination, resource inequities).[57] Learning to see oneself as part of socially defined groups or categories that are stratified and have meaning in society and on one's experiences in the world is a critical next step in students' critical racial consciousness, as well as their understanding of social justice issues.

Dimensions of Self and Society: It's Not ONLY Me, but my Positionality

One of the most pervasive themes that emerged in the narratives of our student participants was that they were treated equally at school, regardless of their race. Taken at face value, this is good news and might suggest that the schools' efforts to create equitable and fair environments had an impact. At the same time, there were contradictions; as reviewed above, the narratives of students of color also contained references to racialized interactions with both peers and teachers. On a few occasions, White students noticed this as well, such as when Sue noted that students who were "ignored" or not considered "part of the community" usually were "not white."

Building on this, while it was also the case that many students alluded to the fact that racial inequality existed in society, they did not have the knowledge or terminology to discuss it in ways that moved beyond generalized references to stereotypes, prejudice, or hate crimes (i.e., a reference to anti-Asian hate), as striking as these examples are. Put another way, students were not able to locate their experiences and perceptions around race in school within the broader dynamics of oppression, privilege, and structural inequality. Indeed, these are difficult concepts for young adolescents to grapple with. However, we can effectively structure and scaffold these conversations in developmentally appropriate ways, by leaning into what they already know.

Examining stereotype, prejudice, and discrimination. Our study findings are consistent with the broader literature that suggests that adolescents are cognizant of group-based stereotypes and that these have the potential to be internalized as prejudices—that is, learned prejudgments or biases about groups to which we don't belong.[58] As well, the fact that student participants often used their perceptions of equal treatment as one rationale for why race and ethnicity did not matter in school provides evidence that they understand that racial prejudice can, in fact, lead to differential treatment. Since there are multiple social categories (e.g., race, gender, nationality, social class, religion) upon which stereotypes, prejudice, and discrimination are derived and enacted, students may already have knowledge or experience with them along many dimensions—especially if they identify as a member of a marginalized group.[59]

Despite their interrelated nature, it is important for students to understand the distinction between stereotype, prejudice, and discrimination; despite their differences, they all have power and impact, both because they are fundamentally unfair and because they also unmask privilege, which can be uncomfortable (e.g., evidence of racial discrimination simultaneously reveals white racial advantage). In short, these concepts are emotional ones, and it is not too early for adolescents to grapple with them, with proper support. In dominant discourse, these terms are often used in diffuse and interchangeable ways, especially as they regard the more structural concept of oppression, often with the intent to undermine conversations around systemic inequity because "everybody has prejudice and discriminates." Conflating these concepts, as well as promulgating the idea that they are inevitable, serves to nullify the need for action.

As our findings suggest, students well understand that stereotypes refer to narrow, over-simplified characteristics attributed to a group.[60] They exist as static and fixed attributions (e.g., all Asian students are smart), and they become activated as prejudice when we add value to them (e.g., Asian students will be the easiest and most enjoyable to teach). Prejudice refers to the internal thoughts, beliefs, and attitudes about members of a group to which one does not belong, based on learned prejudgments and limited knowledge or experience with the group.[61] They can be positive (as in the example above) or negative, but they are always unfair because they are not earned by the individual or group but imposed upon them.

The ways that the imposition and manifestation of stereotypes and prejudices inform our beliefs, assessments, and especially, our interactions with others can also be discussed openly with students in terms of process. For example, when are you more likely to engage in prejudiced thinking? When are you least likely to do so? Where do these ideas come from? What has the potential to reduce or transform a stereotype or prejudice? Do stereotypes—such as all White people can't dance, or all Black people like sweet potato pie—have a uniform impact on racially different people or groups? Although there are many activities aimed at helping students recognize the dynamics of stereotype and prejudice, care should be taken when selecting them. In particular, I do not favor activities in which students are asked to generate lists of prominent stereotypes of various racial, ethnic, or cultural groups; students are likely aware of such stereotypes even in early adolescence, so listing them only serves to spotlight and tokenize target groups in ways that might be uncomfortable.

I do, however, favor an approach where students reflect upon the ways that our ideas and perceptions of people and groups are influenced by our socialization. An activity presented in the book *Is Everyone Really Equal: An Introduction to Key Concepts in Social Justice Education*[62] serves as a good example. Briefly, students are asked to generate a list of actions and personality attributes of people in various occupations, such as teacher, police officer, soldier, farmer, housekeeper, scientist, or politician (or any occupation or societal role). Students must then identify the attributes and associations that come to mind for each; that is, who comes to mind? What is their race or ethnicity? Gender? Education? Language? Physical presentation or ability? Students can compare and discuss their responses, as well as consider the ways their preconceived ideas might influence their interactions with these individuals or their expectations toward them.

A focus on interactions and actions that derive from prejudice is the next critical distinction for students to make. Discrimination occurs when we act upon our prejudices.[63] Without conscious effort and intention, we will act upon our prejudices, especially since many of our biases are unconscious.[64] Often times, young people may associate discrimination with actions that occur in employment settings or in college admissions, since high-profile examples or cases are often widely circulated by the media (as they should be). Although an examination of institutional discrimination (e.g., employment, education, housing, health care) is certainly a necessary and worthwhile area of study, students should also understand that discrimination—or differential treatment of others based on preconceived ideas—can also manifest in everyday behaviors, such as ignoring, avoiding, disinterest, ridiculing, jokes, or insults.[65]

Although the question of whether or not a particular action is rooted in discrimination is often a matter of perception, this matters not; adolescents can certainly appreciate that being the target of these behaviors is hurtful, and there is robust literature that suggests that perceived discrimination is linked to poor outcomes, such as anxiety, depression, obesity, substance abuse, and poor self-esteem, in children and adolescents.[66] The activities around peer storytelling and bearing witness that are presented later in this chapter are ones in which students' experiences with discrimination might be shared with each other. This creates an emotionally laden space that has great potential for listening and empathy-building among students and teachers together, but one that must be facilitated with care, sensitivity, and insight.

Activities such as those suggested in this section support young peoples' understanding that while we cannot avoid prejudice and discrimination, we can become more conscious of our socialized attitudes and behaviors as they regard our respective in-group and out-group memberships. And when we are more conscious of our own biases and perceptions, we can begin to change them. That is, we will be open to new insights, learning, and information that will inform our actions and our interactions with others. This is no less true for adolescents in school settings. Understanding that our attitudes are not immutable, but capable of change, can be an empowering learning moment.

A key takeaway that is important for students to recognize is that we all have prejudices, and we all have the potential to act upon them (i.e., discriminate). Prejudice and discrimination are not only characteristics of "bad" people but also patterns that we all internalize and engage in due to our socialization. Considering this in terms of race, students will be able to appreciate that people of color, for example, may have biases or prejudices about different racial groups (including whites), and may act upon them (discriminate). However, are there contingencies around this? That is, although context is important, will the racial prejudice and discrimination enacted toward a white job applicant by a manager who is a person of color, for example, have the same effect as if this scenario were reversed? A nuanced answer to this question lies in students' accurate understanding of another essential concept: oppression.

Prejudice plus power: Understanding oppression. To a large extent, prejudice and discrimination can be described as individual-level actions; although there are predictable patterns in the way they are enacted (e.g., rooted in dominant stereotypes or past interactions), they occur between people and can be enacted by anyone. Oppression, however, is a group-level phenomenon, and is more than just a situational, individual experience. To provide a basic definition, oppression is the way the dominant group in socially relevant categories (e.g., race, sexuality, gender, class, ability) has the ability to "hold down," exploit, or disenfranchise other groups through a set of policies, practices, traditions, norms, and narratives that become historically embedded in societal institutions.[67] These oppressive relationships are captured by "ism" words that students will be familiar with, such as racism, heterosexism, sexism, classism, and ableism, to name several.

The power between groups in each of these social categories does not shift back and forth in response to situational interactions, unique experiences, or prominent examples (e.g., Barack Obama as the first president of color). This is because oppression has several distinctive features: it is institutional, historical, ideological, and cultural.[68] In making these dimensions of oppression more concrete for students, it is helpful to first clarify what an institution is; that is, those organizing structures in society within which human activity occurs, and within which we live and work. Students can work together to chart some of the major societal institutions—such as government, business/employment, education, legal systems, housing, law enforcement, healthcare—and examine their very interrelated nature. With college students, this activity can take up an entire whiteboard, and it would likely be equally rich with middle school students.

Building on this, the features of oppression can be examined using an accessible, readily identified example, such as the dominance of men within the institution of government (i.e., a prominent example of sexism or gender oppression).[69] Students will notice—and can explore further—the underrepresentation of women in all branches of U.S. government, whose creation and terms were set forth by men, and that this is historically evident and factual; that is, this has been the case throughout history. Further, students can examine the ways that this phenomenon (i.e., sexism) has been justified on both ideological and cultural grounds; that is, the presumption that there are more men in government because they likely worked harder to get ahead (i.e., meritocratic ideology), and that men have characteristics that render them more "well-suited" for positions of power, such as being smarter, more responsible, more driven, and less emotional (i.e., cultural perceptions of government politicians).

In these ways, students can come to understand the ways that oppression can be thought of as prejudice plus power. To return to the question posed above about whether a White person's racial discrimination within the context of employment is the same as that experienced by a person of color, students will now be able to see that while both potential scenarios are unfair, only one group's prejudice and discrimination—White people's—is backed by institutional power, making it inordinately more pervasive and potent. That is, because White people are proportionately more represented in the workforce, and especially in managerial ranks,[70] such actions by a person of color do not contribute to an existing oppressive system. Appreciating the ways that prejudice, discrimination, and oppression are distinct also problematizes the narrative of "reverse racism," which is a powerful insight for students. That is, since racialized systems of oppression are historic and deeply embedded in society and societal structures that privilege White people, they do not "reverse" in response to particular circumstances (even if these seem numerous), or shift back and forth between racial groups.[71] As well, in a broader sense, it is important to recognize that the oppression of one social group inherently benefits or privileges the dominant group in that category. An effective way for students to understand this is by thinking about oppression and privilege as "two sides of the same coin."[72]

The other side of the coin: Privilege. Although the aforementioned reading on white privilege by Peggy McIntosh provides students with a concrete opportunity to reflect upon the ways that racial privilege is embedded in interactions, beliefs, cognitions, and material aspects of daily life, a more conceptual study of the way privilege is defined and used in the context of understanding systemic inequity is very beneficial. A basic definition of privilege used by social justice educators is the "systematically conferred dominance and institutional processes by which the beliefs and values of the dominant group are made 'normal' and universal."[73] Building on this, privilege can be thought of as the power and related advantages one holds as a result of belonging to a dominant or higher status group within the social system; that is, the benefits (such as those in McIntosh's essay) one receives because of their status, identities, or background.[74] In this context, such privileges are neither earned (e.g., through hard work) nor an outcome of being lucky, or things that you can refuse or choose to give up. Instead, they are a result of the way socially relevant categories (e.g., race, social class, gender, ability) are hierarchically constructed in society.

Because the opportunity to earn privileges in many contexts is likely a meaningful reality for most students, such as earning a special treat or privilege as a reward for good behavior, good grades, or doing chores, for example, the concept of unearned privilege can be a hard, confusing, or uncomfortable one for students. This tension should be openly discussed with students, in the context of examining different meanings and functions of the word. When used in conversations about diversity and inclusion, reminding students that the objective is to understand socialized systems of inequity, not demonize individuals or groups for having privileges they did not ask for, is essential. As well, to help students consider the invisibility of privilege for the dominant group—that is, why it is easy to have privilege but not feel or be aware of it—an evolutionary, brain-based perspective can be useful. For example, in humans, our brains are wired to detect threat in the environment and to seek well-being for survival; if our experience has shown us that potential stress or vulnerability is not present in a certain context, it elides our consciousness. Applying this to racial privilege, because of the privileges of being white in society, White people typically do not have to think or worry about how and whether their race will negatively impact their interactions (e.g., with police, teachers, employers, or strangers); hence, it becomes invisible.[75]

Because privilege shapes the way we perceive and interact with the world (and vice versa), it is important for students to understand both its social and institutional dimensions, using concrete examples. Once again, I draw upon the book by Sensoy and DiAngelo (*Is Everyone Really Equal?*) to suggest a compelling strategy for illustrating key dynamics of privilege that I have found to be very impactful among college students, and that can easily be modified for middle school students. Specifically, the authors use ableism (i.e., the privileging of able-bodied/minded people)—a particular oppression that is often neglected—to illustrate what they call external and structural dimensions of privilege, as well as its internal and attitudinal dimensions.[76]

Locating ableism in the context of schools provides a vivid and accessible way for students to examine these dimensions. For example, how does the physical structure of the school privilege able-bodied students? If you are able-bodied, what might you take for granted every day as you move through the school day? Are all spaces and classrooms easily accessible? Does the time between class periods assume anything regarding your ability to avoid lateness? Do the desks or materials favor right-handed people? Are there "special" classrooms for "special," "gifted," or "neurodivergent" students? Where are they located?

Building on the above questions regarding the way able-bodied privilege is embedded in the structure of (certainly most) schools, students can consider its attitudinal dimensions. For example, are differently abled individuals considered "atypical," "inferior," or less important in school? How/which group defines "typical" or "normal"? Are the experiences of able-bodied/minded individuals considered superior? Are the experiences, voices, and perspectives of differently abled individuals legitimized and heard? When does this happen? Should the school cater to able-bodied individuals because they might be the numeric majority, or because one group naturally has to be "on top?"[77] Although these questions are among the many that might be generated in any school context regarding the topic of ableism as an exemplar, they serve to illustrate the way the dynamics of privilege become internalized as normal, natural, and inevitable, and how intentionality is required to uncover it.

It would be remiss not to address what I have found to be a somewhat ubiquitous, yet potentially effective, experiential activity around privilege:

the "privilege walk." There are many iterations of this group activity available; in brief, it consists of arranging individuals in an even line and asking them to take a step forward or backward in response to statements that reflect their experiences of privilege or marginalization in social categories (e.g., race, social class, gender, ability, sexuality), either considered separately or in concert with each other. For example, a question might be, "If one or more of your parents has a college degree, take a step forward." On the one hand, this activity allows participants to appreciate—with their bodies, not their words—the way that privilege functions to help people get ahead and stay ahead; that is, how privilege maximizes the impact of one's "hard work." On the other, it has been criticized for creating a context where only participants in the most privileged spaces benefit at the expense of individuals in marginalized groups, who feel awkward, uncomfortable, or vulnerable, especially when the statements center on a single criterion (i.e., just race).

Although I do not have experience conducting this activity with students, the website "Peace Learner: Cultivating Peace and Nonviolence in the Field of Education" includes a thoughtful rationale and lesson plan for a "privilege walk" for use with adolescent students that focuses on different categories of privilege and marginalization.[78] To some extent, this strategy addresses the abovementioned limitations while reinforcing students' understanding of intersectionality—that members of particular groups might experience privilege or oppression along multiple, intersecting criteria—thereby avoiding debates about which singular group is most oppressed. For example, the statement "if you feel respected for your academic performance, take one step forward,"[79] might be interpreted according to multiple criteria that can be discussed. Other statements, such as "if one or both of your parents has a college degree, take a step forward" or "if you ever been profiled by someone else using stereotypes, take a step back,"[80] focus on social class and race more specifically. Teachers should consider and select statements for the activity as they fit with students' developmental level.

What is effectively underscored in the lesson plan is that for the activity to be meaningful and relevant, there must be adequate familiarity and trust that exist among students and facilitators. Second, it is essential that facilitators debrief with students immediately after the session so that negative or traumatic emotions can be held, processed, and discussed. A list of instructional debrief questions appears on the website and may be of great use and inspiration for those engaged in this work with young people.

Viewing privilege and oppression as two sides of the same coin is a powerful metaphor for understanding the way that everyone is implicated in the maintenance of hierarchically unequal systems (racial or otherwise);

because dominant groups occupy positions of power that confer institutional and social benefits, they receive such privileges at the expense of minoritized groups. Yet, appreciating this interdependence is also critical to our collective ability to envision and work toward equity; that is, in recognizing the ways we hold privilege, we can use our power (e.g., resources, voice, opportunity, access, connections) for the good of everyone. Students can begin their journey toward this endeavor in their schools and communities as they come to understand themselves in society and in relation to others.

Deepening Awareness of the World and Each Other

Sharing, Caring, and Bearing Witness in the Peer and School Context

Storytelling and counter-stories. Few would argue that we do not experience and learn about the world and each other through the stories we tell. It is true that posing the question "how was school today?" to a child or adolescent might often be met with a simple "ok," or "fine." But in their own time, they will tell us about their school lives through stories. Adolescents revel in storytelling among their peers, where their experiences, thoughts, desires, and emotions are captured in vivid narratives during a developmental period in which psychological characteristics such as empathy, trust, and loyalty are privileged aspects of their relationships and friendships. Stories draw us in by capturing our attention in a unique way. Stories also have the potential to build bridges between socioculturally different people, reduce barriers to understanding, make abstract ideas more concrete, and inspire a sense of community. In short, stories "educate us about ourselves and others."[81]

During the process of interviewing students for the studies presented in this book, we reflected often on the way students' answers were often clarified through stories; that is, how they transitioned to personal stories or anecdotes to illustrate their experiences. As the chapters on the narratives of both students of color and White students attest, race, ethnicity, and culture factored importantly in the stories they told about their school lives. Specifically, the salience of race and ethnicity often emerged in both the peer context, evidenced by references to racialized stereotypes, "jokes," or social exclusion in a few cases, as well as the institutional culture of the school. In the latter case, this was manifested in comments around Eurocentrism in the curriculum and school calendar, and the hesitancy with which some teachers were inclined to "stand up" for students in the face of racialized interactions, as perceived by students like Misha.

Structuring time for students to share (at their own discretion—more on this below) the kinds of racialized experiences noted above with each other through anecdotes or stories can provide an opportunity to offer personal testimony and insight into the topics of race and racism. At the same time, it allows students to bear witness to the lived experiences of their classmates. This kind of exercise might best be scaffolded within a content-based unit or lesson, rather than implemented as an open-ended (and seemingly awkward) activity where students of color, for example, are simply asked to share about their racialized experiences.

An excellent framing of this might exist in what writer and novelist Chimamanda Ngozi Adichie refers to as the idea of "single stories." Specifically, in her compelling TED Talk, "The Danger of a Single Story,"[82] Adiche provides insights into the way stereotypes often function as "single stories" of a people, flattening their diverse experiences, as well as the ways that stereotypes influence our perceptions and behaviors. Drawing upon her own life and positionality as a Nigerian American, Adichie also addresses the way that historical power influences the stories that get told, who tells them, how they are told, and whose stories are missing.

After watching and discussing Adichie's TED Talk according to its specific content, students might apply the concept of "single stories" to their own lives, both within and outside school. For example, are there "single stories" around race and ethnicity that exist at school? What are they? Are stereotypes the same as "single stories"? Are there "single stories" that you have heard around your racial or ethnic group? Where did you learn them, and where did they come from? Have you personally had an interaction with someone that you think might have been based on a "single story" of who you or your family are? Can you think of a time when you might have reacted to someone or made a judgment about them based on a "single story" about their race or ethnicity?

Although students from all racial-ethnic backgrounds can benefit from reflecting on "single stories," as students in racially minoritized groups share their lived experiences, they engage in what has been referred to as counter-storytelling. A counter-story is one that "counters" or contradicts dominant ideologies that neutralize the significance of race, such as color-blindness, equal opportunity, or meritocracy, as well as reframes deficit-oriented views of people of color.[83] A counter-story draws explicitly on the lived experiences of individuals of color using personal narratives, stories, or family histories.[84] Counter-stories can also be shared by culturally affirming adult models or guest speakers, who can share their reflections on topics that are highly relevant in middle school, such as school achievement, vocational or college access, or career development. In short, counter-storytelling can provide an invaluable opportunity for students and educatorsto better understand and appreciate the unique, yet diverse, experiences of students of color through deliberate listening and engagement.

It is important to underscore that both vulnerability and courage are required for students to share about themselves and their racialized experiences in a group setting. When teachers model these dispositions in their pedagogy and interactions, students may be more likely to do so themselves. While enacting both dispositions can lead to deeper connections and a stronger sense of kinship among racially and ethnically diverse students,[85] no individual student—from any racial-ethnic group—should ever be expected or forced to share or participate. For students in marginalized groups, in particular, the risks of being emotionally vulnerable may simply be too great. Teachers must use their utmost discretion and skill in facilitating these potentially powerful, but highly sensitive, conversations.

Pursuing multiple perspectives through case studies. The ability to appreciate multiple perspectives and engage in what developmental psychologists call perspective-taking is one of the hallmarks of adolescent cognition. In early adolescence, these abilities are more emergent than they are in later adolescence, so structured activities that scaffold students' growth in this area are very beneficial during this time. As the subject matter of this book attests, content around race, identity, and systemic issues of privilege and oppression is as complex as it is emotional. Learning to see, understand, and navigate the role these issues play in one's life and interactions, and those of others, is tantamount to early adolescents' developing sense of fairness, equity, and social justice. As opposed to simply acquiring new knowledge, this process requires students to engage in critical thinking; that is, to go "below the surface" of what they see around race-based (or other) phenomena, and consider the multiple dimensions and nuances that exists in what might be presented as "objective" and "neutral" information.[86] Examining socially relevant issues using a case study approach or method can be a highly effective pedagogical technique for facilitating these skills.

The case method is an approach whereby a real-life scenario—either actual or contrived—that includes different stakeholders (i.e., people) is used as a topic of inquiry and analysis. Abstract concepts, ideas, or strategies can be considered in the context of the scenario, making them more accessible, concrete, and vivid. Most importantly, because the focus in a case approach is on considering multiple viewpoints, competing needs or agendas, evaluating arguments, considering context, and envisioning diverse outcomes, our tendency to draw premature conclusions or resort to simple solutions to complex issues is challenged in growth-promoting ways.[87]

Although a teacher can certainly write or develop case scenarios around virtually any issue, many resources already exist. I have found Paul Gorski and Seema Pothini's book, *Case Studies on Diversity and Social Justice Education*[88] to be a particularly effective and excellent way for college students to flesh out and discuss the inherent complexities embedded in issues around equity, access, and representation, especially as it bears upon applied practice in educational settings. This book is a collection of case scenarios related to educational equity and social justice developed by the authors, based upon their own experiences as K–12 and higher education practitioners, as well as outside testimony. The case scenarios are organized in clusters according to various dimensions of difference, including race, ethnicity and culture, poverty and socioeconomic status, religion, (dis)ability, language, immigration status, sexuality, and gender. They address topics such as school culture, curricular content, bullying, institutional policies, and family engagement. Each case includes multiple stakeholders—students, teachers, administrators, community members, or families—and involves a scenario where an issue of possible injustice or inequity might be at play. The cases are vivid, relatable, and designed to be used flexibly with different age groups.[89]

The authors provide a framework to guide case analyses—what they term the equity literacy framework.[90] In this framework, seeking equity, which refers to fairness, is imperative, and is fundamentally different from seeking equality, which refers to sameness. This is a distinction that our student research participants often did not make, as seen in chapters 2 and 3. In brief, the equity literacy framework is a series of seven steps that help individuals recognize, respond, and redress bias and inequity, with the goal of creating sustainable and affirming learning environments. For example, a case entitled "Diverse Friends Day" presents a scenario in which a teacher organizes a day in which students are encouraged to interact with classmates with whom they would not normally interact, especially in terms of race.[91] Although the teacher has good intentions (e.g., cross-racial contact), their efforts are met with some resistance among several students of color—resistance that the teacher finds perplexing and confusing. To examine the nature of the tensions in the case, one must consider the biases and inequities present (step 1), the various perspectives among stakeholders (step 2), challenges and opportunities present (step 3), just and equitable outcomes (step 4), and short and long-term solutions and actions (steps 5–7).

Because the students in my courses are often pre-service teachers, counselors, or youth workers, the practice implications of a case such as the one above resonate deeply with them. For students in middle school, a stronger focus might be placed on identifying the biases and inequities in the case, along with the various perspectives, challenges, and opportunities that are present. It is also likely that some cases are more developmentally appropriate and relevant for this age group than others. Regardless, working from case studies provides a wonderful opportunity for students to consider issues of power, equity, and representation around race, as well as other categories of difference, outside of what might be their own personal context, allowing them to relate, empathize, and grapple with social justice content in a less threatening, but no less real, way.

Engagement with History and the Sociopolitical World

The relevance of history. At present, the teaching of history in U.S. schools has become increasingly contentious, as the spate of restrictive laws and book bans that have proliferated in many states across the nation attests.[92] However, scholars of race have long observed the contradictory and selective way that the topic of history and its importance is used in dominant discourse in the United States. For example, the bravery, insights, fortitude, and resistance of the founding fathers and early explorers are to be valorized. The establishment of our country's independence is joyfully commemorated annually by a federal holiday. As these examples presume, knowing our history is relevant and important. Yet, when the more troubling aspects of our nation's history are brought into the conversation, history is considered irrelevant, best relegated to something "in the past," or more pointedly, cast as "un-American." This is especially true when the topics of race and racism are brought to bear.[93]

As people who play key roles in building students' intellectual and historical knowledge, as well as their ability to be productive, engaged citizens who know and care about each other, who know and care about inclusion and affirmation, and who know and care about racial justice, teachers must stand firm against these or related claims that teaching a more complete, albeit fraught, history is "un-American," "divisive," or "partisan." Instead, teachers must give voice and expertise to the teaching of an accurate history—one that is deeply flawed and often depraved, yet still innovative and often beautiful—that inspires and guides us in the creation of a truly equitable democracy. Students need and deserve this kind of inspiration and guidance. Teachers hold the privilege, power, and awesome potential to be among those who provide this to them.

It would be impossible and beyond the scope of this or any chapter in this book to provide an exhaustive accounting of the instantiation of white supremacy and racial oppression in the Unites States and globally. Instead, I seek only to underscore that these fundamental concepts can be illustrated by innumerable examples in U.S. history. In reflecting upon this history, it might be true that two examples lie at the core of the country's formation, economic expansion, and global power: the colonization of Indigenous peoples by Europeans and African slavery. Such content also has obvious relevance to other historic and contemporary examples of racial holocaust and genocide throughout the world. Teachers have an ethical responsibility to address these topics in ways that are diligent, honest, and developmentally appropriate, where "inconvenient" historical facts are neither sanitized nor removed, and curricular materials and books are not censored.

From a critical multicultural perspective, the teaching of history should also be unlinked from what is often a traditional, Eurocentric curricular viewpoint; for example, a singular focus on the conditions under which Abraham Lincoln sought to end slavery. Although it is important to understand this, students should also study examples of the innovation, strength, and commitment of Black people to secure their own freedom.[94] Indeed, in a democratic society, students have a right to learn about and appreciate the nuance and complexity of history, and to acquire the analytic skills to investigate historical and contemporary phenomena. In short, they have a right to be educated in a way that is both truthful and empowering.[95]

The current backlash around the teaching of history, and especially its intersection with race, begs the question of how teachers can engage in this content with legitimacy in states where restrictive laws or legislation have been enacted. There are many emerging narratives on how to do this that can be drawn from multiple sources and venues (e.g., online forums, public scholarship, school districts, community and nonprofit organizations), and I encourage readers to partner with colleagues to seek them out. For example, in the interactive *New York Times* piece, "What's Actually Being Taught in History Class"[96] that was referenced in chapter 1, several history teachers from high schools across the country articulate their resolve in teaching a more complete U.S. history. They share their strategies for doing so and often speak from their own local context or positionality. As the piece illustrates, because much of the actual language of various divisive concepts laws enacted is very broad, teachers can accurately address historic racism within topics such as free market capitalism and the concept of liberty, examining content from multiple perspectives.[97]

In this regard, maintaining a sense of agency that is strategic and intentional is important. At a recent academic conference, I was privileged to hear about a university-school partnership aimed at supporting K–12 teachers in teaching social justice content, in a state with a considerable number of banned books.[98] A striking example that was shared in the session was the practice of "hacking" books; that is, engaging with the content of "approved" books or texts in the curriculum in ways that consider alternate plots, characters, illustrations, viewpoints, life experiences, or perspectives. For example, what if the race-ethnicity of the characters in this story were different—would the plot, issues, or outcomes change? What if the location or setting were different? How might we interpret this story in light of current events? Whose voices are absent from the story? From whose perspective is the story told?

This kind of creative restructuring of "sanctioned" curricular content does not mean we won't cover what is "expected"—only that we open the material up to new interpretations, perspectives, and possibilities, especially regarding their implications for equity.

As mentioned above, it is critical not to center the study of racial oppression only through the lens of pain; that is, examples of strength, resistance, and advocacy among racially marginalized groups, as well as their white allies, are also prominent throughout history.[99] Once again, because of the pervasiveness of whiteness and Eurocentrism across all aspects of the curriculum, exposure and study of the adaptive characteristics, traditions, values, and circumstances of groups that have been racially and culturally marginalized in U.S. history are often minimal or outright lacking in schools. Several of our study participants across all schools commented on the absence of their ethnic history or traditions in the curriculum, such as when Yolanda lamented that "we should learn about our [Puerto Rican] heroes" during her conversation on this topic with Alfredo. In the context of schooling, not examining the strengths-based narratives around education that have existed among historically marginalized groups serves to perpetuate and uphold whiteness, while at the same time depriving students of color of essential knowledge of their respective histories; for example, the fervent belief held by Black and other groups of color that literacy and education were things that communities fought for and gave their lives for, as they sought to engage in "the practice of freedom."[100]

The inclusion of ethnic and indigenous studies content in school curricula is a logical and empirically supported mode by which students explore the histories, cultures, intellectual, and political traditions of people of color in the United States.[101] An established body of research has documented that well-designed and well-taught ethnic studies content confers multiple benefits for both students of color and White students: cross-cultural understanding, critical consciousness, empathy, increased academic engagement and performance, increased school attendance, and ethnic, racial, and cultural affirmation.[102] Formal ethnic studies courses exist more commonly at the high school level, and California is currently the only U.S. state with a mandated K–12 ethnic studies curriculum. However, the momentum around decentering whiteness, while acknowledging the disconnect between the traditional, Eurocentric curriculum and the growing population of K–12 students of color, many of whom are first-generation immigrants, continues to grow.[103]

Yet, having formal ethnic studies courses or electives is not required for middle school teachers to adopt core ethnic studies principles, such as representation, equity, and racial justice, in their exploration of the diverse characteristics of different racial-ethnic groups. Although resources and curricula (such as California's Ethnic Studies Model Curriculum[104]) are available, teachers can begin with their own school, classroom, and community populations, using interdisciplinary approaches and units that include text, film, literature, oral histories, art, and music. Once again, working in teams and in community is key; in particular, materials chosen for pedagogical use should not be tokenistic, but be informed, written, or produced by people of color who have firsthand knowledge of their group's experiences with oppression and resistance.[105]

As a powerful aspect of inclusive teaching, ethnic studies content provides students with a deeper (and necessary) understanding of the diversity of our nation, in the service of challenging the structural inequities that still exist. That is, the sociocultural and political struggles around race, ethnicity, representation, and inequity from the past are still seen in the present. Students in middle school are not too young to grapple with this reality as it manifests in current events and popular culture. Teachers are well positioned to help them do so with information, sensitivity, and insight.

Race, racism, and advocacy in current events. As I have argued in this book, early adolescents are highly attuned to the social environment and equipped with more sophisticated cognitive abilities that allow them to consider and reflect upon local and global events with more sophistication than in middle childhood. This developmental advantage has an even greater impact when we consider adolescents' frequent and varied media usage, which virtually ensures that they are going to be exposed to contemporary issues as they unfold. As the opening quotation in chapter 4 by sixth-grade student Agatha attests, students appreciate opportunities to discuss such issues with teachers, rather than have them "pretending like it's [current event] not going on." It is not an overstatement to say that issues of race, racism, and identity are frequently centered in both local and global conflicts, which attests to the way they are deeply woven into the fabric of our society and to our ideas about racial justice and equity. To not acknowledge or ignore the complex manifestations of race in societal events with young people is not only fallacious but profoundly short-sighted, since it perpetuates a continued silencing around race, thereby reinforcing the belief that it is a "taboo" topic, especially among White people.

From a practical point of view, it is also true that learning is enhanced when material is local and relevant, and adolescents are no exception to this. Using local, national, and global circumstances to examine and apply difficult concepts around race, racism, privilege, and oppression—that is, virtually all the topical material presented in this chapter—is an excellent strategy that is worthwhile on several fronts. Along with the opportunity to concretize the material, examining the salience of race and its many dimensions as it presents in current and popular culture helps young people to become more engaged in their world, fosters critical awareness and thinking, and encourages them to be more civic-minded. Events that have currency for students in this regard will undoubtedly exist at both the national and local levels.

Race at the national level: (Only a few) possible examples. Recent tragedies such as the 2015 massacre at the historic Mother Emanuel African American Episcopal Church sparked a nationwide movement to remove Confederate monuments, memorials, flags, and other symbols that pay homage to the Confederacy from public spaces. Educational settings are not removed from this, and the number of K–12 schools and buildings on college campuses that are named for Confederate icons (e.g., Robert E. Lee, Jefferson Davis) is quite large.[106] In school spaces, early adolescent students should become knowledgeable about this issue, and be ready to engage in the conversation. Indeed, in some cases, the issue may implicate their own school buildings, street names, or counties.

Despite the renaming or removal of almost 400 Confederate memorials from communities across the United States,[107] such actions continue to be contested political flashpoints, where demands for the removal of Confederate symbolism and its racially oppressive underpinnings are frequently met with backlash, characterized as a resistance to "erase" history and heritage. But understanding the history around why so many schools were named after Confederates in the wake of the *Brown* decision, for example, along with the broader motivation (historically and presently) behind the dedication of Confederate memorials, is critical to students' emerging racial literacy. So too must they be able to grapple with and formulate answers to critical questions around the nature of the "history" being memorialized by Confederate iconography, whether some history is being ignored or trivialized, who benefits from Confederate representations or traditions, how different racial groups are impacted, and whether the standards of the present or the past should be used to judge and evaluate this issue.

A similar conversation around history and the power of representation can also be held around the topic of racialized mascots in sports, an issue that is likely to hold a strong appeal for many adolescents due to the pervasive role of sports in social, school, and cultural life. Although both contingencies and the potential of sports can be examined along many dimensions (e.g., race, gender, access, social class) with students, interrogating the common and widespread use of Native American mascots and team names in high school, college, and professional teams is a particularly important topic to address. In the classroom, students can be guided to go "below the surface" of the seemingly benign and simple rationale that Native American monikers are meant to honor and show respect for Native Peoples and their history. They should be able to speak with insight on not only why the Washington Redskins football team moved to change their name in 2020, for example, but also why it took so long to do so, despite the term "redskin" being deeply offensive to many Native Americans (of course, why most people are unaware of this association is also an important question). In doing so, they must engage with many important facts (e.g., team owners and athletes are not typically Native American, nor are most teams located in areas with large Native American populations), social dynamics (e.g., who has the power to designate something an "honor," and whether it is perceived as such by recipient groups, current status and treatment of Native Americans in the United States), and stereotypes (e.g., Native American iconography in sport as savage or cartoonish) that are relevant to this historic practice.[108]

Racial justice messaging in sport is also a compelling topic for students to discuss. Race-based athletic activism (e.g., calling attention to systemic racism) in the last decade has increased in prominence and scope.[109] Although the striking example of football player Colin Kaepernick "taking a knee" during the playing of the national anthem that was headline news in 2016 occurred when current early adolescent students were very young, it is part of a much broader wave of race-based activism in sport and among professional athletes that exists today. Indeed, contemporary adolescents can witness such activism via representations, such as justice-focused messages or phrases (e.g., #SayHerName, End Racism) on the court or displayed on players' pre-game jerseys, or in examples of solidarity among players and their organizations, such as equity-oriented initiatives, formal public statements, or collective and individual advocacy or nonprofit work among players.

If early adolescents take this kind of public advocacy in sport for granted, many (adults) do not; that is, claims that sport and sport figures should be neutral and apolitical are not uncommon. So too do many (adults) argue that sport should serve merely as a source of entertainment and fun, not social advocacy. Once again, there are rich opportunities for students to go "below the surface" of these lamentations, and to gather more information about the way that sports has never been apolitical; for example, sport has been used to maintain racial hierarchies, such as the practice of barring African American athletes from sports leagues and professional teams, and racialized stereotypes are promulgated across sport domains. As well, asking students to consider, once again, the questions of "who benefits" or "whose interests are served" when sport or high-profile athletes are relegated to purely entertainment, rather than advocacy roles, is a meaningful and worthwhile perspective-taking exercise which illustrates key dynamics of oppression. Cast in vivid imagery, what are the emotions that might arise from different racial groups when a player takes a knee in protest? How are racial comfort and equilibrium disrupted? Whose comfort is being privileged in the contention that such behaviors are disrespectful? Is respect being defined in the same way?

Race at the community level. Community and local events that have (or are perceived by some to have) racialized dimensions or implications can be particularly compelling for students to discuss and examine, although they must be facilitated with great care since students, families, and the entire school may be invested in them on a more personal level. Since we can never predict how, when, and during which time such issues will emerge, I consider the process and impact of these conversations to be iterative ones. Specifically, although a fundamental understanding of the nature of social inequality will undoubtedly contribute to students' ability to notice and analyze the extent to which racial (or other) inequities are present in any given situation, the dynamics of inequity (e.g., oppression and privilege) can also be revealed through grappling with situational events in classroom community.

To clarify further, respectful discussion of a local event or incident that is relevant to students and their families need not be avoided because certain concepts around inequity have not been fully addressed. However, consistent with my argument in chapter 4, this does underscore the need for teachers themselves to be ready to draw upon critical multicultural knowledge and praxis in ways that are informed, flexible, and adaptive. It is a truism that students' lives outside of school impact their experiences and interactions in school. Although schools and teachers do not have control over much of this—for example, they cannot control racism, xenophobia, or identity-based discrimination that students and their families might experience in the community—school personnel should at least be aware of these conditions, and how they might be affecting the lives of children, youth, and families.[110]

I reflected upon this insight many times this academic year, as a local situation that was part of a national issue played out in my own suburban, majority-white community. Like many municipalities across the United States, our relatively small town in the Northeast received and provided shelter for a significant number of migrant families and children who were seeking asylum status over the course of the 2023–2024 school year. In following the events, and through conversations with town officials, I learned that newcomer students were learning together in relatively segregated, mixed-age classrooms at our local elementary school, with the support of bilingual instructors who were fluent in the native language of the children. There were frequent updates throughout the school year that the students were "doing well." Although I chose to remain hopeful about the validity of this statement, I continued to wonder about it; that is, from whose assessment was this conclusion drawn? Furthermore, I continued to wonder about the newcomer students' reception in school, as well as that of their families, especially after becoming aware of some significant local tensions around the issue. Were resident students informed about the situation, as well as the larger context around family migration to the United States, in developmentally appropriate ways? Were teachers and school staff scaffolding these conversations? Were conversations with resident students (again, mostly White) even happening at all?

During a recent fall semester, a first-year student in one of my college classes brought a compelling issue that had occurred in her home community to our classroom space. The issue centered on representation and free speech; specifically, a very large Confederate flag had been draped across the outside of a home that directly abutted the high school football field, such that the flag was visible from most angles of the field. Requests to remove the flag by school administrators were ignored by the homeowner, who viewed this as an issue of free speech and property rights. Although we discussed the issue as a college classroom, we wondered about the kinds of conversations that were happening with the people who were most affected by the issue in real time—the students, families, and community members who regularly attended the football games. Were middle and high school students engaged in such conversations in the classroom? Did they understand and appreciate the complexity of the issues that were at play?

There is nothing particularly unique about either of these examples; that is, similar situations could, and likely have, occurred in communities across the nation. But the salience of race in both cases is part of what makes them ubiquitous. I present them here only to illustrate that the intersection of race, community, and school-based content is likely inevitable and will show up in the classroom. How we choose to engage with students in understanding the nature of such intersections as they bear upon their lived experiences is a testament to our commitment to a more holistic, relational, and antiracist pedagogy.

CONCLUSION

As shown in this chapter, middle school classrooms can become creative, innovative spaces where adolescents develop an understanding—or build upon their existing knowledge—of the dynamics of race, privilege, and oppression through an exploration of their own racial identity and positionality, an examination of the construct of race in history, and through bearing witness to the lived experiences of their racially similar and different peers. Although struggle, tension, discomfort, and strong emotions are inexorable parts of this process, it is important to recognize that none of the classroom activities presented are meant to make students feel shamed, guilty, or maligned because of their race. However, all of the activities have as their ultimate goal the opportunity for students to see their own humanity in each other, and to be inspired to work toward positive change. Indeed, teachers have the power to activate these processes and must hold fast to this power, even when it appears to be under threat.

Chapter 6

Do What's in Your Power to Do

(Re) Claiming our Agency in Making the Case for Race in Middle School

> I feel like my teachers have to be able to teach well. Like, when I'm learning at an appropriate pace for my level, and everyone else is as well, but we're also being engaged with on a personal level. Like they will know you well enough to where you're comfortable and then make jokes with you or laugh with you. They won't cross the line with you either, like being disrespectful. Like, if someone were to insult my ethnicity, and then I were to say I was offended, and they [teachers] didn't stop that. (Ana, Chinese, eighth-grade student)

If you look back at many of the student quotations that have opened each chapter of this book, it becomes clear that students in the middle grades are able to define the characteristics of a good teacher with great insight, garnered from their school experiences. Although content knowledge and learning are clearly important, we can see that "personal" and "comfortable" relationships with teachers that feel respectful are also paramount. In the segment above, Ana brings forth another dimension of what it means to "teach well": the teacher's willingness or readiness to intervene in the face of an ethnic "insult." When I first began to engage in teaching, research, learning about race, racism, and systems of oppression, it was comments from students of color like Ana that moved me the most as a White teacher. They still do move me, of course, but I have come to a deeper awareness that issues of race-ethnicity, discrimination, and oppression are as much about bringing White students and White teachers to new levels of racial consciousness and understanding as they are about supporting students of color.

In this book, I have explicitly positioned a critical multicultural praxis aimed at supporting racial consciousness in adolescence as an essential element of good teaching for all students, during a developmental period of dramatic cognitive, social, and affective growth and change. Moreover, I consider teaching and consciousness-raising around race and social justice issues an ethical responsibility and right of educators, all of which are integral to maintaining a democratic society.[1] As I have argued, antiracist and anti-oppressive teaching requires more than good intentions, goodwill, or the simple hope that our love for children will translate into an identity-affirming pedagogy—it requires critically informed knowledge about the historic and systemic nature of racial oppression and privilege, as well as deep reflection about how we—as individuals, teachers, and educators—are implicated in this complicated web. To be transparent, writing about these issues during a time when they have come under renewed attack at the federal, state, and local levels often gave me pause and caused me to question my own agency in making an argument for the inclusion of race-based content in school. Along with ongoing support and fellowship with colleagues, I drew inspiration during these times of hesitation from an interview I listened to with author Barbara Kingsolver, who noted that writing must not only reflect reality, but also push against it. As a White educator, this book is my bold and humble attempt to do just that, in the service of more just and equitable schools for young people, and a more just and equitable society.

Toward these ends, it is my hope that the student narratives, points of professional and personal reflection, and classroom strategies and activities around the history, construct, and manifestation of race in society that were presented in this book will serve as sources of possibility and inspiration, and that they gain momentum in your classroom and with your students as you implement them in creative, contextually relevant ways. After all, when we begin to internalize a critical multicultural perspective and stance, it impacts everything we do in the classroom and everything we teach. We are not always successful in our efforts, and in fact, we often fall short, but we come to see that these conversations begin to move from the periphery of the curriculum, and closer to the center of it. To be clear, when we commit to racial equity, critical consciousness, and social justice as core educational values, we will move differently in the classroom than we did before.[2]

But I want to do more than hope in this final chapter, and instead, shift the focus more squarely to our potential for action; that is, our ability to "move differently" in the classroom. Returning to the opening quotation as one example, we could think of this as the confidence with which we take action to address or "stop" the kind of racially or ethnically offensive behavior that Ana makes note of. Would you provide scaffolding, questions, or advocacy in that situation, or ignore it and let students work it out themselves? In many ways, this comes down to our sense of confidence, power, and agency in addressing racialized issues head on with students. Coming to terms with our role in this complicated and unpredictable process, amidst what often feels like public scrutiny and disparagement around any mention or legitimization of race in school and in classroom practice is difficult work, to say the least.

In this regard, we each have our own power as teachers, but that power is far from the same. We have different racial and ethnic histories, statuses, and intersectional positionalities. We teach in different states and school contexts, with varying degrees of support, as well as varying sources of resistance or censure of curricular content. We have different personal, familial, health, and financial circumstances that influence our lives outside (and inside!) the classroom. And although I do believe that a teaching context that is overtly hostile to social justice ideals and values may not be the right fit for an equity-minded educator, the choice to simply leave a paid teaching position in search of a better one is likely not one that most teachers can easily rely upon. Hence, I will not put forth here what I consider to be a privileged argument that teachers must make the case for teaching race in school even if it means putting their jobs at risk or losing their jobs altogether. Beyond the impracticality of this stance, it positions virtually all the material presented in this book in a bifurcated way; that is, that there exist discrete teaching contexts where conversations around race *can* happen, and those where they just *cannot*.

Instead, I frame what I hope is read as sources of agency and inspiration as presented in this chapter using a line from what is arguably an unexpected source: the 1998 movie *American History X*. The movie follows the journey of a family that must grapple with their eldest son Derek's radicalization by local neo-Nazi groups. Derek serves time for the voluntary manslaughter of two Black men. One of his former high school teachers, Dr. Sweeney—himself a Black man—becomes involved in his subsequent healing and rehabilitation both in prison and upon his release. As part of this rehabilitation, Derek agrees to work with Dr. Sweeney and local authorities in their attempts to infiltrate and disband the neo-Nazi group by offering them inside information and key informants. In one scene, Derek rages against the compromising and dangerous position he is in, shouting, "What do you expect me to do?" Dr. Sweeney calmly and steadfastly asserts, "I want you to do what's in your power to do."

Do what's in your power to do. That phrase, that imperative, kept returning to my mind as I moved through the chapters of this book about making a case for the teaching of race and supporting critical racial consciousness among adolescents in the face of the current sociopolitical resistance. Indeed, it is often hard to connect with our own power or to remember that we have any in such times. But our agency as teachers comes from knowing that when we close our classroom doors, we have a certain pedagogical power that nobody can take from us. As equity-minded educators, we have the insight, creativity, and innovation to make contextually relevant choices and decisions—decisions that might be different from a teacher in another community and another context, but that are no less committed to children's learning about these critical issues.

From this view, we don't need to be in some sort of idealized teaching context to do this work, with idealized colleagues and administrators who provide us with a safe and foolproof roadmap for moving forward with an antiracist teaching ethos. When we believe and stand firm in our power and agency as teachers, a critical multicultural praxis is something *every* teacher who is committed to these values can enact, in *any* teaching context, with *varying* levels of content and degrees of complexity. What we trust is that we have done the necessary work required for this kind of affirming pedagogy. What we trust is the knowledge around race and social justice that we have gained through listening, intentional study, or lived experience. As we seek to prepare young people to work toward and find their place in a more inclusive world, we do what is in our power to do, every day.

DOING WHAT'S IN OUR POWER TO DO: DECONSTRUCTING THE STRATEGY AROUND THE RESISTANCE

Strategy is also important as we seek to assert our power and agency in the classroom as it serves equity goals. In chapter 1 and throughout this book, I have referenced the various federal and state legislative efforts designed to regulate or restrict the ways that the nation's teachers can discuss racism, sexism, and issues of systemic inequity in the classroom, including the way that CRT has been misused and leveraged as the newest buzzword designed to promote fear and angst about social justice and equity initiatives in schools. In an ideological sense, a great deal of this resistance is grounded in aspirational but patently false notions of color-blindness in a country that is constructed on the codification of racial differences. Yet, conservative rhetoric has co-opted the language of color-blindness, stripping it from the way it was used by civil rights leaders to challenge apartheid laws and policies, in order to stimulate hyper-race-consciousness among White people[3]—including parents. Among other things, such a strategy activates white racial anxiety and discomfort.

As it applies to schools, the motivation for presumably color-blind, anti-CRT, and "divisive concepts" legislation is also practical and more immediate: to silence teaching about race and racism in order to protect the inequitable racial status quo or face varying consequences.[4] In this context, it is understandable and not surprising that, according to the 2023 State of American Teacher Survey by the RAND Corporation, 65% of teachers nationally reported that they chose to limit discussions of social and political issues like race and gender in the classroom, including in states without laws restricting such instruction.[5]

As I noted at the beginning of this chapter, although I am deeply empathetic toward the range of contextual circumstances under which teachers attempt to do this work, I am also mindful of the recommendations of a panel of teacher educators from different states who delivered a session at a 2024 international conference of educators that I attended, entitled "Dismantling Systems and Reimagining Equity in Politically Hostile Learning Contexts,"[6] who cautioned against "over-interpreting" our response to restrictive legislation that applies to public school curricula, such as the 2021 Texas House Bill 3979 (HB 3979). That is, from their view, we should not let fear minimize or eliminate our resolve to give students the kind of engaging, honest, and civically rich education that they need and deserve. Reimagining ways to prioritize equity in the teaching and learning process is possible. It is still happening in schools and classrooms throughout the country, despite the challenges.

But it is not easy. In considering the discursive practices that are used to justify legislation against the teaching of social justice and equity issues, I argue that they are delivered in a way that is meant to put administrators, school personnel, and teachers on the defensive. Put another way, although many educators may sense that the bills are unjust, they lack the necessary background to express their concerns with confidence.[7] As educators, it behooves us to be able to deconstruct some of the core elements of the rationale for silencing equity-based content as it applies to both our pedagogy and our relationships with parents and families. Our ability to respond to these attacks—not seek to avoid or retreat from them—is critical to our ability to sustain a critical multicultural pedagogy. In my view, such attacks often weaponize three widely held, hegemonic ideas about the role and positionality of teachers in educating children: the issue of indoctrination, political neutrality, and parental involvement and rights. Although I have touched upon these issues in various chapters of this book, I bring them together here because they illuminate particularly salient dimensions of the resistance to equity work that is targeted at teachers in particular.

Claims of Indoctrination

Contemporary movements that frame public schools as sites of indoctrination have as one of their aims an attempt to silence equity, diversity, and inclusive content and modes of teaching. Such efforts threaten to weaken the very institutions that prepare students to become informed citizens in a diverse and pluralistic democracy.[8] Being able to articulate the difference between instruction and indoctrination (despite its nuance within social science disciplines) is important in fighting back against such attempts. First, teaching and education involve imparting information from a particular point of view, school of thought, or historical body of work. This involves introducing and reinforcing concepts through a gradual process of transmitting information to students and teaching them to engage with it through reading, thinking, discussion, questioning, and analysis.

In this way, expecting students to comprehend and apply ideas that have been accepted as truth within a discipline through research and study of observable data, patterns, and evidence constitutes legitimate instruction, not indoctrination.[9] However, when ideas that have not been tested are presented as truth, or when instructors *insist* that propositions that are contestable within a discipline be accepted *without* allowing students to question their validity or pose alternative understandings, indoctrination is at play.[10] Preliminary findings from a national study by the American Historical Association show very little evidence of indoctrination among U.S. middle and high school history teachers, who report that they draw upon multiple sources to develop critical thinking, questioning, and analytical skills among students, and that open inquiry is a core dimension of their pedagogy.[11]

Second, it is fascinating and enlightening to consider which kinds of subject matter or content are often considered fodder for indoctrination claims from conservative groups. For example, sharing the relevance and role that Confederate monuments have in "honoring" heroes of the past is considered simply teaching and preserving our "patriotic" history, but if a teacher exposes students to the complicated reasons and racialized initiatives behind the impetus to construct and preserve such monuments in our history, it is suddenly labeled *indoctrination*. Presenting Christopher Columbus as a valiant discoverer of the "new world" and the "first" Thanksgiving as a purely celebratory, peace-building tradition is teaching history (consider how many of us were taught these things in our grade school years). Yet when the brutalization and genocide of Indigenous peoples of the Americas as part of that history is added to the discussion, it becomes *indoctrination*. As a community of educators, it is critically important that we expose and give voice to such contradictions.

Teachers as Apolitical and Neutral

The contention that teachers must maintain both an apolitical and neutral stance in the classroom is related to claims of subject matter indoctrination. Once again, these claims are emotionally triggering for teachers and serve to neutralize (no pun intended) their agency in addressing contemporary issues, events, and circumstances that have a real impact on the lives of children, families, and communities. First, it is important to acknowledge the fact that the U.S. education system is inherently political; it is governed by law and by federal and state boards of education, as well as local school boards and administrators who are beholden to larger structural imperatives. Such imperatives include the policies that guide teachers' work, curricular mandates, the choice of textbooks, and the organization of the school day and calendar.[12] At present and in our more recent history, the various "divisive concepts" laws and COVID-19 school protocols are vivid examples of the politicized nature of schools. Further back in history, debates around the teaching of evolution, the recitation of the Pledge of Allegiance, and the end of legal school segregation in the wake of the *Brown* decision attest to the political nature of schools.[13] As outlined in the first chapter, race is implicated in many (if not most) of the kinds of examples listed above. Being able to articulate that politics are already at play in schools provides necessary perspective on this issue and dampens the sensationalized claim that teachers "bring their politics into the classroom."

Of course, there are human and relational dimensions to this issue. Since we are all members of the body politic, both students and teachers bring their backgrounds, views, and beliefs into the classroom; as a teacher, in being your authentic self with students, you are teaching your politics.[14] Second, it is imperative that we consider what we are teaching students when we ignore contemporary issues or events that are political in nature, and how students will be harmed in different ways by our silence. This does not mean that teachers should tell students which political candidate their families should vote for, or which political party students should aspire to be part of. But remaining silent about sociopolitical events as they are unfolding in the world not only reinforces complacency and civic disengagement for students but also eliminates the opportunity to engage in conflict or dialogue. In a political—not partisan—classroom, students learn to analyze and debate political questions, build their knowledge on what makes communities democratic, and acquire the skills they will need to make their interactions in the community better.[15]

For sure, supporting students' ability to engage in critical thinking involves examination of multiple sources, an analysis of multiple perspectives and dimensions, comparison and synthesis of information and arguments, and the freedom to share their experiences and perspectives. At the same time, being an advocate for social justice and equity often requires that we choose a side—that is, that we are not indifferent in the face of injustice. To be clear, our students must see us—their teachers and mentors—taking a stand against oppression and oppressive practices. If we seek to be authentic in our relationships with students as we espouse a critical multicultural praxis, our commitment to equity must be visible and clear to them. As the opening quotation from Ana attests, students from racially marginalized groups are watching us carefully in the classroom, making note of how and whether we respond to or address issues of discrimination or oppression; that is, whether we stay neutral, or whether we speak out against the status quo. A strict adherence to neutrality in the face of unjust events that impact the lives and realities of students with marginalized identities can risk alienating them in a classroom space that is supposed to be affirming. For students in all identity groups, they lose out on the ability to witness what an anti-oppressive teaching stance can look and sound like. The book *Teaching on Days After: Educating for Equity in the Wake of Injustice* by Alyssa Hadley Dunn contains moving and inspirational narratives from teachers and students on their actual classroom experiences as they pushed past their fears and anxieties to grapple together on the "days after" unjust national and local events, such as school shootings, racial violence, or gender injustice, occurred.[16] Their real-life stories are a testament to teacher and student agency.

Finally, as noted in the first chapter of this book, it is important to remember that silence and neutrality are political choices in themselves. Moreover, in a recent ethnographic study with social studies teachers in a predominately White school, observation of their classroom practices revealed how their purported neutrality often functioned as a passive endorsement of conservative views, such as American imperialism and resistance to affirmative action. In follow-up interviews, students did not characterize such examples as right-leaning but neutral.[17] This reveals yet another compelling irony that is often at play both inside and outside schools: if an idea supports the dominant ideological point of view (e.g., meritocracy, equal opportunity), it is deemed *neutral*, but if it challenges or pushes against the status quo (e.g., naming systemic inequity), it is deemed *political*. Once again, we must question what is being protected by these characterizations, and how power and hegemony are at play.

In my work with college students, I am explicit about the fact that my coursework and my views are grounded in the values of equity and social justice. I state clearly when I am not neutral on a particular issue, even when it is controversial, and that my view is informed by an amalgamation of research, study, life experience, and core values. I encourage them to ask questions, consider opposing views, and reflect upon the relevance of positionality and lived experience in the construct and interpretation of diverse perspectives. This strategy puts the tensions around neutrality directly on the table, while at the same time, it models a commitment to justice in the classroom. Ultimately, although the style of any strategy for navigating these complexities with students should be at the discretion of the instructor,[18] in an equity-oriented, anti-racist classroom, a commitment to social justice should be seen, heard, and felt.

Parents' Involvement and Rights

As teachers, we have always known that parents and families are integral to students' health, wellness, and school success. Indeed, most pre-service teacher licensure programs require coursework and study on strategies for facilitating parent involvement and engagement. Educational books and literature on parent involvement and engagement are voluminous and have become richly nuanced in the way that the definitions of involvement—as well as family engagement strategies—have become more inclusive, as well as more contextually and culturally responsive.

However, the inherent value of strong partnerships with parents and families that is arguably part of our consciousness as teachers has been undermined in recent years, as parents and the issue of "parental rights" have been strategically brought into the fight against "divisive concepts" in schools. In yet another obvious example of the political nature of schools, K–12 schools, teachers, and parents have been pitted against each other as enemies by some conservative lawmakers and politicians, as they continue to promote the narrative that teachers seek to indoctrinate children with anti-American, "woke" ideas (read: race, diversity, equity, and inclusion content and advocacy). This has culminated in legislative action; for example, the Parents' Bill of Rights Act (H.R.5), which was passed in the House in 2023 (but does not have Senate approval) would add language to existing federal legislation (i.e., the 1965 Education and Secondary Education Act, 1974 Family Educational Rights and Privacy Act), requiring schools to notify parents that they have the right to review school curricula or books, school budgets, and mandate a minimum number of teacher meetings, to name several aspects of the bill, presumably as a way of providing more "transparency and accountability to education."[19]

At the state level, Florida's controversial Parental Rights in Education bill, referred to by critics as the "Don't Say Gay" bill, requires district school boards to adopt procedures by which parents must be notified of "a change in services or monitoring" related to a child's mental, emotional, or physical health (e.g., if children disclose information about their sexual or gender identity) and prohibits classroom discussion of sexuality or gender issues in certain grade levels.[20] Many other states have considered or passed similar legislation to restrict discussions around race, gender identity, or sexual identity in school. Such efforts have run alongside the emergence and advocacy of a spate of "parental rights" groups and organizations, such as the nonprofit group Moms for Liberty,[21] whose co-founder warned at its second annual Joyful Warriors National Summit in 2023 that "we are also warriors, meaning, if someone is demonstrably harming our children, we are going to come together to fight to protect them."[22] What, exactly, children are being "protected" from is reflected in the work of such groups, which have influenced hundreds of school board elections by supporting candidates who oppose DEI initiatives, spearheaded campaigns against teachers, and whose advocacy has resulted in the removal of books with LGBTQ+ characters and characters of color from schools and school libraries.[23] In fact, in 2023, the Southern Poverty Law Center included Moms for Liberty in its annual "Year in Hate & Extremism 2022" report, citing the group as promoting an antistudent inclusion agenda, and drawing comparisons between them and parent groups that attempted to re-segregate public schools during the civil rights movement.[24]

It appears very clear, as many educational leaders have observed, that the various initiatives of the legislative actions and parents' rights groups briefly outlined above represent a coordinated response to efforts by schools to teach students about race, racism, and inclusivity and to provide protections for LGBTQ+ students.[25] Such efforts sow division and mistrust between schools and families, as they undermine public education writ large. However, many administrative leaders point out that parental rights legislation is based on fallacious assumptions; that is, many, if not most, of the requirements in the bill are already in place in public schools, such as the ability to view curricular materials or books, access to the school budget, and the opportunity to speak at public school board meetings.[26] At the classroom level, being available and responsive to parents has always been considered a best practice, and teachers often use their own unpaid time outside of the school day to communicate with families.

In this context, it is important for teachers not to lose sight of the fact that despite the way the platform of groups like Moms for Liberty has been elevated by the reach and connections of wealthy donors, conservative foundations, and media outlets, they do not constitute the majority views of parents of children in K–12 school spaces. Hence, once again, it is critical that we not over-interpret their power and take heart in the fact that most parents, as well as the general public, see teachers as professionals who should be trusted to make curricular decisions. For example, the PDK Poll of the Public's Attitudes Toward the Public Schools is a national, representative random sample of U.S. adults that has been disseminated since 1969. Considered a trusted source of public opinion about K–12 education due to its content (i.e., range of questions) and methodological rigor, results of the 55th Annual PDK Poll in 2023 showed strong and continued support and empathy for teachers. Specifically, although just over half of adults surveyed (51%) did support state laws that restrict teaching content, a wider majority of adults (66%) felt that teachers should have a substantial say in what is taught in public schools, more so than school boards, local residents, or lawmakers. Also, 75% of respondents noted that teachers are undervalued in society, and 67% were in support of increasing local public school teacher salaries by raising property taxes.

We have always known that we need the support of parents and families to serve children best. Regarding the teaching of race, social justice, and equity content in school, we must believe and know there are parents who also deeply value these things and that they *will* support what we are doing. They trust our expertise and recognize the care we give, and will advocate and fight for us because they see the impact we are having on their children (and perhaps they are tired of hearing our names over and over at home!). Those parents are there, and we need to create opportunities in our classrooms and our schools to bring them together in collective advocacy.[27]

But for those parents who *won't* or *can't* support our work, we cannot give up on them. They are part of our classroom and school community. We need to continue to engage with them, not avoid their phone calls or emails. Certainly, some parents will have concerns, worries, or strong opinions that come from many places—past experiences, different understandings, religious or personal beliefs, lack of knowledge, biases, or contextual realities. Grounded in the confidence that comes from knowing our curricular content, our values, and ourselves, we must commit also to facilitating understanding among parents and families, as we do with our students. We must not be afraid to let them know *what* we are doing to support equity, diversity, and inclusion in our classroom, *why* we are doing it, and *why* it is important. We need to answer their questions, and we need to ask questions of them. In many ways, bringing parents to new understanding, empathy, and closer solidarity with us, and with each other, can be an exciting outcome of doing what's in our power to do as teachers. A renewed narrative about racial equity and inclusion in school can be promoted—one that teachers, families, and communities create together.

CONCLUSION: NURTURING EMOTIONAL SUSTENANCE

As a teacher, making the case for teaching race in school isn't just a curricular or intellectual argument. Because we bring our various identities and our full selves into the classroom, it is deeply emotional work. Although the content and valence of any teacher's emotions around race and racial equity are not the same, suffice it to say that no teacher can do this work alone. Because our day-to-day tasks as teachers are both unique to our own classrooms and students, as well as all-encompassing, we often isolate ourselves as we strive to make it all work. Although we all need alone time in our classroom spaces at the end of the school day, we need connection and community to sustain ourselves and each other as we work to create socially just schools.

Inside the building and within your school district, seek out other teachers who value and are also committed to equity, diversity, and inclusion goals, and brainstorm ideas and strategies that are both big and small. Together, push your administrators to listen and ask for their support and resources. Negotiate with them, but also be familiar with your rights as they regard your teaching and advocacy. Find school board officials who support this work and dialogue with them. As we reflect upon educational issues that have had historic precedent, such as the delivery of special education services and school desegregation, we must never lose sight of the integral and essential role that parents and families have played in fighting for an equitable, just, and inclusive education for their children. Believe in their ability to serve as powerful allies.

As noted by Bettina Love, conflict is a part of racial justice and equity work, and as we know from history, there will always be potent resistance to it.[28] Although we should be strategic and creative in the way we frame our equity-based initiatives, we must always be honest in our intentions, and we must seek to understand the intentions of those who resist. For example, questions like "what does equity and justice mean to you?" or "what elements of teaching about race, identity, or inclusion are you uncomfortable with?" or "what kind of society do you want, or dream can happen?" can reveal not only sources of misunderstanding and fear but also places of potential alignment. What is imperative is that we learn how to dig deep within ourselves to build from conflict and navigate resistance and to do so in coalition with others.

In this regard, it behooves us to reflect once again on the idea of safety and risk as we move forward in this work. Consider the words of the renowned writer and civil rights activist James Baldwin:

> Now, it is true that the nature of society is to create, among its citizens, an illusion of safety; but it is also absolutely true that the safety is always necessarily an illusion. Artists are here to disturb the peace.[29]

As teachers, we are also artists—we create lessons, we offer lively instruction, we facilitate spaces of learning, potentiality, and possibility. In developing critical racial consciousness in our students and ourselves, we are making a choice to disturb what is, for many a "peaceful" façade of color-blindness in school and in society. We make such a choice because we seek to confront the legacy of racism and white supremacy in America with honesty and integrity. We make such a choice during this developmental period because we believe in the resilience and empathy of youth and in their ability to imagine, create, and demand a more equitable democracy and a more equitable world.

We do what is in our power as educators to make a case for race in middle school because we believe in the power of education to be transformative. In doing so, we join a fight against oppression that is historic and ongoing, sustained by an indefatigable belief in justice, freedom, and equity. The possibilities that exist when teachers and adolescents engage with these ideals in classroom communities are dynamic, inspiring, and simply beautiful to imagine. The result is a kind of educational justice that is anything but divisive; it is hopeful, unifying, and fundamentally humanizing.

Notes

CHAPTER 1

1. All student first names used throughout this book are assigned pseudonyms. The racial-ethnic descriptors used throughout the book to identify student quotations were those used by the students themselves as they self-identified during individual interviews.

2. Byrd, C.M. (2021). Cycles of development in learning about identities, diversity, and equity. *Cultural Diversity & Ethnic Minority Psychology, 29*(1), 43–52.

3. Freire, P. (1996). *Education for critical consciousness*. Continuum.

4. Race is a socially constructed phenotypic category and is distinct from ethnicity, which refers to cultural group membership. As per the guidelines of the American Psychological Association (APA; 7th ed.), in this book, racial and ethnic groups are designated by proper nouns and are capitalized, such as White, Black, or Asian. The term "Caucasian" is never used as an alternative to "White," because it originated as a way of classifying the White race as biologically superior. "People/communities of color" refers to groups from diverse ethnocultural backgrounds not classified as racially White according to U.S. Census categories.

5. Sleeter, C.E. (2017). Critical race theory and the whiteness of teacher education. *Urban Education, 52*(2), 155–169. DOI: 10.1177/0042085916668957

6. Roberts, S.O., & Rizzo, M.T. (2021). The psychology of American racism. *American Psychologist, 76*(3), 475–487. DOI: 10.1037/amp0000642

7. Eurocentric refers to an orientation and worldview that is centered on Western civilization; it indicates a tendency to interpret phenomena from the point of view of Europeans or European people. Eurocentrism, by definition is derived from imperialism and colonialism, wherein non-Western/European societies are considered inferior and in need of Western intervention.

8. Picower, B. (2021). *Reading, writing, and racism: Disrupting whiteness in teacher education and in the classroom*. Beacon Press.

9. Singh, A.A. (2019). *The racial healing handbook: Practical activities to help you challenge privilege, confront systemic racism, and engage in collective healing.* New Harbinger Publications.

10. Suyemoto, K.L., Donovan, R.A., & Kim, G.S. (2022). *Unraveling assumptions: A primer for understanding oppression and privilege.* Routledge.

11. As defined by APA, the term "people of color" refers to non-White racial and ethnic groups collectively. Since it is a broad-based label that does not function as a proper noun (such as the designations White or Hispanic racial or ethnic groups, respectively), it is not capitalized in this book. Similarly, "students of color" is not capitalized for the same reasons.

12. McClure, S.M., & Harris, C.A. (Eds.). (2022). *Getting real about race* (3rd ed.). Sage Publications, Inc.

13. Euroethnic refers to those groups whose ethnic ancestry is located in Europe.

14. Singh, A.A. (2019). *The racial healing handbook: Practical activities to help you challenge privilege, confront systemic racism, and engage in collective healing.* New Harbinger Publications.

15. Leonardo, Z. (2009). *Race, whiteness, and education* (Critical Social Thought). Routledge.

16. Picower, B. (2021). *Reading, writing, and racism: Disrupting whiteness in teacher education and in the classroom.* Beacon Press.

17. Roediger, D. (2007). *The wages of whiteness: Race and the making of the American working class* (New edition). Verso.

18. Gorski, P. (2016). Rethinking the role of "culture" in educational equity: From cultural competence to equity literacy. *Multicultural Perspectives, 18*(4), 221–226. DOI:10.1080/15210960.2016.1228344

19. Durand, T.M., & Tavaras, C.L. (2020). Countering complacency with radical reflection: Supporting White teachers in the enactment of critical multicultural praxis. *Education & Urban Society, 53*(2). DOI: 10.1177/0013124520927680

20. Gay, G. (2018). *Culturally responsive teaching* (3rd ed.). Teachers College Press.

21. Ibid.

22. Ladson-Billings, G. (2021). *Critical race theory in education: A scholar's journey.* Teachers College Press.

23. Hadley Dunn, A. (2022). *Teaching on days after: Educating for equity in the wake of injustice.* Teachers College Press.

24. Tatum, B.D. (2007). *Can we talk about race? And other conversations in an era of school resegregation.* Beacon Press.

25. Bonilla-Silva, E. (2021). *Racism without racists: Color-blind racism and the persistence of racial inequality in America* (6th ed.). Rowman & Littlefield.

26. Sensoy, O., & DiAngelo, R. (2017). *Is everyone really equal? An introduction to key concepts in social justice education* (Multicultural Education Series) (2nd ed.). Teachers College Press.

27. Suyemoto, K.L., Donovan, R.A., & Kim, G.S. (2022). *Unraveling assumptions: A primer for understanding oppression and privilege.* Routledge.

28. Delgado, R., & Stefancic, S. (2017). *Critical race theory: An introduction* (3rd ed.). NYU Press.

29. Love, B. (Foreword). In Picower, B. (2021). *Reading, writing, and racism: Disrupting whiteness in teacher education and in the classroom.* Beacon Press.

30. Walsh, M. (2023, June). *Supreme court ends affirmative action in college admissions in decision watched by K–12.* EdWeek. https://www.edweek.org/policy-politics/supreme-court-ends-affirmative-action-in-college-admissions-in-decision-watched-by-k-12/2023/06

31. Students for Fair Admissions, Inc., *v* President and Fellows of Harvard College, No. 20–199. *Supreme Court of the United States.* https://www.supremecourt.gov/opinions/22pdf/20-1199_hgdj.pdf

32. Ibid.

33. Delgado., R. & Stefancic, S. (2017).

34. Saric, I. (2023, June). *Affirmative action's end spells more isolation for students of color.* Axios. https://www.axios.com/2023/06/29/affirmative-action-overturned-students-minorities

35. Bonilla-Silva, E. (2021). *Racism without racists: Color-blind racism and the persistence of racial inequality in America* (6th ed.). Rowman & Littlefield.

36. Ladson-Billings, G. (2018). The social funding of race: The role of schooling. *Peabody Journal of Education, 93*(1), 90–105. https://www.teachingworks.org/images/files/Ladson-Billings_The_Social_Funding_of_Race_The_Role_of_Schooling.pdf

37. Clotfelter, C.T. (2006). *After Brown: The rise and retreat of school desegregation.* Princeton University Press.

38. Spring, J. (2012). *Deculturalization and the struggle for equality: A brief history of the education of dominated cultures in the United States* (7th ed.). McGraw-Hill Education.

39. Flores, N., Tseng, A., & Subtirelu, N. (Eds.) (2020). *Bilingualism for all? Raciolinguistic perspectives on dual language education in the United States.* Multilingual Matters.

40. Morgan, H. (2020). Misunderstood and mistreated: Students of color in special education. *Voices of Reform: Educational Resources to Inform and Reform, 3*(2). https://files.eric.ed.gov/fulltext/ED610548.pdf

41. Moss, J. (2016, summer). Where are all the teachers of color? *Harvard Graduate School of Education: Ed Magazine.* https://www.gse.harvard.edu/ideas/ed-magazine/16/05/where-are-all-teachers-color

42. Heitzeg, N.A. (2016). *The school-to-prison pipeline: Education, discipline, and racialized double standards.* Praeger.

43. Gay, G. (2018). *Culturally responsive teaching* (3rd ed.). Teachers College Press.

44. Love, B.L. (2020). *We want to do more than survive: Abolitionist teaching and the pursuit of educational freedom.* Beacon Press.

45. Freire, P. (1996). *Education for critical consciousness.* Continuum.

46. Pollack, M. (2019). Standing up against hate. In L. Delpit (Ed.), *Teaching when the world is on fire* (pp. 26–32). The New Press.

47. Delpit, L. (2019). *Teaching when the world is on fire*. The New Press.

48. Pitts, J. (2019). Don't say nothing. In L. Delpit (Ed.), *Teaching when the world is on fire* (pp. 81–85). The New Press.

49. Anderson, C. (2016). *White rage: The unspoken truth of our racial divide*. Bloomsbury.

50. Fenwick, L.T. (2022, May). The ugly backlash to *Brown v. Board of Ed* that no one talks about. *Politico*. https://www.politico.com/news/magazine/2022/05/17/brown-board-education-downside-00032799

51. Dorrien, G. (2018). The backlash this time: Obama, Trump, and the American trauma. *CrossCurrents, 68*(1), 54–72. DOI:10.1353/cro.2018.a782655

52. The word "woke" in contemporary vernacular refers to being mindful and well-informed on progressive issues around inequity, oppression, and privilege. However, it originated within Black culture and the Black community and was used to connote the need to stay vigilant in the face of discrimination, in the spirit of advocacy.

53. Delgado, R., & Stefancic, S. (2017). *Critical race theory: An introduction* (3rd ed.). NYU Press.

54. López, F., & Sleeter, C.E. (2023). *Critical race theory and its critics: Implications for research and teaching* (Multicultural Education Series). Teachers College Press.

55. Chen, G. (2023, June). Changing demographics will alter the diversity of public schools. *Public School Review*. https://www.publicschoolreview.com/blog/changing-demographics-will-alter-the-diversity-of-public-schools

56. López, F., & Sleeter, C.E. (2023). *Critical race theory and its critics: Implications for research and teaching* (Multicultural Education Series). Teachers College Press.

57. Ibid.

58. Ibid.

59. Zinaty, G. (2023, August). *Does diversity, equity, and inclusion training work?* Forbes. https://www.forbes.com/sites/forbescoachescouncil/2023/08/22/does-diversity-equity-and-inclusion-training-work/?sh=53c163df5a00#:~:text=DEI%20ballooned%20into%20a%20priority,bias%2C%20discrimination%20and%20systemic%20behavior

60. Wallace-Wells, B. (2021, June). How a conservative activist invented the conflict over critical race theory. *The New Yorker*. https://www.newyorker.com/news/annals-of-inquiry/how-a-conservative-activist-invented-the-conflict-over-critical-race-theory

61. Exec. Order (EO) No. 13950 3 C.F.R. (2020). https://trumpwhitehouse.archives.gov/presidential-actions/executive-order-combating-race-sex-stereotyping/

62. Wallace-Wells, B. (2021, June).

63. Waxman, O.B. (2023, April). Exclusive: New data shows the anti-critical race theory movement is "far from over." *Time*. https://time.com/6266865/critical-race-theory-data-exclusive/

64. UCLA School of Law, Critical Race Studies; *CRT Forward Tracking Project*. https://crtforward.law.ucla.edu/wp-content/uploads/2023/04/UCLA-Law_CRT-Report_Final.pdf

65. Waxman, O.B. (2023, April). Exclusive: New data shows the anti-critical race theory movement is "far from over." *Time*. https://time.com/6266865/critical-race-theory-data-exclusive/

66. Meehan, K., & Friedman, J. (2023, April). Banned in the USA: State laws supercharge book suppression in schools. *Pen America*. https://pen.org/report/banned-in-the-usa-state-laws-supercharge-book-suppression-in-schools/

67. Banks, J.A. (Series Foreword). In López, F., & Sleeter, C.E. (2023). *Critical race theory and its critics: Implications for research and teaching* (Multicultural Education Series). Teachers College Press.

68. Fortin, J. (2021, November). *Critical race theory: A brief history*. The New York Times. https://www.nytimes.com/article/what-is-critical-race-theory.html

69. Ibid.

70. Delgado, R., & Stefancic, S. (2017). *Critical race theory: An introduction* (3rd ed.). New York University Press.

71. Ibid.

72. Ward, L. (2022). The real "boogeyman": How White legal logic is used to create educational gag order laws in U.S. higher education. *Philosophy & Theory in Higher Education, 4*(3), 13–27. DOI:10.3726/ptihe.032022.0002

73. Delgado, R., & Stefancic, S. (2017). *Critical race theory: An introduction* (3rd ed.). New York University Press.

74. Ladson-Billings, G. (2021). *Critical race theory in education: A scholar's journey*. Teachers College Press.

75. Picower, B. (2021). *Reading, writing, and racism: Disrupting whiteness in teacher education and in the classroom*. Beacon Press.

76. López, F., & Sleeter, C.E. (2023). *Critical race theory and its critics: Implications for research and teaching* (Multicultural Education Series). Teachers College Press.

77. Dixon, A.D. (2018). "What's going on?" A critical race theory perspective on Black Lives Matter and activism in education. *Urban Education, 53*, 231–247.

78. Anderson, J. (2022, February). The state of critical race theory in education. *EdCast: Harvard Graduate School of Education*. https://www.gse.harvard.edu/ideas/edcast/22/02/state-critical-race-theory-education

79. National Association of School Psychologists (NASP). (n.d.). *The importance of addressing equity, diversity, and inclusion in schools*. https://www.nasponline.org/resources-and-publications/resources-and-podcasts/diversity-and-social-justice/social-justice/the-importance-of-addressing-equity-diversity-and-inclusion-in-schools-dispelling-myths-about-critical-race-theory

80. López, F., & Sleeter, C.E. (2023). *Critical race theory and its critics: Implications for research and teaching* (Multicultural Education Series). Teachers College Press.

81. Reynolds Lewis, K. (2023, September). Schools spend billions on training so every student can succeed. They don't know if it works. *USA Today*. https://www.usatoday.com/story/news/education/2023/09/14/flawed-equity-efforts-us-schools-teachers/70679911007/

82. American Psychological Association. (2021). *Inclusive language guidelines.* https://www.apa.org/about/apa/equity-diversity-inclusion/language-guidelines

83. Bracken et al. (2022, August). What's actually being taught in history class. *The New York Times.* https://www.nytimes.com/interactive/2022/08/17/us/teaching-critical-race-theory.html

84. Marrun, N.A., Clark, C., Beach, K., Morgan, M., Chiang-López, C., González, C., & McCadney, O. (2023). Indifferent, (un)critical, and anti-intellectual: Framing how teachers grapple with bans on teaching truth about race and racism, and critical race theory. *Race Ethnicity and Education.* DOI:10.1080/13613324.2023.2203935

85. Love, B.L. (2023, July). No, public education isn't too woke. It's barely even awake. *EdWeek.* https://www.edweek.org/leadership/opinion-no-public-education-isnt-too-woke-its-barely-even-awake/2023/07

86. Wong Chin, C.B., Baran, J.N., Mauer, G.M., & Jhee, C.J. (2021). Coming together: Family reflections on racism. *Sesame Workshop.* https://sesameworkshop.org/our-work/research-and-insights/reflections-on-racism-study/

87. Equal Justice Initiative. (2020). *Black children are six times more likely to be shot to death by police.* https://eji.org/news/black-children-are-six-times-more-likely-to-be-shot-to-death-by-police/

88. Umaña-Taylor, A.J., Quintana, S.M., Lee, R.M., Cross Jr, W.E., Rivas-Drake, D., Schwartz, S.J., Yip, T., & Ethnic and Racial Identity in the Twenty-first Century Study Group. (2014). Ethnic and racial identity during adolescence and into young adulthood: An integrated conceptualization. *Child Development, 85*(1), 21–39. DOI: 10.1111/cdev.12196

89. Steinberg, L. (2015). *Age of opportunity: Lessons from the new science of adolescence.* Harper Paperbacks.

90. References to ethnic-racial identity (ERI) used throughout this book draw upon the conceptualization of these constructs used by the Ethnic and Racial Identity in the Twenty-first Century Study group.

CHAPTER 2

1. The reader is reminded that although the hyphenated term "racial-ethnic" is used throughout as a meta-construct that captures ethnic heritage experiences, as well as those that result from racially ascribed categories/groups in the United States, ethnic-racial identity (ERI) is the term used for identity-based references, as per the Ethnic and Racial Identity in the Twenty-first Century Study Group (Umaña-Taylor et al., 2014).

2. The use of the term "youth" varies both contextually and globally. Although both the United Nations (UN) and the Organisation for Economic Cooperation and Development (OECD) formally define "youth" as beginning at the age of 15 and extending into the 20s, it will be used in this and in subsequent chapters to include children in early adolescence (approximately the ages 11–14).

3. Waters, M.C. (2007). Optional ethnicities: For Whites only? In M.A. Andersen & P.H. Collins (Eds.), *Race, class, & gender: An anthology* (6th ed.) (pp. 198–207). Thomson Higher Education.

4. Office of Juvenile Justice and Delinquency Prevention. (2014). https://ojjdp.ojp.gov/model-programs-guide/literature-reviews/positive_youth_development.pdf

5. Bell, L.A. (2019). *Storytelling for social justice: Connecting narrative and the arts in antiracist teaching* (2nd ed.). Routledge.

6. Perry, T., Steele, C., & Hilliard, Asa III. (2004). *Young, gifted, and Black: Promoting high achievement among African-American students*. Beacon Press.

7. Byrd, C.M. (2021). Cycles of development in learning about identities, diversity, and equity. *Cultural Diversity & Ethnic Minority Psychology, 29*(1), 43–52.

8. Graham, S. (2018). Race/ethnicity and social adjustment of adolescents: How (not if) school diversity matters. *Educational Psychologist, 53*(2), 64–77.

9. Saleem, F.T., & Byrd, C.M. (2021). Unpacking school ethnic-racial socialization: A new conceptual model. *Journal of Social Issues, 77,* 1106–1125.

10. Voight, A., Hanson, T., O'Malley, M., & Adekanye, L. (2015). The racial school climate gap: Within-school disparities in students' experiences of safety, support, and connectedness. *American Journal of Community Psychology, 56*(3–4), 497–527.

11. Roeser, R.W., & Eccles, J.S. (1998). Adolescents' perceptions of middle school: Relation to longitudinal changes in academic and psychological adjustment. *Journal of Research on Adolescence, 88,* 123–158.

12. Singh, A.A. (2019). *The racial healing handbook: Practical activities to help you challenge privilege, confront systemic racism, and engage in collective healing.* New Harbinger Publications.

13. United Negro College Fund (UNCF). (n.d.). *K–12 disparity facts and statistics.* https://uncf.org/pages/k-12-disparity-facts-and stats#:~:text=Students%20of%20color%20are%20often,Spending%20on%20Students%20of%20Color

14. Williamson, V., & Gelfand, I. (2019). Trump and racism: What do the data say? *Brookings.* https://www.brookings.edu/articles/trump-and-racism-what-do-the-data-say/

15. Umaña-Taylor, A.J., Quintana, S.M., Lee, R.M., Cross Jr, W.E., Rivas-Drake, D., Schwartz, S.J., Yip, T., & Ethnic and Racial Identity in the Twenty-first Century Study Group. (2014). Ethnic and racial identity during adolescence and into young adulthood: An integrated conceptualization. *Child Development, 85*(1), 21–39. DOI: 10.1111/cdev.12196

16. Durand, T.M. (2020). Overcoming stereotypes to "master our dreams": The salience of ethnic climate and racial diversity among students of color in middle school. *Journal of Early Adolescence, 40*(8), 1029–1060; Durand, T.M., & Skubel, A. (2022). Narratives of Puerto Rican middle school students regarding school context and identity: Contradictions and possibilities. *Journal of Adolescent Research.* Advance online publication. DOI:10.1177/07435584221096446; Durand, T.M., & Blackwell, R. (2022). Dimensions of belonging and "othering" in middle school: Voices of immigrant and island-born Puerto Rican adolescents. *Journal of Education for Students Placed at Risk.* Advance online publication.

17. Darling-Hammond, L. (2010). *The flat world and education: How America's commitment to equity will determine our future*. Teachers College Press.

18. Juvonen, J., Kogachi, K., & Graham, S. (2018). When and how do students benefit from ethnic diversity in middle school? *Child Development, 89*(4), 1268–1282.

19. Hughes, D., Way, N., & Rivas-Drake, D. (2011). Stability and change in private and public ethnic regard among African American, Puerto Rican, Dominican, and Chinese American early adolescents. *Journal of Research on Adolescence, 21*(4), 861–870. http://blog.glorialopez.com/wp-content/uploads/2017/02/Stability-and-Change-in-Private-and-Public-Ethnic-Regard-Among-African-American-Puerto-Rican-Dominican-and-Chinese-American-Early-Adolescents.pdf

20. Jackson, A., Colson-Fearon, B., & Versey, H.S. (2022). Managing intersectional invisibility and hypervisibility during the transition to college among first-generation women of color. *Psychology of Women Quarterly, 46*(3). https://journals.sagepub.com/doi/full/10.1177/03616843221106087#body-ref-bibr11-03616843221106087

CHAPTER 3

1. Wong, H.L. (2023, November). New "Latino" and "Middle Eastern or North African" checkboxes proposed for U.S. forms. *NPR*. https://www.npr.org/2023/01/26/1151608403/mena-race-categories-us-census-middle-eastern-latino-hispanic

2. Smithsonian. (n.d.). *Talking about race: Whiteness*. https://nmaahc.si.edu/learn/talking-about-race/topics/whiteness

3. Wilson, J., & Flanagan, A. (2022, May 17). The racist "great replacement" conspiracy theory explained. *Southern Poverty Law Center*. https://www.splcenter.org/hatewatch/2022/05/17/racist-great-replacement-conspiracy-theory-explained

4. Sensoy, O., & DiAngelo, R. (2017). *Is everyone really equal? An introduction to key concepts in social justice education* (Multicultural Education Series) (2nd ed.). Teachers College Press.

5. Odabas, M., & Aragão, C. (2023, April 4). School district mission statements highlight a partisan divide over diversity, equity, and inclusion in K–12 education. *Pew Research Center*. https://www.pewresearch.org/social-trends/2023/04/04/school-district-mission-statements-highlight-a-partisan-divide-over-diversity-equity-and-inclusion-in-k-12-education/

6. Byrd, C.M. (2021). Cycles of development in learning about identities, diversity, and equity. *Cultural Diversity & Ethnic Minority Psychology, 29*(1), 43–52.

7. Rivas-Drake, D., & Umaña-Taylor, A.J. (2019). *Below the surface: Talking with teens about race, ethnicity, and identity*. Princeton University Press.

8. Sensoy, O., & DiAngelo, R. (2017). *Is everyone really equal? An introduction to key concepts in social justice education* (Multicultural Education Series) (2nd ed.). Teachers College Press.

9. Moffit, U., Rogers, L.O., & Dastrup, K.R.H. (2021). Beyond ethnicity: Applying Helms' white racial identity development model among White youth. *Journal of Research on Adolescence, 32*(2), 1140–1159.

10. Satterthwaite-Freiman, M., Sladek, M.R., Wantchekon, K.A., Rivas-Drake, D., & Umaña-Taylor, A.J. (2023). Examining ethnic-racial identity negative affect, centrality, and intergroup contact attitudes among White adolescents. *Journal of Youth and Adolescence, 52*, 61–75.

11. Grossman, J.M., & Charmaraman, L. (2009). Race, context, and privilege: White adolescents' explanations of racial-ethnic centrality. *Journal of Youth and Adolescence, 38*(2), 139–152. DOI: 10.1007/s10964-008-9330-7

12. Dull, B.D., Hoyt, L.T., & Chaku, N. (2022). White adolescents' racial contexts: Associations with critical action. *Child Development, 93*, 1698–1712. DOI: 10.1111/cdev.13812

13. Glover, C.S., Varner, F., & Holloway, K. (2022). Parent socialization and antiracist ideology development in White youth: Do peer and parenting contexts matter? *Child Development, 93*, 653–667.

14. Freire, P. (1970). *Pedagogy of the oppressed.* Continuum.

15. Ibid.

16. Diemer, M.A., Rapa, L.J., Park, C.J., & Perry, J.C. (2017). Development and validation of the critical consciousness scale. *Youth & Society, 49*(4), 461–483.

17. Heberle, A.E., Wagner, A.C., & Hoch, N. (2022). Adolescent mental health in relation to anti-racism critical action. *Journal of Youth and Adolescence, 51*, 832–847.

18. Dull, B.D., Hoyt, L.T., & Chaku, N. (2022). White adolescents' racial contexts: Associations with critical Action. *Child Development, 93*, 1698-1712. DOI: 10.1111/cdev.13812

19. Woolverton, G.A., & Marks, A.K. (2022). An integrative model for the development of anti-racist behavior in White adolescents. *Journal of Adolescent Research*, 1–33. DOI:https://doi.org/10.1177/07435584221091492

20. Ibid.

21. Roberts, S.O., & Rizzo, M.T. (2021). The psychology of American racism. *American Psychologist, 76*(3), 475–487. DOI: https://doi.org/10.1037/amp0000642

22. Thomann, C.R.B., & Suyemoto, K.L. (2018). Developing an antiracist stance: How White youth understand structural racism. *Journal of Early Adolescence, 38*(6), 745–771. DOI:https://doi.org/10.1177/0272431617692443

23. Bonilla-Silva, E. (2021). *Racism without racists: Color-blind racism and the persistence of racial inequality in America* (6th ed.). Rowman & Littlefield.

24. Durand, T.M. (2020). Overcoming stereotypes to "master our dreams": The salience of ethnic climate and racial diversity among students of color in middle school. *Journal of Early Adolescence, 40*(8), 1029–1060; Durand, T. M., & Skubel, A. (2022). Narratives of Puerto Rican middle school students regarding school context and identity: Contradictions and possibilities. *Journal of Adolescent Research.* Advance online publication. DOI:https://doi.org/10.1177/07435584221096446; Durand, T.M., & Blackwell, R. (2022). Dimensions of belonging and "othering" in middle school: Voices of immigrant and island-born Puerto Rican adolescents. *Journal of Education for Students Placed at Risk.* Advance online publication.

25. Woolverton, G.A., & Marks, A.K. (2022). An integrative model for the development of anti-racist behavior in White adolescents. *Journal of Adolescent Research*, 1–33. DOI:https://doi.org/10.1177/07435584221091492

26. Byrd, C.M. (2021). Cycles of development in learning about identities, diversity, and equity. *Cultural Diversity & Ethnic Minority Psychology, 29*(1), 43–52.

CHAPTER 4

1. Pendharker, E. (2022, October 17). Legal challenges to "divisive concepts" laws: An update. *Education Week.* https://www.edweek.org/policy-politics/legal-challenges-to-divisive-concepts-laws-an-update/2022/10
2. Paulsen, K. (September 19, 2023). *Divisive concepts.* https://firstamendment.mtsu.edu/article/divisive-concepts/
3. Ibid.
4. Anderson, G., & Cohen, M.I. (2015). Redesigning the identities of teachers and leaders: A framework for studying new professionalism and teacher resistance. *Education Policy Analysis Archives, 23*(85), 1–29.
5. Ibid.
6. hooks, b. (2003). *Teaching community: A pedagogy of hope.* Routledge.
7. Taie, S., & Lewis, L. (2022). *Characteristics of 2020–2021 public and private K–12 school teachers in the United States: Results from the national teacher and principal survey first look* (NCES 2022–113). U.S. Department of Education. National Center for Education Statistics. https://nces.ed.gov/pubsearch/pubsinfo.asp?pubid=2022113
8. Ibid.
9. Cherng, H.S., & Halpin, P.F. (2016). The importance of minority teachers: Student perceptions of minority versus White teachers. *Educational Researcher, 45*(7), 407–420.
10. Egalite, A.J., Kisida, B., & Winters, M.A. (2015). Representation in the classroom: The effect of own-race teachers on student achievement. *Economics of Education Review, 45,* 44–52.
11. Picower, B. (2009). The unexamined whiteness of teaching: How white teachers maintain and enact dominant racial ideologies. *Race Ethnicity & Education, 12*(2), 197–215.
12. Sensoy, O., & DiAngelo, R. (2017). *Is everyone really equal? An introduction to key concepts in social justice education* (Multicultural Education Series) (2nd ed.). Teachers College Press.
13. Picower, B. (2009). The unexamined whiteness of teaching: How white teachers maintain and enact dominant racial ideologies. *Race Ethnicity & Education, 12*(2), 197–215.
14. Dillard, C. (2020). The weaponization of whiteness in schools. https://www.learningforjustice.org/magazine/fall-2020/the-weaponization-of-whiteness-in-schools
15. Utt, J., & Tochluk, S. (2020). White teacher, know thyself: Improving antiracist praxis through racial identity development. *Urban Education, 55*(1), 125–152. DOI:https://doi.org/10.1177/0042085916648741

16. Ayers, W. (2019). I shall create! Teaching toward freedom. In L. Delpit (Ed.), *Teaching when the world is on fire* (pp. 3–15). The New Press.

17. hooks, b. (2003). *Teaching community: A pedagogy of hope*. Routledge.

18. Schick, C. (2000). "By virtue of being white": Resistance in anti-racist pedagogy. *Race Ethnicity and Education, 3*(1), 83–101. DOI:https://doi.org/10.1080/713693016

19. Morrison, M.S. (2013, spring). Becoming trustworthy white allies. *The Future of Race*. https://reflections.yale.edu/article/future-race/becoming-trustworthy-white-allies

20. Durand, T.M., & Tavaras, C.L. (2020). Countering complacency with radical reflection: Supporting white teachers in the enactment of critical multicultural praxis. *Education & Urban Society*, 1–17. https://journals.sagepub.com/doi/10.1177/0013124520927680

21. Duncan-Andrade, J. (2009). Note to educators: Hope required when growing roses in concrete. *Harvard Educational Review, 79*(2), 181–194. DOI:10.17763/haer.79.2.nu3436017730384w

22. Leonardo, Z. (2009). *Race, whiteness, and education*. Routledge.

23. Gay, G. (2018). *Culturally responsive teaching* (3rd ed.). Teachers College Press.

24. Gorski, P. (2016). Rethinking the role of "culture" in educational equity: From cultural competence to equity literacy. *Multicultural Perspectives, 18*(4), 221–226. DOI:10.1080/15210960.2016.1228344

25. Kemmis, S., & Smith, T.J. (Eds.). (2008). *Enabling praxis: Challenges for pedagogy*. Sense Publishers.

26. Banks, J.A. (2021). Multicultural education: History and dimensions. In J.A. Banks (Ed.), *Transforming multicultural education policy & practice* (pp. 42–52). Teachers College Press.

27. Ibid.

28. Gorski, P. (2016). Rethinking the role of "culture" in educational equity: From cultural competence to equity literacy. *Multicultural Perspectives, 18*(4), 221–226. DOI:10.1080/15210960.2016.1228344

29. Banks, J.A. (2021). Multicultural education: History and dimensions. In J.A. Banks (Ed.), *Transforming multicultural education policy & practice* (pp. 42–52). Teachers College Press.

30. Ordway, D.M. (2021, January 25). Multicultural education: How schools teach it and where educators fall short. *The Journalist's Resource: Informing the News*. https://journalistsresource.org/education/multicultural-education-schools/

31. Sleeter, C.E., & McLaren, P. (2000). Origins of multiculturalism. *Rethinking Schools, 15*(1). https://rethinkingschools.org/articles/the-origins-of-multiculturalism/

32. Ibid.

33. Gorski, P. (2016). Rethinking the role of "culture" in educational equity: From cultural competence to equity literacy. *Multicultural Perspectives, 18*(4), 221–226. DOI:10.1080/15210960.2016.122834834,4

34. Zhou, M., & Tran, V. (2022). "Asians are doing great, so that proves race really doesn't matter anymore." The model minority myth and the sociological

reality. In S.M. McClure & C.A. Harris (Eds.), *Getting real about race* (3rd ed., pp. 145–153). Sage.

35. May, S., & Sleeter, C.E. (2010). *Critical multiculturalism: Theory and praxis.* Routledge.

36. Sensoy, O., & DiAngelo, R. (2017). *Is everyone really equal? An introduction to key concepts in social justice education* (Multicultural Education Series) (2nd ed.). Teachers College Press.

37. Allport, G.W. (1954). *The nature of prejudice.* Addison-Wesley.

38. Gorski, P. (2016). Rethinking the role of "culture" in educational equity: From cultural competence to equity literacy. *Multicultural Perspectives, 18*(4), 221–226. DOI:10.1080/15210960.2016.1228344

39. May, S., & Sleeter, C.E. (2010). *Critical multiculturalism: Theory and praxis.* Routledge.

40. Ibid.

41. Sensoy, O., & DiAngelo, R. (2017). *Is everyone really equal? An introduction to key concepts in social justice education* (Multicultural Education Series) (2nd ed.). Teachers College Press.

42. Ibid.

43. Freire, P. (1993). *Pedagogy of the oppressed.* Penguin. First published in 1970.

44. Ibid.

45. Ibid.

46. Ibid.

47. Byrd, C.M. (2023). Cycles of development in learning about identities, diversity, and equity. *Cultural Diversity and Ethnic Minority Psychology, 29*(1), 43–52. DOI:https://doi.org/10.1037/cdp0000389

48. May, S., & Sleeter, C.E. (2010). *Critical multiculturalism: Theory and praxis.* Routledge.

49. Sensoy, O., & DiAngelo, R. (2017). *Is everyone really equal? An introduction to key concepts in social justice education* (Multicultural Education Series) (2nd ed.). Teachers College Press.

50. Freire, P. (1993). *Pedagogy of the oppressed.* Penguin. First published in 1970.

51. May, S. & Sleeter, C.E. (2010). *Critical multiculturalism: Theory and praxis.* Routledge.

52. Ibid.

53. Ibid.

54. Ibid.

55. Jupp, J.C., Berry, T.R., & Lensmire, T.J. (2016). Second-wave teacher identity studies: A review of White teacher identity literatures from 2004 through 2014. *Review of Educational Research, 86*(4), 1151–1191.

56. Leonardo, Z. (2009). *Race, whiteness, and education.* Routledge.

57. Yamato, G. (2004). Something about the subject makes it hard to name. In M.L. Anderson & P. Hill Collins (Eds.), *Race, class, and gender* (5th ed.). Wadsworth.

58. Love, B.L. (2020, February 6). White teachers need anti-racist therapy. *Education Week.* https://www.edweek.org/teaching-learning/opinion-white-teachers-need-anti-racist-therapy/2020/02

59. Bonilla-Silva, E. (2021). *Racism without racists: Color-blind racism and the persistence of racial inequality in America* (6th ed.). Rowman & Littlefield.

60. Sensoy, O., & DiAngelo, R. (2017). *Is everyone really equal? An introduction to key concepts in social justice education* (Multicultural Education Series) (2nd ed.). Teachers College Press.

61. Bronson, P., & Merryman, A. (2009). See baby discriminate: Kids as young as 6 months judge each others based on skin color. What's a parent to do? *Newsweek, 154*(11), 55–60.

62. Emdin, C. (2016). *For white folks who teach in the hood . . . and the rest of y'all too: Reality pedagogy and urban education.* Beacon Press.

63. Gorski, P. (2021). Embracing a structural view of poverty and education: Ditching deficit ideology and quitting grit. In J.A. Banks (Ed.), *Transforming multicultural education policy & practice* (pp. 315–325). Teachers College Press.

64. Ibid.

65. Picower, B. (2021). *Reading, writing, and racism: Disrupting whiteness in teacher education and in the classroom.* Beacon Press.

66. DiAngelo, R., & Sensoy, O. (2010). Ok, I get it! Now tell me how to do it! Why we can't just tell you how to do critical multicultural education. *Multicultural Perspectives, 12*(2), 97–102.

67. Matias, C.E. (2013). Check yo' self before you wreck yo' self and our kids: Counterstories from culturally responsive white teachers? . . . To culturally responsive white teachers! *Interdisciplinary Journal of Teaching and Learning, 3*(2), 68–81.

68. DuBois, W.E.B. (1989). *The souls of black folk.* Penguin. First published in 1904.

69. Leonardo, Z. (2009). *Race, whiteness, and education.* Routledge.

70. Ibid.

71. Ibid.

72. Ibid.

73. Utt, J., & Tochluk, S. (2020). White teacher know thyself: Improving antiracist praxis through racial identity development. *Urban Education, 55*(1), 125–152. DOI: 10.1177/0042085916648741

74. Matias, C.E. (2013). Check yo' self before you wreck yo' self and our kids: Counterstories from culturally responsive white teachers? . . . To culturally responsive white teachers! *Interdisciplinary Journal of Teaching and Learning, 3*(2), 68–81.

75. Ibid.

76. Dillard, C. (2020). The weaponization of whiteness in schools. *SPLC: Learning for Justice in Schools.* https://www.learningforjustice.org/magazine/fall-2020/the-weaponization-of-whiteness-in-schools

77. Ibid.

78. Bell, M. (2021). *Whiteness interrupted: White teachers and racial identity in predominately Black schools.* Duke University Press.

79. Picower, B. (2021). *Reading, writing, and racism: Disrupting whiteness in teacher education and in the classroom.* Beacon Press.

80. Utt, J., & Tochluk, S. (2020). White teacher know thyself: Improving antiracist praxis through racial identity development. *Urban Education, 55*(1), 125–152. DOI:10.1177/0042085916648741

81. Gay, G. (2018). *Culturally responsive teaching* (3rd ed.). Teachers College Press.

82. Ibid.

83. Sacks, A. (2019, September). What makes a great teacher: Pedagogy or personality? *Education Week.* https://www.edweek.org/teaching-learning/opinion-what-makes-a-great-teacher-pedagogy-or-personality/2019/09

84. Sleeter, C.E. (2017). Critical race theory and the whiteness of teacher education. *Urban Education, 52*(2), 155–169.

85. Ladson-Billings, G. (2006). It's not the culture of poverty, it's the poverty of culture: The problem with teacher education. *Anthropology & Education Quarterly, 37*(2), 104–109.

86. Gay, G. (2018). *Culturally responsive teaching* (3rd ed.). Teachers College Press.

87. Ibid.

88. Sleeter, C.E. (2017). Critical race theory and the whiteness of teacher education. *Urban Education, 52*(2), 155–169.

89. Gay, G. (2018). *Culturally responsive teaching* (3rd ed.). Teachers College Press.

90. Ibid.

91. Banks, J.A. (2021). Multicultural education: History and dimensions. In J.A. Banks (Ed.), *Transforming multicultural education policy & practice* (pp. 42–52). Teachers College Press.

92. Sleeter, C.E. (2017). Critical race theory and the whiteness of teacher education. *Urban Education, 52*(2), 155–169.

93. Banks, J.A. (2021). Multicultural education: History and dimensions. In J.A. Banks (Ed.), *Transforming multicultural education policy & practice* (pp. 42–52). Teachers College Press.

94. Ladson-Billings, G. (2006). It's not the culture of poverty, it's the poverty of culture: The problem with teacher education. *Anthropology & Education Quarterly, 37*(2), 104–109.

95. Ibid.

96. Singh, A.A. (2019). *The racial healing handbook: Practical activities to help you challenge privilege, confront systemic racism, & engage in collective healing.* New Harbinger Publications.

97. Matias, C.E. (2013). Check yo' self before you wreck yo' self and our kids: Counterstories from culturally responsive white teachers?. . .To culturally responsive white teachers! *Interdisciplinary Journal of Teaching and Learning, 3*(2), 68–81.

98. DiAngelo, R. (2018). *White fragility: Why it's so hard for white people to talk about racism.* Beacon Press.

99. Harris, C. (1993). Whiteness as property. *Harvard Law Review, 106*(8), 1709–1795.

100. Love, B.L. (2020, February 6). White teachers need anti-racist therapy. *Education Week.* https://www.edweek.org/teaching-learning/opinion-white-teachers-need-anti-racist-therapy/2020/02

101. Jensen, R. (2005). *The heart of whiteness: Confronting race, racism, and white privilege.* City Lights Publishers.

102. Stefaniak, A., & Wohl, M.J.A. (2022). In time, we will simply disappear: Racial demographic shift undermines privileged group members support for marginalized groups via collective angst. *Group Process Intergroup Relations, 25*(3). https://www.ncbi.nlm.nih.gov/pmc/articles/PMC9036153/

103. Jensen, R. (2005). *The heart of whiteness: Confronting race, racism, and white privilege.* City Lights Publishers.

104. Singh, A.A. (2019). *The racial healing handbook: Practical activities to help you challenge privilege, confront systemic racism, & engage in collective healing.* New Harbinger Publications.

105. Ibid.

106. Ibid.

CHAPTER 5

1. Will, M., Heubeck, E., Najarro, I., Prothero, A., & Schwartz, S. (2024, March). The "difficult, beautiful" work of teaching. *EducationWeek.* https://www.edweek.org/teaching-learning/the-difficult-beautiful-work-of-teaching/2024/03

2. Pollack, M. (2019). Standing up against hate. In L. Delpit (Ed.), *Teaching when the world is on fire* (pp. 26–32). The New Press.

3. Kahne, J., & Middaugh, E. (2008). Democracy for some: The civic opportunity gap in high school. *Circle working paper 59. Center for Information and Research on Civic Learning and Engagement* (CIRCLE).

4. Flanagan, C.A., Cumsille, P., Gill, S., & Gallay, L.S. (2007). School and community climates and civic commitments: Patterns for ethnic minority and majority students. *Journal of Educational Psychology, 99*(2), 421. DOI:10.1037/0022-0663.99.2.421

5. Vygotsky, L.S. (1978). *Mind in society: The development of higher psychological processes.* Harvard University Press.

6. Ibid.

7. Ellerbrock, C.R., Main, K., Falbe, K.N., & Franz, D.P. (2018). An examination of middle school organizational structures in the United States and Australia. *Education Sciences, 8*(168). https://eric.ed.gov/?id=EJ1201001

8. Banks, J.A. (2021). Multicultural education: History and dimensions. In J.A. Banks (Ed.), *Transforming multicultural education policy & practice* (pp. 42–52). Teachers College Press.

9. Hurd, E., & Weilbacher, G. (2018). Developing and using a co-teaching model within a middle level educational program. *Current Issues in Middle Level Education, 23*(1). https://eric.ed.gov/?id=EJ1191655

10. Ellerbrock, C.R., Main, K., Falbe, K.N., & Franz, D.P. (2018). An examination of middle school organizational structures in the United States and Australia. *Education Sciences, 8*(168). https://eric.ed.gov/?id=EJ1201001

11. Byrd, C.M. (2021). Cycles of development in learning about identities, diversity, and equity. *Cultural Diversity & Ethnic Minority Psychology, 29*(1), 43–52.

12. Tatum, B.D. (1992). Talking about race, learning about racism: The application of racial identity development theory in the classroom. *Harvard Educational Review, 62*(1), 1–24.

13. Wing Sue, D. (2016). *Race talk and the conspiracy of silence: Understanding and facilitating difficult dialogues on race.* Wiley.

14. Leonardo, Z., & Porter, R.K. (2010). Pedagogy of fear: Toward a Fanionian theory of "safety" in race dialogue. *Race Ethnicity and Education, 13*(2), 139–157.

15. Steinberg, L. (2015). *Age of opportunity: Lessons from the new science of adolescence.* Harper Paperbacks.

16. Hammond, Z. (2015). This is your brain on culture: Understanding how culture programs the brain. In Z. Hammond, *Culturally responsive teaching & the brain* (pp. 36–50). Corwin.

17. Tatum, B.D. (1992). Talking about race, learning about racism: The application of racial identity development theory in the classroom. *Harvard Educational Review, 62*(1), 1–24.

18. Graham, S. 2018. Race/ethnicity and social adjustment of adolescents: How (not if) school diversity matters. *Educational Psychologist, 53*(2), 64–77.

19. Flynn, J.E. (2010). Discussing race and culture in the middle-school classroom: Scaffolding critical multiculturalism. In S. May & C.E. Sleeter (Eds.), *Critical multiculturalism: Theory and praxis* (pp. 165–175). Taylor & Francis.

20. Ibid.

21. Sensoy, O., & DiAngelo, R. (2017). *Is everyone really equal? An introduction to key concepts in social justice education* (Multicultural Education Series) (2nd ed.). Teachers College Press.

22. Rodríguez, M.D. (2014, December). No way but through. *TedXTalk.* https://www.youtube.com/watch?v=2orqr-nOIPk

23. Sensoy, O., & DiAngelo, R. (2017). *Is everyone really equal? An introduction to key concepts in social justice education* (Multicultural Education Series) (2nd ed.). Teachers College Press.

24. Elkind D. (1967). Egocentrism in adolescence. *Child Development, 38*, 1025–1034. DOI:10.2307/1127100

25. Sensoy, O., & DiAngelo, R. (2017). I*s everyone really equal? An introduction to key concepts in social justice education* (Multicultural Education Series) (2nd ed.). Teachers College Press.

26. Ibid.

27. Ibid.

28. Ibid.

29. Ibid.

30. Arao, B., & Clemens, K. (2013). From safe spaces to brave spaces: A new way to frame dialogue around diversity and social justice. In L. Landreman (Ed.),

The art of effective facilitation: Reflections from social justice educators (pp. 135–150). Stylus Publishing.

31. Ibid.

32. Leonardo, Z., & Porter, R. (2010). Pedagogy of fear: Toward a Fanonian theory of "safety" in race dialogue. *Race Ethnicity and Education, 13*(2), 139–157.

33. Ahenkorah, E. (2020). Safe and brave spaces don't work (and what you can do instead). *Medium.* https://medium.com/@elise.k.ahen/safe-and-brave-spaces-dont-work-and-what-you-can-do-instead-f265aa339aff

34. Gannon, L., & Nguyen, J. (n.d.). Accountable spaces: Transforming the early years sector into an accountable space. *Strive.* https://www.striveswo.ca/blog-posts/accountable-spaces-transforming-the-early-years-sector-into-an-accountable-space

35. Byrd, C.M. (2021). Cycles of development in learning about identities, diversity, and equity. *Cultural Diversity & Ethnic Minority Psychology, 29*(1), 43–52.

36. Sensoy, O., & DiAngelo, R. (2017). *Is everyone really equal? An introduction to key concepts in social justice education* (Multicultural Education Series) (2nd ed.). Teachers College Press.

37. Ibid.

38. Lynch, E.W., & Hanson, M.J. (2011). *Developing cross-cultural competence: A guide to working with children and their families* (4th ed.). Paul Brookes Publishing.

39. Cammarota, J., & Romero, A. (2006, Winter). A critically compassionate intellectualism for Latino/a students: Raising voices above the silencing in our schools. *Multicultural Education.* https://www.appstate.edu/~nelsenpj/rcoe/2400Spring11/Week2Readings/CammarotaRomero.pdf

40. Suyemoto, K.L., Donovan, R.A., & Kim, G.S. (2022). *Unraveling assumptions: A primer for understanding oppression and privilege.* Routledge.

41. Ibid.

42. Ibid.

43. Umaña-Taylor, A.J., Quintana, S.M., Lee, R.M., Cross Jr, W.E., Rivas-Drake, D., Schwartz, S.J., Yip, T., & Ethnic and Racial Identity in the Twenty-first Century Study Group. (2014). Ethnic and racial identity during adolescence and into young adulthood: An integrated conceptualization. *Child Development, 85*(1), 21–39. DOI: 10.1111/cdev.12196

44. Suyemoto, K.L., Donovan, R.A., & Kim, G.S. (2022). *Unraveling assumptions: A primer for understanding oppression and privilege.* Routledge.

45. Moffit, U., Rogers, L.O., & Dastrup, K.R.H. (2021). Beyond ethnicity: Applying Helms' White racial identity development model among White youth. *Journal of Research on Adolescence, 32*(3), 1140–1159.

46. McIntosh, P.K. (1989, July–August). White privilege: Unpacking the invisible knapsack. *Peace and Freedom Magazine.* https://www.nationalseedproject.org/images/documents/Knapsack_plus_Notes-Peggy_McIntosh.pdf

47. Cebulko, K. (2022). If they cared about their kids, they wouldn't have broken the law: Historical and contemporary implications of citizenship and immigration. In S.M. McClure & C.A. Harris (Eds.), *Getting real about race* (3rd ed., pp. 271–284). Sage.

48. Ibid.

49. Rico, B., Jacobs, P., & Coritz, A. (2023). 202 Census shows increase in multiracial population in all age categories. *U.S. Census Bureau.* https://www.census.gov/library/stories/2023/06/nearly-a-third-reporting-two-or-more-races-under-18-in-2020.html

50. Donella, L. (2016). All mixed up: What do we call people of multiple backgrounds? *NPR: CodeSw!tch.* https://www.npr.org/sections/codeswitch/2016/08/25/455470334/all-mixed-up-what-do-we-call-people-of-multiple-backgrounds

51. Dalmage, H. (2013). Patrolling racial borders: Discrimination against mixed race people. In M. Adams, W. Blumenfeld, C.R. Castañeda, H.W. Hackman, M.L. Peters, & M. Zuñiga (Eds.), *Readings for diversity and social justice* (3rd ed., pp. 96–101). Routledge.

52. Ibid.

53. Root, M. (1993–1994). *The bill of rights for people of mixed heritage.* https://www.apa.org/pubs/videos/4310742-rights.pdf

54. Hud-Aleem, R., & Countryman, J. (2008). Biracial identity development and recommendations in therapy. *Psychiatry, 5*(11), 37–44. https://www.ncbi.nlm.nih.gov/pmc/articles/PMC2695719/

55. Thompson, A. (2004). Caring and Colortalk: Childhood innocence in white and black. In V.S. Walker & J.R. Snarey (Eds.), *Race-ing moral formation: African American perspectives on care and justice* (pp. 23–37). Teachers College Press.

56. Byrd, C.M. (2021). Cycles of development in learning about identities, diversity, and equity. *Cultural Diversity & Ethnic Minority Psychology, 29*(1), 43–52.

57. Suyemoto, K.L., Donovan, R.A., & Kim, G.S. (2022). *Unraveling assumptions: A primer for understanding oppression and privilege.* Routledge.

58. Sensoy, O., & DiAngelo, R. (2017). *Is everyone really equal? An introduction to key concepts in social justice education* (Multicultural Education Series) (2nd ed.). Teachers College Press.

59. Byrd, C.M. (2021). Cycles of development in learning about identities, diversity, and equity. *Cultural Diversity & Ethnic Minority Psychology, 29*(1), 43–52.

60. Sensoy, O., & DiAngelo, R. (2017). *Is everyone really equal? An introduction to key concepts in social justice education* (Multicultural Education Series) (2nd ed.). Teachers College Press.

61. Ibid.

62. Ibid.

63. Ibid.

64. Ibid.

65. Ibid.

66. American Psychological Association. (2016). *Talking to kids about discrimination.* Author. https://www.apa.org/topics/racism-bias discrimination/kids#:~:text=Use%20age%2Dappropriate%20language%20children,as%20they%20come%20up%20naturally

67. Sensoy, O., & DiAngelo, R. (2017). *Is everyone really equal? An introduction to key concepts in social justice education* (Multicultural Education Series) (2nd ed.). Teachers College Press.

68. Ibid.
69. Ibid.
70. Bureau of Labor Statistics. https://www.bls.gov/opub/reports/race-and-ethnicity/2020/home.htm
71. Sensoy, O., & DiAngelo, R. (2017). *Is everyone really equal? An introduction to key concepts in social justice education* (Multicultural Education Series) (2nd ed.). Teachers College Press.
72. Suyemoto, K.L., Donovan, R.A., & Kim, G.S. (2022). *Unraveling assumptions: A primer for understanding oppression and privilege* (p. 44). Routledge.
73. Sensoy, O., & DiAngelo, R. (2017). *Is everyone really equal? An introduction to key concepts in social justice education* (Multicultural Education Series) (2nd ed., p. 80). Teachers College Press.
74. Suyemoto, K.L., Donovan, R.A., & Kim, G.S. (2022). *Unraveling assumptions: A primer for understanding oppression and privilege*. Routledge.
75. Ibid.
76. Sensoy, O., & DiAngelo, R. (2017). *Is everyone really equal? An introduction to key concepts in social justice education* (Multicultural Education Series) (2nd ed.). Teachers College Press.
77. Ibid.
78. Peace Learner. (2016, March 14). *Privilege walk lesson plan*. https://peacelearner.org/2016/03/14/privilege-walk-lesson-plan/#comments
79. Ibid.
80. Ibid.
81. Gay, G. (2018). *Culturally responsive teaching* (3rd ed., p. 3). Teachers College Press.
82. Adiche, C.N. (n.d.). The danger of a single story. *TED Talk*. https://www.youtube.com/watch?v=D9Ihs241zeg
83. Solórzano, D.G., & Yosso, T. J. (2002). Critical race methodology: Counter-storytelling as an analytical framework for education. *Qualitative Inquiry, 8*(1), 23–44.
84. Ibid.
85. Bettez, S.
86. Sensoy, O., & DiAngelo, R. (2017). *Is everyone really equal? An introduction to key concepts in social justice education* (Multicultural Education Series) (2nd ed.). Teachers College Press.
87. Gorski, P.C., & Pothini, S.G. (2018). *Case studies on diversity and social justice education* (2nd ed.). Routledge.
88. Ibid.
89. Ibid.
90. Ibid.
91. Ibid.
92. Abdul-Alim, J., & Mahal, J. (2023, July 3). How new state laws and book ban movements have made the teaching of US history contentious: Five essential reads. *The Conversation*. https://theconversation.com/how-new-state-laws-and-book-ban-movements-have-made-the-teaching-of-us-history-contentious-5-essential-reads-208576

93. Jensen, R. (2005). *The heart of whiteness: Confronting race, racism, and white privilege*. City Lights books.

94. Brosbe, R. (2023, February 15). Q & A: Teaching racial justice in schools. *U.S. News & World Report*. https://www.usnews.com/education/k12/articles/q-a-teaching-racial-justice-in-schools

95. Sonnenberg, R. (2022, September 2). Unbanning history: Georgia teen organizers fight back against school censorship. *SPLC*. https://www.splcenter.org/news/2022/09/02/georgia-students-fight-back-against-school-censorship

96. Bracken et al. (2022, August 17). What's actually being taught in history class. *The New York Times*. https://www.nytimes.com/interactive/2022/08/17/us/teaching-critical-race-theory.html

97. Brundage, W.F. (n.d.). How teachers can stay true to history without breaking new laws that restrict what they can teach about racism. *The Conversation*. https://theconversation.com/how-teachers-can-stay-true-to-history-without-breaking-new-laws-that-restrict-what-they-can-teach-about-racism-205452

98. Brown, C., Price-Dennis, D., & Rabb, C. (2024, April 14). *Book bans in teaching and teacher education* [Conference presentation]. Annual Meeting of the American Educational Research Association, Philadelphia, PA.

99. Brosbe, R. (2023, February 15). Q & A: Teaching racial justice in schools. *U.S. News & World Report*. https://www.usnews.com/education/k12/articles/q-a-teaching-racial-justice-in-schools

100. Perry, T., Steele, C., & Hilliard, A. (2003). *Young, gifted, and Black: Promoting high achievement among African-American students*. Beacon Press.

101. Nguyen, H.P. (2021, May 21). Through ethnic studies, schools push to include marginalized perspectives. *Edutopia*. https://www.edutopia.org/article/through-ethnic-studies-schools-push-include-marginalized-perspectives/

102. Sleeter, C.E., & Zavala, M. (2020). What the research says about ethnic studies. *National Education Association (NEA)*. https://www.nea.org/sites/default/files/202010/What%20the%20Research%20Says%20About%20Ethnic%20Studies.pdf

103. Nguyen, H.P. (2021, May 21). Through ethnic studies, schools push to include marginalized perspectives. *Edutopia*. https://www.edutopia.org/article/through-ethnic-studies-schools-push-include-marginalized-perspectives/

104. California Department of Education, Sacramento. (2022). *Ethnic studies model curriculum*. Author. https://www.cde.ca.gov/ci/cr/cf/documents/ethnicstudiescurriculum.pdf

105. Nguyen, H.P. (2021, May 21). Through ethnic studies, schools push to include marginalized perspectives. *Edutopia*. https://www.edutopia.org/article/through-ethnic-studies-schools-push-include-marginalized-perspectives/

106. Southern Poverty Law Center. (2022, February 1). *Whose heritage? Public symbols of the confederacy* (3rd edition). https://www.splcenter.org/20220201/whose-heritage-public-symbols-confederacy-third-edition

107. Ibid.

108. Williams, D.M. (2022). "But it's honoring! It's tradition!" The persistence of racialized Indian mascots in sports. In S. McClure & C.A. Harris (Eds.), *Getting real about race* (3rd ed., pp. 155–165). Sage.

109. Harper, S. (2022). Advancing and sustaining racial justice in pro sports. *USC Race and Equity Center.* https://rossierapps.usc.edu/facultydirectory/publications/231/Harper-2022-Pro-Sports-Report.pdf

110. Gorski, P.C., & Pothini, S.G. (2018). *Case studies on diversity and social justice education* (2nd ed.). Routledge.

CHAPTER 6

1. National Council of Teachers of English (NCTE). (2022, March 7). *Educators' right and responsibilities to engage in antiracist teaching.* Author. https://ncte.org/statement/antiracist-teaching/

2. McCoy, W., Nichols, S., López, F., King, N., Frankenberg, E., & Burnett, M. (2024, April 14). *Dismantling systems and reimagining equity in politically hostile learning contexts* [Conference presentation]. Annual Meeting of the American Educational Research Association.

3. Hannah-Jones, N. (2024, March 13). Five takeaways from Nikole Hannah-Jones's essay on the "colorblindess" trap. *The New York Times.* https://www.nytimes.com/2024/03/13/magazine/nikole-hannah-jones-colorblind-racial-justice.html

4. Contreras, R., & Ortiz, K. (2023, February 1). Black history month arrives as teachers' fears mount. *Axios.* https://www.axios.com/2023/02/01/black-history-month-teacher-fears-crt-ban-books

5. Najarro, I. (2024, February 15). Teachers censor themselves on socio-political issues, even without restrictive state laws. *EducationWeek.* https://www.edweek.org/teaching-learning/teachers-censor-themselves-on-socio-political-issues-even-without-restrictive-state-laws/2024/02?utm_source=nl&utm_medium=eml&utm_campaign=eu&M=9048014&UUID=47df0c2e7fce2a3abea7283ba5aa5d51&T=11972520

6. McCoy, W., Nichols, S., López, F., King, N., Frankenberg, E., & Burnett, M. (2024, April 14). *Dismantling systems and reimagining equity in politically hostile learning contexts* [Conference presentation]. Annual Meeting of the American Educational Research Association.

7. National Council of Teachers of English (NCTE). (2022, March 7). *Educators' right and responsibilities to engage in antiracist teaching.* Author. https://ncte.org/statement/antiracist-teaching/

8. American Association of University Professors (AAUP). (2023, October 30). *Defending the freedom to learn.* Author.

9. American Association of University Professors (AAUP), Committee A on Academic Freedom and Tenure (2007, September–October). *Freedom in the classroom.* Author.

10. Ibid.

11. Banerji, O. (2024, March 20). History group finds little evidence of "indoctrination." *EducationWeek.* https://www.edweek.org/teaching-learning/history-group-finds-little-evidence-of-k-12-indoctrination/2024/03

12. Walker, T. (2018, December 11). "Education is political": Neutrality in the classroom shortchanges students. *NEA Today.* https://www.nea.org/nea-today/all-news-articles/education-political-neutrality-classroom-shortchanges-students

13. Sensoy, O., & DiAngelo, R. (2017). *Is everyone really equal? An introduction to key concepts in social justice education* (Multicultural Education Series) (2nd ed.). Teachers College Press.

14. Ferlazzo, L. (2020, October 11). "Classrooms are political." *EducationWeek*. https://www.edweek.org/teaching-learning/opinion-classrooms-are-political/2020/10

15. Ibid.

16. Hadley Dunn, A. (2022). *Teaching on days after: Educating for equity in the wake of injustice*. Teachers College Press.

17. Sánchez Loza, D. (2023). Political neutrality as ideal, right-wing pedagogy in practice: Hegemony and civic learning opportunities in predominately White schools. *The Peabody Journal of Education, 98*(5), 562–576. DOI:10.1080/0161956X.2023.2261327

18. American Association of University Professors (AAUP), Committee A on Academic Freedom and Tenure. (2007, September–October). *Freedom in the classroom*. Author.

19. Lonas, L., & Schnell, M. (2023, March 24). House Republicans pass Parents Bill of Rights. *The Hill*. https://thehill.com/homenews/house/3916114-house-republicans-pass-parents-bill-of-rights/

20. Florida House of Representatives. (n.d.). *Parental rights in education*. https://www.myfloridahouse.gov/Sections/Bills/billsdetail.aspx?BillId=76545

21. *Moms for Liberty*. (n.d.). https://www.momsforliberty.org/about/

22. Justice, T. (2023, July 10). *Tiffany justice at the 2023 Moms for Liberty summit* [Video]. YouTube. https://portal.momsforliberty.org/news/summit23-tiffany-justice/

23. Stanford, L. (2023, August 31). Parents' rights groups have mobilized. What does it mean for students? *EducationWeek*. https://www.edweek.org/leadership/parents-rights-groups-have-mobilized-what-does-it-mean-for-students/2023/08

24. Southern Poverty Law Center. (2023, June 6). *The year in hate and extremism 2022*. Author. https://www.splcenter.org/year-hate-extremism-2022

25. Yousef, O. (2023, June 7). Moms for Liberty among conservative groups named "extremist" by civil rights watchdog. *NPR*. https://www.npr.org/2023/06/07/1180486760/splc-moms-for-liberty-extremist-group

26. Stanford, L. (2023, August 31). Parents' rights groups have mobilized. What does it mean for students? *EducationWeek*. https://www.edweek.org/leadership/parents-rights-groups-have-mobilized-what-does-it-mean-for-students/2023/08

27. Durand, T.M., & Perez, N.A. (2013). Continuity and variability in the parental involvement and advocacy beliefs of Latino families of young children: Finding the potential for a collective voice. *School Community Journal, 23*(1), 49–79.

28. Love, B. (2024, April 12). *Intersectional organizing, solidarity-building, and educational justice: A town hall conversation with scholars and community organizers* [Conference presentation; AERA Presidential Session]. Annual Meeting of the American Educational Research Association.

29. Standley, F.L., & Pratt, L.H. (Eds.). (1989). *Conversations with James Baldwin*. University Press of Mississippi.

Index

accountable spaces, 119–21
Adichie, Chimamanda Ngozi, 140
adolescent egocentrism, 118
Ahenkorah, Elise, 120
American History X (Film), 155
American identity, 125–28
American Psychological Association (APA), 15
anti-racist behavior: among White adolescents, 59–60. *See also* An Integrative Model for the Development of Anti-racist Behavior in White Youth
Arbery, Ahmaud, 11

Baldwin, James, 164
Banks, James, 87, 102, 112
Bell, Derrick, 13
Bell, Marcus, 98
Biden, Joseph, 82
"Bill of Rights for People of Mixed Heritage" (Root), 129
Black Lives Matter (BLM) movement, 10
Bonilla-Silva, Eduardo, 7, 94
Brown v. Board of Education, 9, 147
Byrd, Christy, 121

Carlson, Tucker, 11
Case Studies on Diversity and Social Justice Education (Gorski & Pothini), 142–43
color-blindness: approach in schools, 110, 140; classroom resistance strategies, 130–31; expressed by adolescent research participants, 50, 69; as ideology, 5–8, 94, 154, 170; as used in conservative rhetoric, 156; as viewed in CRT, 21
Coming Together: Family Reflections on Racism Study, 16
confederate iconography: as free speech, 150; removal of, 147
conscientização, 1
counter-story: as classroom activity, 140–41; in CRT perspective, 21
Crenshaw, Kimberlé, 13
critical action among adolescents: in critical consciousness, 58–60. *See also* An Integrative Model for the Development of Anti-racist Behavior in White Youth
critical consciousness, 1, 58–59, 91
critical multicultural approach, 3–4, 92; difficulties implementing, 92–93. *See also* critical multiculturalism; critical multicultural praxis

Critical Multiculturalism: Theory and Praxis (May & Sleeter), 90
critical multiculturalism: definition of, 90–92
critical multicultural praxis, 79, 106–7; pedagogical possibilities and classroom strategies, 109; rationale for, 153–54
critical pedagogy: as a "third space" for reflection, 97; definition of, 91; Freire's conceptualization, 91–92
critical race theory (CRT): definition, 13–15; as the new "villain," 10–13, 156–57; as research framework, 62
Critical Race Theory and its Critics: Implications for Research and Teaching (López & Sleeter), 10, 15
Critical Race Theory in Education: A Scholar's Journey (Ladson-Billings), 14
critical racial consciousness: definition, 17; identity-based scaffolding around, 122–31; rationale for in adolescents, 164; relational and community-based scaffolding around, 131–50
Cullors, Patrice, 10
Culturally Responsive Teaching: Theory, Research, & Practice (Gay), 4, 100
Culturally Responsive Teaching and the Brain: Promoting Authentic Engagement and Rigor Among Culturally and Linguistically Diverse Students (Hammond), 114
cultural neutrality: in teaching and schools, 100–103
"Cycles of Development in Learning About Identities, Diversity, & Equity" (Byrd, article), 121–22

"The Danger of a Single Story" (Adiche), 140
Delgado, Richard, 13
Delpit, Lisa, 9, 110
democratic education, 82
demographics of K–12 teachers, 83

DiAngelo, Robin, 54, 103–4, 117–19
discrimination: classroom strategies around, 133–36; definition, 133
diversity, equity, & inclusion (DEI): conflation with CRT, 15; definition and curricular focus, 11, 15; opposition to, 161; workplace training, 11
divisive concepts: laws or legislation, 12, 81–82, 156–57
Domenech Rodríguez, Melanie, 117
Donovan, Roxanne, 6
DuBois, W. E. B., 96
Duckworth, Angela, 95
Duncan-Andrade, Jeffrey, 85

equity literacy framework, 142
Equity Literacy Institute, 89
ethnic/indigenous studies content, 89, 145
Ethnic and Racial Identity in the Twenty-first Century Study Group, 26, 170n1, 170n90
ethnic-racial identity (ERI): classroom strategies, 113–15, 122–28; construct, 170n1, 170n90; research literature on White youth, 55–60; supporting biracial identity, 128–30; views of research participants of color, 19, 40–52; views of White research participants, 53–54, 67–78
Ethnic Studies Model Curriculum (California), 145–46
Eurocentric or Eurocentrism: within CRT studies, 14; within the curriculum, 5, 8, 35, 101–3, 115; definition, 165n7
Executive Order (EO) 13950, 11, 82

Floyd, George, 11
Freire, Paulo, 1, 8, 58–59, 91–92

Garza, Alicia, 10
Gay, Geneva, 4, 100–102
Gorski, Paul, vii–x, 89, 95, 141–42
Graham, Sandra, 22

Grit: The Power of Passion and Perseverance (Duckworth), 95

Hadley Dunn, Alyssa, 160
Hammond, Zaretta, 114
Harris, Kamala, 119
The Heart of Whiteness: Confronting Race, Racism, and White Privilege (Jensen), 104–5
Helms, Janet, 56, 99
history, subject area: avoidance or backlash in schools, 99, 110, 144; curricular relevance of, 9, 143; teaching of, 15, 128–29, 143–50
hooks, bell, 82, 84
hypervisibility, racial, 49–52

"I AM . . ." poems, 124–25
iceberg of culture, 123
Index of School Book Bans (PEN America), 12
indoctrination: claims of, 10, 157–58; definition of, 157–58
institutional nature of race, 94–96
An Integrative Model for the Development of Anti-racist Behavior in White Youth: conceptual model and framework, 63; discussion of, 61–64, 121–22
invisibility, racial, 51–52
Is Everyone Really Equal? An Introduction to Key Concepts in Social Justice Education (Sensoy & DiAngelo), 54–55, 133, 137
"It's Not the Culture of Poverty, It's the Poverty of Culture" (Ladson-Billings, article), 102

Jensen, Robert, 104

Kim, Grace, 6
Kingsolver, Barbara, 154

Ladson-Billings, Gloria, 14–15, 102
latent curriculum, 102

Leonardo, Zeus, 93, 97
López, Christina, 10, 15
Love, Bettina, 15, 94, 95, 104, 164

manifest curriculum, 102
Marks, Amy, 61
Martin, Trayvon, 10
Matias, Cheryl, 96–98
Matsuda, Mari, 13
May, Stephen, 88, 90–91
McIntosh, Peggy, 127, 136
McLaren, Peter, 87
meritocracy: as ideology, 5–8, 92, 97, 140, 160; as viewed in CRT, 21. *See also* neutrality
microaggressions, 116
Moms for Liberty, 12, 161–62
Mother Emanuel African American Episcopal Church, 147
multicultural education (MCE): Banks' dimensions of, 87; celebratory approach to, 3–4, 88; conceptualization and use in schools, 86, 88, 112; equity-oriented roots of, 86–87; liberal multicultural approach in schools, 88–90

National Association of School Psychologists (NASP), 15
National Center for Education Statistics (NCES), 83
National Teacher and Principals Survey 2020–2021, 83
neutrality: in law, 13–14; in teaching, 4–5, 158–60. *See also* cultural neutrality
"No Way but Through" (Rodríguez), 117

Obama, Barack, 119, 135
oppression: classroom strategies around, 134–36; definition, 134–35

parental involvement in schools: conservative rhetoric around, 161–62; rationale for, 160–63
Parental Rights in Education bill (Florida), 161

Parents' Bill of Rights Act (H.R.5), 161
PDK Poll of the Public's Attitudes Toward the Public Schools, 162
"Peace Learner: Cultivating Peace and Nonviolence in the Field of Education" (website), 138
Pedagogy of the Oppressed (Freire), 91
Picower, Bree, 99
politicization of schools, 5–6, 158–60
Pollack, Mica, 110
Positive Youth Development (PYD), 21
Pothini, Seema, 142
praxis: definition of, 86
prejudice: classroom strategies around, 133–34; definition, 132–33
privilege: able-bodied, 137; classroom strategies around, 137–38; definition, 136–37; "privilege walk" activity, 138
problem-posing pedagogy, 91–92

race: agency in teaching, 153–64; classroom application to community events, 148–49; classroom application to national events, 147–48; definition, 165n4; institutionalized in schools, 7–8; social construction of, 125–27; in sports, 147–48
RACE: The Power of an Illusion (film), 125
Race, Whiteness, and Education (Leonardo), 97
racelessness, feelings of: among White adolescents, 55–56, 73–74
racial-ethnic climate: definition and salience of, 22–23
racial healing, 105–6
The Racial Healing Handbook: Practical Activities to Help you Challenge Privilege, Confront Systemic Racism, & Engage in Collective Healing (Singh), 105–6
radical reflection: contextual use and application, 85–86; outcome of, 101; in practice, 86

Reading, Writing, and Racism: Disrupting Whiteness in Teacher Education and in the Classroom (Picower), 99
"reverse racism," 136
Roediger, David, 97
Root, Maria, 129
Rufo, Christopher, 10–11

school climate: definition of, 22
sensitive period: in early adolescent development, 17
Sensoy, Öslem, 54, 117–19
sheltered English immersion (SEI) classrooms, 32
Singh, Anneliese, 103, 105–6
Sleeter, Christine, 10, 15, 87–88, 90–91
"Something about the Subject Makes it Hard to Name" (Yamato, essay), 93
State of American Teacher Survey, 2023 (RAND Corporation), 156–57
stereotypes: classroom strategies around, 133–34; definition, 132. *See also* "The Danger of a Single Story"
Stop Asian Hate, 45–46
Students for Fair Admissions, Inc. v. President & Fellows of Harvard College, 6–7
Students for Fair Admissions, Inc. v. University of North Carolina, 6–7
Suyemoto, Karen, 6
systemic racism: defined, 2. *See also* institutional nature of race

Tatum, Beverly Daniel, 113
Taylor, Breonna, 11
Teaching on Days After: Educating for Equity in the Wake of Injustice (Dunn), 160
Teaching When the World is on Fire: Authentic Classroom Advice, from Climate Justice to Black Lives Matter (Delpit), 9, 110
Texas House Bill 3979 (2021; HB 3979), 157

Tometi, Opal, 10
Trump, Donald, 11, 82

Unraveling Assumptions: A Primer for Understanding Oppression and Privilege (Suyemoto et al.), 6

Vygotsky, Lev: zone of proximal development (ZPD), 111–12

Waters, Mary, 20
"What's Actually Being Taught in History Class" (*New York Times*), 15, 144
white emotionalities, 103–6
white fragility, 103–4
white identity among White adolescents: research findings on, 55–58
whiteness: association with white identity, 53–54; awareness of by students, 75–76; curricular tools of, 99; defined, 3, 96–97; interrogation of, 96–98; normativity of, 20, 52; as weaponized, 83, 98–99

Whiteness Interrupted: White Teachers and Racial Identity in Predominately Black Schools (Bell), 98–99
"White Privilege: Unpacking the Invisible Knapsack" (McIntosh), 127–28
white racial identity development (WRID) model, 56–57, 99
white racial positionality: author reflections on, xii, 84; salience for White teachers, 84–86
white replacement, 54
white supremacy: defined, 3; emotional investment in, 10, 103–6; as socialized, 60
Wing Sue, Derald, 113
Woolverton, Genevieve Alice, 61

Yamato, Gloria, 93
"Year in Hate and Extremism 2022" (Southern Poverty Law Center), 161–62

Zimmerman, George, 10

About the Author

Tina M. Durand, PhD, is a clinical associate professor of applied human development at Boston University, Wheelock College of Education and Human Development. She is a developmental psychologist who teaches courses on anti-oppressive practices and the psychology of race, and a former K–12 public school teacher. She has published widely in the areas of critically conscious teacher pedagogy, home and school contextual factors that promote student success, and the development of ethnic and racial consciousness and advocacy among adolescents.

www.ingramcontent.com/pod-product-compliance
Lightning Source LLC
Chambersburg PA
CBHW051059230426
43667CB00013B/2368